Route to Financial Success

Build Wealth, Keep it and Live a Life Free of Money Worries

by

Faiz Versey

TELEMACHUS PRESS

Route to Financial Success: Build Wealth, Keep It And Live a Life Free of Money Worries

Cover concept by Umtul Versey
Cover design by Telemachus Press, LLC

Cover art:
Copyright © iStock/25945439/CraigNeilMcCausland
Copyright © iStock/35073136/FooTToo
Copyright © iStock/35204078/AngiePhotos
Copyright © iStock/36505896/sigurcamp

Interior art:
Copyright © iStock/28441364/sunstock

Four Steps Millionaire Formula™ and Four Ways Business Formula™ are trademarks of Versey & Associates (Pty) Ltd.

The source for the Dow Jones Industrial Average graph is The Federal Reserve Bank of St. Louis. It has been reprinted with permission. The Dow Jones Industrial Average is proprietary to and is calculated, distributed and marketed by S&P Opco, LLC (a subsidiary of S&P Dow Jones Indices LLC), its affiliates and/or its licensors and has been licensed for use. S&P® is a registered trademark of Standard & Poor's Financial Services LLC, and DJIA®, Dow Jones Industrial Average® and Dow Jones® are registered trademarks of Dow Jones Trademark Holdings LLC. ©2014 S&P Dow Jones Indices LLC, its affiliates and/or its licensors. All rights reserved.

Published by Telemachus Press, LLC
http://www.telemachuspress.com

Visit the author website:
http://www.RouteToFinancialSuccess.com

ISBN: 978-1-941536-10-0 (eBook)
ISBN: 978-1-941536-11-7 (Paperback)

Library of Congress Control # 2014951153

Version 2015.01.05

Printed in the United States of America

10 9 8 7 6 5 4 3 2 1

Disclaimer:

The purpose of this book is to raise the awareness and financial literacy of the readers. It is not the intention of the author that a well thought out financial plan be discarded. When in doubt let the reader seek a qualified second opinion. This work contains the author's views and opinions, which are current as of the date of publication. The information presented in this work will be influenced by changing conditions, and therefore, the author reserves unto himself all rights and especially the right to change any of the material represented in this work in line with changing conditions. While the information contained herein was obtained from sources believed to be reliable, neither the author nor his affiliates/partners or successors in title assume any responsibility for any action based on it.

The basis of this work are many experiences of myself, my family and my clients. Certain facts have, however, been altered for educational purposes.

Please note that this book contains word spelling and punctuation consistent with traditional British style of English.

All terms in this book that are denoted with an asterisk* are defined in Appendix VII—Frequently Asked Questions.

Visit our Website at: www.RouteToFinancialSuccess.com

DEDICATED to my wife, without whose support this book would never have seen the light of day.

Table of Contents

About The Author

FAIZ VERSEY, CPA, CA, CIM, FCSI, FCA, RFC® is a Chartered Accountant and personal finance expert. He started his career in financial services in 1989 after he graduated with a B.Comm from the University of Toronto. He has devoted twenty-five years to financial services, including seven as an auditor and one and a half decades as a financial intermediary. He now teaches people about matters of personal finance so that they can acquire and retain financial independence.

In the book, Faiz makes several references to God. In this regard, he would like to take a moment to explain why Muslims prefer to use the term Allah when referring to God:

This is not a book on religion, but I am mildly religious. For those of you who could not get this fact from my name, I am a Muslim. And when it comes to making reference to the term *God*, Muslims prefer to use the term *Allah*. Since there seems to be a lot of misconception around this term (*Allah*), let me just take a moment to give a brief clarification. Muslims prefer to use the term *Allah* when referring to God because *Allah* denotes the specific iteration of God as mentioned in the Holy Quran, the holy scriptures of the Muslims. Probably (and please note that I am no expert in theology) Allah is the same God as that of many other religions; or the same *Higher Power* that many of the people on this earth believe in. However, because various religions and cultures refer to multiple Gods, Muslims feel it is safer to say *Allah* when referring to God so as not to create any confusion in either their own ears or that of their listeners.

There, I hope I have laid rest to some of the misconceptions with respect to the term *Allah*. And if I have said something incorrect or offensive in the preceding paragraph my heartfelt apologies, right away, to whoever might feel aggrieved. I respect all religions. The purpose of this book is not to debate religion, just to be mindful of it in the sense that many of us believe in a God, and call upon Him in times of need, especially financial need. Now that I have clarified the use of the term Allah as used by Muslims, for the rest of this book I will use the term *God* whenever it is my intention to refer to the *Higher Power*.

Route to Financial Success

Build Wealth, Keep it and Live a Life
Free of Money Worries

Introduction:

I am worried about you. Are you financially independent, or will you become financially independent during your lifetime? I hope so, but, unfortunately, the statistics are not in your favour. According to Graydon Watters, a Canadian financial author, statistics compiled in 1991 suggest that of people who reach the age of 65, only three percent will be financially successful.[1] A 2011 *Wall Street Journal* article indicates that only one percent of the individuals in the U.S. are millionaires.[2] Even in Botswana, where I live, I came across a newspaper story in 2012 in which the reporter estimated that five percent of the country's population holds the majority of the wealth.[3]

Therefore, it would seem to me that the poor vastly outnumber the rich. This is the problem that the 'Occupy Wall Street' movement harkened to in 2011. For those of you not familiar with the Occupy Wall Street movement, it started in New York City, late in 2011, and spread across the country. It was a protest against social and economic inequality in the U.S. The movement promulgated that 99 percent of the country is poor and one percent is rich.

This scenario applies not only to the U.S., but also to the rest of the world. So, the bad news is that financially you are probably in trouble.

Of course, that's not the end of it. It's the "reason why" for this book: I want to present you with a plan to get out of this mess. If you are young enough, you have a really good chance of achieving financial independence. If you are already late in your years, then it becomes more difficult, but it may still be treatable. Read on, as I have specifically addressed the needs of several age groups in this book, starting from teens all the way up to post-retirees (80 years young and above).

The reason for my addressing such a broad group is that, in my financial advisory career, I have served clients from the ages of fifteen to eighty-plus. So I am quite familiar with the hopes, needs and aspirations of each of these age groups. In each group, and also among the individuals in each group, the hopes, needs and aspirations differ significantly. I am aware of that. But there is also much common ground that needs to be taught to all age groups, such as the need to understand how inflation works, where it comes from and how it could impact your future financial well-being, no matter what your age. For instance, did you know that the U.S. dollar has lost over 80 percent of its value in the last fifty years?[4] What if it loses another 80 percent in the next fifty years? If you happen to live to a ripe old age, how will that impact your ability to survive financially? We will discuss this important problem and how to tackle it in Chapter 11 (*Trap #3: The US Fed*).

Because of the huge changes that the world has seen in the last fifty years, the knowledge of how to become financially independent has become even more important than it was, say, in the middle of the twentieth century. In those days you could expect to work for a large organisation—for instance, government or a large corporation—for life. It would feed you during your working years, and by providing a pension plan, also take care of you in your retirement years.

The problem that has emerged in recent times is that with the advent of the computer chip, the world has changed. Large organisations are downsizing* or disappearing altogether, and in the process are laying-off thousands of people. There is no more job security. In addition, after President Nixon cut the link between gold and the U.S. dollar in 1971, there has been the advent of massive monetary manipulation by many of the central banks of the world. This is a point that is little understood by the average person, and I will deal with it at length later in this book.

The new reality is that you have to rely on your own efforts, whether that means you have to think of new ways to contribute to your job, or think of how to start your own business. You also need to possess the financial education needed to create your own income security. It also means that the faster you become "money-wise," the better it will be for you.

So there you have it. One of the driving forces that motivated me to write this book is the desire to teach people how to become financially independent. Most of the people on mother earth currently have financial problems, and I want to do everything in my power to help those people.

I should also add that if you are a one-percenter, you, too, need to read this book, as you may be wealthy today, but it's so easy for you to lose your wealth and slip into the 99 percent. As one of the richest men in Botswana once told me:

"Faiz, do you know why I'm rich?"

"No," I said.

"It's because I take care of my money." What? Here's a rich man telling me that he *takes care* of his money. That is valuable advice, one that I will expand on later in this book.

Another reason I decided to write this book is to attack the inaccurate advice that I currently see being dispensed in the world today. I started my financial advisory career selling financial products in Toronto, Canada, in 1996. At that time I offered the conventional financial advice that the financial services industry teaches its advisors to offer their clients: Invest in mutual funds for the long term, buy a retirement account, work until you're sixty-five and then retire (if you're not dead already). Such conventional financial advice has caused more harm than good. There is a better way to become financially independent.

Which knowledge I stumbled upon totally by accident.

As fate would have it, in 1998, I had to leave Toronto, Canada and move to Gaborone, Botswana, where I re-established a financial advisory practice. Here I had the incredibly amazing opportunity to meet and work with, what we call in our industry—High Net Worth (HNW) clients. Just a fancy way to say "rich people." The financial services industry is so steeped in lies that it hates to say things in a simple way, in a way that even dumb people—meaning most of us—can understand. Over a period of time, to my great surprise, I learned that my HNW clients knew very little about "conventional" financial advice—investing* in mutual funds for the long-term, buying retirement accounts, and the like—and yet were rich. Come recession or no recession,* they would just keep on making money.

I studied them and started to do what they were doing. And voilà—well, not that fast, there were a few hiccups along the way—over a period of thirteen years, I too became a self-made "half-millionaire." (My net worth probably went over a million U.S. dollars in 2011. However, at the time of going to print I estimate that my current net worth is probably less. This is because Botswana's currency has since depreciated against the U.S. dollar. As well I have been busy investing copious amounts of money into this book project rather than engendering earnings! Hence, to be conservative, I estimate my net worth is "half a million" U.S. dollars). When I first arrived in Gaborone, Botswana, in 1998, I had just a small amount of money. Over the next thirteen years I had created a reasonable nest egg for my family.

Hence, this book: To teach people two things—first, how to become financially independent as fast as possible, and, second, how to protect themselves from the bad financial advice out there. It is the story of what I learned along the way while on my journey to create and protect wealth. There are three perspectives included:

- First, from the perspective of my formal education in personal finance, which I shall call "conventional" financial wisdom.

- Second, from the perspective of my rich clients' strategies, which I shall call "non-conventional" financial wisdom.

- Third, from my own experiences on the road to becoming a self-made "half-millionaire."

None of these approaches is flawless. All have pluses and minuses. Yet all have great lessons to offer in terms of what to do and what not to do; what works and what is likely to fail horribly.

I have put together the lessons from the three sources cited above to come up with a recipe that is practical, comprehensive and works in multiple situations across borders and continents. Of course, I can't say that the system is foolproof. Whether or not you will become financially independent will depend on your own hunger for financial success and how much effort you are willing to put into it. But if you do the things mentioned in this book, there is every chance that you will end up financially successful in your life, if not outright rich, keep your wealth, and live a life free of money worries.

And the reason you should be able do this is simple. It's called the Law of Cause and Effect,[5] which says if you want to achieve the "Success" that someone has achieved, then work backwards and figure out the "Cause" of it. Reverse-engineer the process. That way, once you know the steps, it stands to reason that all you have to do is follow the same steps, and you, too, should achieve the same result.

That is, do what the wealthy do, and then you can have wealth, too.

The problem is you may not have had a lot of contact with rich people. So it may be hard for you to know the steps. That's where I come into the picture. I have had a lot of contact with rich people. So I've done the work for you. I've provided you with the steps in this book. In fact, I used them myself to become a self-made "half-millionaire" by the time I reached my mid-forties. Most of my clients have become self-made millionaires using the exact same steps (only a few of my clients inherited their wealth). I call these steps the Four Steps Millionaire Formula, and you can read about them in Chapter 4 (*The Four Steps Millionaire Formula*). Most importantly, neither my clients nor I are extraordinary people. We are just ordinary folks, with average intelligence, but with a big hunger for wealth creation. If we've created wealth, you can do it, too.

Here is a question for you: If tomorrow, somehow, by accident, you became wealthy, how would that change your life? If you are sitting with someone, I want you to turn to that person and tell him or her, how your life would be different. You have one minute. Go.

Done? Did you find the life you were describing disappointing or appealing? If you found it appealing, then just keep on reading. In this book I am going to show you how to become financially independent so that you can get what you want out of life.

Book Overview:
This book is divided into seven parts.

In Part I, I open up the new world to you. There have been some big changes going on and most people have missed them. It's still not too late to catch the train, but you have to hurry. I also tell you why it's imperative that you learn how to become financially independent.

In Part II, we go into the details of how to become financially independent. This is a hugely important topic that needs to be understood by everyone in the world today. There are two reasons that many of the people in the world today are poor: First, it's because they just don't know how to become financially independent. This is a serious issue. Therefore, the main objective of this book is to show you how to become financially independent.

Second, it's because people have imbibed the misinformation put out by the financial services industry—for instance, investment companies telling people that to get rich they should invest in mutual funds (mutual funds are described in detail in Chapter 7: *How to Invest Money*). Nothing could be farther from the truth. Investing in mutual funds only makes the mutual funds companies rich. Specifically, these companies take fees even if the mutual fund returns are negative. Therefore, I need to debunk this myth and tell you how the rich really get rich.

Once you know the secret of how to become financially independent, you'll see how feasible it is for anyone on this planet to become rich, including you. You just need to know how. And not only does it have nothing to do with investing in mutual funds, it has everything to do with *not* investing in mutual funds.

In Part III, I talk about the traps to avoid on your march to financial independence. If you know about these traps, you can protect yourself from their deleterious effects. Not losing money is just as important as making it.

On the flip side of the coin, once you know how the traps operate, you can figure out how to profit from them. I cover this aspect in Chapter 30 (*In defense of the Gruesome Trifecta*)

In Part IV, I apply what we've learned in Parts I to III to the specific stage of the "life cycle" that you may find yourself in. I also bring up other financial matters, which could be relevant to you as you pass through one of these life stages.

Although, at first blush it may appear that not every chapter in this book is relevant to you, I urge you to read the entire book. This will give you a perspective for the wealth of information contained herein. Then pick out the areas that are most relevant to your particular situation in life, and use those sections to guide your current financial moves. In this way, you may find that there are sections that are relevant to your loved ones, and you may wish to refer the book to them.

For example, if you are a teenager and want to learn how to get rich, then you will need to read all the chapters in Part II—*Acquiring Wealth*. But you will also want to read the whole book because it will give you the perspective on what financial problems seventy-year olds have to deal with. And what you can do *today* so that you don't have to deal with such problems when you turn seventy ... as you surely will if you live long enough.

Similarly, if you are in your thirties and are looking to get out of debt, then focus your attention for now on Chapter 16 (*Young Adult*).

If you are in your fifties and simply want to achieve a comfortable retirement, and getting rich is not your thing, then focus your attention on chapters 17 (*Pre-retirement*) and 18 (*Retirement*).

You get the idea.

In Part V, I have specially provided financial advice for certain groups that I think need advice for their specific circumstances. These are excellent case studies for everyone and you may find that there is information therein, which may help you better understand your current or future situation. So don't skip these chapters, even though the title of the chapter may not be talking to you specifically.

Also, the reason I didn't think it necessary to write a separate personal finance book for the groups of people mentioned in Part V at the moment, but, God willing, I might in the future, is that parts I-IV cover the essential personal financial knowledge that I think *everyone* needs to know. That is the foundation from which we can start in order to build to your particular financial situation and address your particular financial concerns; and that includes the groups of people mentioned in Part V.

In Part VI, I address some tips for financial success that I want to impart to readers before they stop reading and start taking action.

In Part VII, the conclusion, I give you some final takeaways.

Before I move on to Chapter One, please note that whenever I use the term *men*, please understand that I also mean to include women. It would be cumbersome to write "men and women" each time. I truly want both men and women to benefit from what I am teaching because it is relevant to both genders.

As well, for an explanation of all starred words (*) please see Appendix VII, Frequently Asked Questions.

Becoming financially independent should be high on your priority list. The faster you get there, the more you will be able to get out of life, whether it's simply to enjoy it, help your loved ones or change the world. Or all of the above.

Part I: The Penny Drops

Chapter 1: The New World

In the last one hundred and fifty years man has made more progress than he has ever made before in his history. Just a century and a half ago people had to work a lot harder to obtain some of the material benefits that we take for granted today. They had to trudge miles to get water and then they had to boil it to make it safe to drink. We get potable water on tap. They had to go out and buy kerosene to light their lamps for nighttime illumination. We get light at the push of a button. They died from simple diseases. Today many of those diseases can be easily and quickly cured. Compared to the lives of people living in the nineteenth century, we all live like kings.

With such an increase in our standard of living, why then do we have a situation such as "99 percent versus one percent?" Why do we have a great part of the world living in abject poverty? Why do we have food insecurity? Why is the middle class being hollowed out (meaning: gone! That's no good.)? Why do we have money problems in marriages? What went wrong?

What has gone wrong is that the world has changed in two important ways and people have not yet bothered to connect the dots and figure out how these changes are having an impact on them.

The first change is the advent of the computer chip.[6] Computing power has grown immensely in the last fifty years. It is said that the computing power of microchips doubles every eighteen months. So going forward we can only expect more technological advancements, not fewer. What this means is that the way work is done on the planet has changed. With all this technology available to us, we actually need fewer human beings to get results.[7] This transformation is known as "automation" and is the name of the game in business today, resulting in the decreased need for human labour. That is, "jobs."

One of the clients from my former financial advisory practice gave me an excellent example of how automation is adversely affecting the need for human labour. He is in the hardware business. He told me that ten years ago he would need ten people to offload a truck carrying cement bags. Today a forklift can do the job in a fraction of the time using a fraction of the labour. The trend towards automation is increasing in every industry, enabling more and more work to be done by machines. Just look around you. Are there as many tellers in your bank as there used to be? No, much less, because they are no longer necessary. Bank customers can get much of their banking done through an ATM and on the Internet. How about accounting personnel? No longer are hordes of accounting personnel needed to crunch the numbers. Computers do it by brute force.

Because of the use of outsourcing, microchip technology has also inspired the downsizing of corporations. As information becomes easier and less expensive to transmit electronically, there is less and less reason to have costly in-house staff to perform tasks that can be outsourced. Such is the case with call centres and accounting staff. Your local institution may be getting the work done in a different country[8] where the cost of labour is much cheaper. As a result, many people in the developed world have lost their jobs.

Another effect of computer technology is that industries that previously required large capital investment don't require it any more. The same work can be done less expensively. For example, take the case of publishing. It used to be the exclusive domain of large companies. Publishing required large equipment and people to run that equipment. Now all the work can be done on a computer. We don't even need to buy printed material. We can get a lot of our reading done on the Internet. Hence, Newsweek magazine, for example, ended its eighty-year run in print in 2012,[9] and many other "legacy" (in computer lingo, meaning not up-to-date with current computer technology) magazines are going the same way, having to reinvent themselves in the digital era.

As a result of this decrease in the cost of doing business, entrepreneurial companies have become easier to startup. Individuals can now do the work that previously required huge capital investment, which formerly placed those ventures exclusively in the domain of large organisations. Hence, again, there is less and less need for large organisations and their legions of employees.

You've seen these changes happening. Many of the large companies that existed ten or fifteen years ago are no more or have downsized. As a result thousands of people have lost their jobs. Take the example of Kodak, the photography giant. It used to be that we all desired a "Kodak moment" in our lives. However, Kodak failed to keep up with digital technologies and filed for bankruptcy in 2012.[10]

What does all this mean for the average person? It means that the idea of lifetime employment with one employer is gone. Gone along with that is the idea of being taken care of by a large corporation during one's working years, and thereafter in retirement with plush pension plans. Whereas our parents and grandparents were able to fashion their lives on the idea of having a dependable source of income all their lives, we do not.

So people find themselves out of a job, which they thought they would have for life. Unfortunately, the concept of job security is now history. People have to recognise this and act accordingly. But this huge change in how the world works seems to have caught most people by surprise. In fact, judging by the public's constant clamouring in the media for the government to create jobs, I think that most people are not even *aware* that the whole concept of a "job," of having a permanent income, is gone. "Not being aware of a problem" is an awful situation. Because if you can't identify the problem in the first place, how will you ever come up with a solution for it? We will address the problem of disappearing jobs and the related solution in Chapter 5 (*How to Make Money*).

The second change, along with the microchip revolution, is that there has been the advent of massive monetary manipulation by many of the central banks around the world. We will discuss this in more detail in Chapter 11 (Trap #3: *The US Fed*). Although the manipulation started approximately at the turn of the twentieth century, essentially, it gathered steam after President Nixon cut the link between gold and the U.S. dollar in 1971.[11] After that day, central banks around the world had the mechanism to print unlimited amounts of money, which many did.

It set off a process of credit creation.[12] Massive amounts of credit were created, credit that was subsequently foisted onto the unsuspecting public. The problem is that, in this way, the printing of money causes a cycle of boom and bust, wherein a credit bubble* builds up and then implodes, monetarily crushing millions of people. The central banks repeat the cycle, pumping it up again, and then it implodes again, crushing additional millions of people. As I write this book, nobody knows when this cycle of terror will end, or what form it will take when it ends. But it is likely to end very badly for the whole world.

Bottom line, you need to get prepared for a new world. Grandma's world doesn't exist anymore.

So what lies ahead? Is it all doom and gloom from here on in? The bad news is that for the people who refuse to get financially educated, it is. Most people don't do what they have to do to succeed. However, for those who are willing to put in the time and effort to learn the ins-and-outs of the money game, not only will they survive, they will prosper.

In this new world we are heading into, I want to show you what you need to do, first, just to survive, and then, second, to prosper. Unfortunately, I don't think that buying mutual funds will make you rich. If mutual funds were the great financial solution, do you think we'd have the 99 percent versus one percent problem? Clearly, the old paradigms have not worked.

We need a new approach.

There is a saying that goes: when you are in a hole, stop digging. Basically, what humans need to do is to stop digging themselves further into the hole that they are already in and find a way out.

This book provides the way out. Those who will find their way out are those who will not only understand how to protect themselves from the system that is currently in place, but also how to profit from it. As it turns out, the system is global. It's everywhere, in every country around the world. The reason for this is simply that English has more or less become the language of business around the world. And along with that the use of British financial laws has spread. Accordingly, the principles contained in this book are universally applicable. Sure, there will be minor differences from country to country, but if you understand the principles behind the financial strategy, you'll figure out how to make it work for you in your country.

Who will win and who will lose in this new world?

The winners will be people who will not enter the playing field blindfolded. They will understand the game being played by Government, Big Business and Financial Services—a group that I have dubbed "The Gruesome Trifecta"—and these winners will know how to protect themselves from the injurious actions of these institutions. On the flip side of the coin, they will also have figured out how to profit from the favourable economic circumstances created by this group. This book will show you both sides of the coin.

The losers will be people who refuse to increase their financial education. More than ever before, this is the time to increase one's financial education. As well, it's not just the education, but also the implementation of that education, which will enable people to beat the mass poverty that is about to descend on all of mankind.

Shortly after I moved to Botswana, I set up my own financial advisory practice. It was tough going in the beginning, but soon I broke into the High Net Worth (HNW) circles and started working almost exclusively with them. It was a lucky break. Not only because my financial advisory practice grew, but because I started to see firsthand how the rich were building and managing their wealth. It was an eye-opener. I started to use their techniques myself, and soon my wealth started to grow.

If you don't want to be just road kill on the road of life, you need to know these techniques.

Chapter 2: How I discovered
the secret to wealth

I've always wanted to be rich. Ever since I was a child. I tried many entrepreneurial endeavours, but nothing seemed to stick. In the meantime I
continued with my studies, earning a B.Comm degree from the University
of Toronto and a Chartered Accountancy designation from the Institute
of Chartered Accountants of Ontario.

In 1996, I had my first serious stab at starting a successful business. I
joined a financial services firm in Canada, Midland Walwyn, which later
became Merrill Lynch Canada. I became a broker (a commissioned salesman) offering financial products such as stocks, bonds, mutual funds, options and life insurance. It seemed to be the way to wealth for me.

I immersed myself in the opportunity and after three years of hard work I
was managing about 25 million Canadian dollars on behalf of investors.
These were reasonable numbers. However, as fate would have it, in 1998 I
had to move to Botswana. My parents lived there, and being the only son
in the family, I decided to join my parents. I was lucky that my wife was
one hundred percent behind this major life-move.

In Botswana, after a short stint with a local financial advisory firm, I created my own financial advisory practice. It was hard going at first, and I

almost didn't make it. At the end of the first year, I was down to my last $100 of savings. The day I counted my last $100 also happened to be the beginning of a long weekend. And as it turned out, early in the morning that day, my mother called me and said, "Your dad and I want to go for a holiday to Cape Town. Are you coming?"

Whoops! I put the phone on my chest and looked at my wife. It didn't take her a moment to tell me "Say yes."

"OK, Mom, we're coming," I said to my mother.

We spent our last $100 on that trip. As we returned home, and just as I was slipping the key into the front door to my house, thinking about how I was going to have to go out and look for a job the next day, my cell phone rang, and a familiar voice on the other end said, "Faiz, you know that investment plan you talked to me about? Well, I have some funds (money) to invest. When can you come by to see me?"

I felt like saying, "How about now?" but I held back my excitement and made an appointment for the next day. It was the turning point in my career. Literally, from that day onwards my practice started to gain traction.

Thereafter, came a big break in my life. Through client introductions I started to work almost exclusively with HNWs (High Net Worth clients). At first, I didn't pay much attention to what these people were doing to get wealthy. But slowly, it started to dawn on me that the HNWs were doing something mighty different in creating wealth than what I had been taught in my personal finance courses. They were not getting rich by buying mutual funds. The only reason they bought mutual funds at all was that I would bug them to death to do it. Of course, I would be thinking all the while that I was being mighty useful to them—helping them to "manage their wealth"—as I'd put it in those days.

However, as I started to learn more about what my wealthy clients were doing to build wealth, I started to implement the same strategies in my life. And sure enough, my wealth started to grow.

Then, along the way, came the great global financial crisis of 2007.

At first I thought that the global financial crisis was just a temporary event and that things would right themselves shortly. In fact, in May 2007, Ben Bernanke, Chairman of the Federal Reserve, the USA's central bank, said the increasing mortgage problems (for a brief explanation of "mortgage" and the "subprime mortgage problem" please see FAQ) would not seriously harm the US economy.[13]

Shortly thereafter, in September 2007, the DOW (a US stock market index) hit an all-time high of approximately 14,000 points (basically, this is good news). However, by then the crisis had started to spread beyond the borders of the USA. It steadily got worse and the reality of the subprime problem started to unfold. By 2008, major financial institutions were in trouble. Lehman Brothers, the fourth largest investment bank in the country, went under causing one of the biggest bankruptcies, (for explanation of "bankruptcy" see FAQ) 639 billion dollars, in U.S. history.

In October 2008, the global financial system had pretty much frozen up. Imagine that. Imagine going to the bank one day and finding that your paycheque, which had been credited to your bank account the previous day, was no longer there. Because the bank had gone belly-up. What would you do? Dive into your savings? Well, guess what? That too would have gone up in smoke, because if your savings were in the same bank that received your paycheque, then that money would have disappeared, too.

Imagine if that happened to everyone in your town, your country, the continent you lived on and on every continent around the world. What would have happened? Mass chaos. People coming out onto the streets everywhere. Riots. Mayhem.

To avert such a political catastrophe, the central banks of the world jumped in. They pumped billions and billions of dollars into the bankrupt banking system, in order to avoid a huge potential crisis and, perhaps, it could even go unobserved.

However, I became curious. I started to dive deeply under the surface to try and figure out what was really going on.

I had chosen to sell products offered through the investment platforms of large investment companies. Before offering these products to my clients I would do a lot of due diligence. I'd watch how the products would perform for a period of time, and then grill the sales representatives of the companies offering the products. The questions I asked these companies were always met with responses where the positive was accentuated while the potential pitfalls were trivialised.

Notwithstanding the due diligence that I performed the severity of the financial meltdown that took place after the 2007 global financial crisis took me and many others by surprise, especially when funds were frozen due to liquidity issues.

Because of this I started to question conventional investments. Therefore, I lost my passion to sell financial products. So I chose to withdraw from the financial intermediary profession and closed my practice.

That juncture was also my "Aha" moment. It started to dawn on me that the stuff the financial industry promoted was dubious. Investments could decline steeply, get suspended or go up in smoke altogether. There was no guarantee that the upside would be permanent. If you are dependent on your investment portfolio for retirement income, there could be trouble brewing. This is an important theme in this book—assessing the security of the source of your retirement income—and we will discuss it in detail later on.

I also started to realize that the growth that some of my clients were achieving in their personal estates through their private efforts was better than the growth the financial industry products at the time could offer.

I have been extremely fortunate to learn how the rich get rich. I learned this from three different perspectives. First, I realized that my formal education in personal finance had not helped me figure out how to create wealth in the real world. As I've said before, buying mutual funds just does not cut it if you're trying to get rich.

Second, I learned from working with rich people as their financial advisor. Therein, I had the fantastic opportunity to peer into their business lives. That gave me a firsthand view of how they were building their wealth.

And third, from implementing, for myself, the wealth-building techniques I learned from my rich clients. Over a period of thirteen years I created wealth for my family starting from a small sum and grew it to over half a million U.S. dollars. Please do not consider this bragging. Quite the opposite; I am sharing my story to convince you that if I can start with practically nothing and create half a million dollars of wealth, then in all likelihood, so can you. I am just an ordinary person. And so were most of my wealthy clients.

Shortly I am going to tell *you* how to get wealthy. I will reveal the secret in Chapter Four (*The Four Steps Millionaire Formula*).

Chapter 3: Route to Financial Success—summary of the financial solution

What I'm giving you in this book is the entire menu of what you need to know to succeed financially. Thereafter, if you need more tutelage on certain topics, you are welcome to search for it. But this is the first time that anyone has put together, in one place, in an easy to read and understand manner, everything you need to know about succeeding financially. It's the path. So that's why this book is called the *Route to Financial Success*. The whole path is set out for you.

The *Route to Financial Success* strategy consists of five parts. Let's briefly go over each of them.

Acquiring Financial Independence (discussed in Part II)
Here we will go on the most critical journey of all—how to get rich. It has become imperative for people around the world to get rich. Or at least know enough about the subject. If you are rich, or progress significantly towards getting rich, you will improve your lifestyle. Globally, we have moved away from the former trend of large organisations taking care of people for their entire lives—their working years and their retirement years. These large organisations face the sword at the hands of the twin

destroyers of yesteryear—the microchip and the global manipulation of the monetary system. You now face a brand new world. You have to become financially savvy yourself, and take care of your own personal finances, rather than depend on an external party to do it for you. In this section, I will tell you how to get rich. It is an important subject that was not taught to us in school.

Mind the Trap (discussed in Part III).
There are forces that contrive to snatch your financial security from you. You have to be aware of who or what they are and how they operate. Once you are aware of the damage that these forces can inflict on you, then you will know how to consciously protect yourself. On the flip side, you also need to know how to profit from these forces, so that you become the *house*. If you play the game according to the rules of the house you win.

What stage of the life cycle are YOU in (discussed in Part IV)?
This book will find different people at different stages of their life cycle. Your dreams, opportunities and abilities will be different according to the stage of the life cycle that you are in. You have to adjust accordingly. If you are facing financial difficulties, do not hide from them. Face the truth. If you have made mistakes recognise them, so you don't repeat them. Use the gifts of knowledge that these problems give you and apply the gifts of knowledge to figure out solutions to your problems. It is your best chance at recovering from a weak financial position.

Financial Advice for Certain Groups of People (discussed in Part V)
In this section, I provide financial advice for certain groups of people. You may be one of the groups specifically mentioned. If not, you should read this part anyway, because the advice has a broad spectrum of application.

This section is comprised of case studies that could enhance your understanding of how to manage your own financial life. By studying them you will learn more about your own financial management process.

More Tips for Financial Success (discussed in Part VI)

I want to give you more tips that can help you to round out the financial knowledge we have covered previously in the book. In this way, we will have covered most of the important financial topics that people around the world need to know about.

This is the *Route to Financial Success*. It is what you need to know to create financial success in your life. The lessons can be composed into an acronym as follows:

Where:

(Part II): A = $\mathbf{A}$cquiring Financial Independence.

(Part III): M = $\mathbf{M}$ind the Trap.

(Part IV): Y = What Stage of the life cycle are $\mathbf{Y}$OU in?

(Part V): A = Financial $\mathbf{A}$dvice for Certain Groups of People

(Part VI): T = More $\mathbf{T}$ips for Success

The Biggest Obstacles

As you go through the book you may feel that becoming financially independent is beyond your reach. We need to identify these obstacles and help you get over them.

Obstacle #1: You don't believe you can do it

Why is 99 percent of the world poor? First, it's because they just don't know how to become financially independent. However, we will eliminate that problem. By the time you finish this book you will know how to become financially independent. That will eliminate the biggest problem standing in your path.

Second, you may find that doubts start to creep up, inhibiting the implementation of what you learned in the book. This is just as bad as the first problem. Financial independence is not just going to fall into your lap. You have to *do* stuff to become financially independent.

Consider this: If everybody believed that they couldn't do it, there would be no financially independent person on this earth. But if one percent of the earth's people *are* financially independent, and there are seven billion people on this planet, it means seventy million people are financially independent. Huh? Don't you think you could be ONE of those seventy million people, especially if you are armed with the information in this book?

I didn't have this book when I started on my road to financial independence, yet after thirteen years I grew my family's wealth from a small figure to a significant one. Just by learning what's in this book, you are light-years ahead of where I was. So honour your journey. Trust in this book. Your chances for financial success are much better than you think.

Obstacle #2: But I don't have any mentors
That makes sense. You need a mentor when embarking on a long, unknown and dangerous journey. A mentor will be your guide on that path. I get it. For instance, I am a camping enthusiast. I love to go into the wilds of Botswana. But the wilds of Botswana are no Garden of Eden. With lions, elephants, snakes and scorpions in constant attendance, if you don't know what you're doing, you can die. So before going on a trip I read books, watch videos and talk to other people who have already been to the place that I want to visit. I always take my family with me. So there is a huge responsibility on my shoulders to get my family to our destination and back safely.

I seek out mentors, books, videos and people who can guide me there and back.

That is the reason I wrote this book. I can serve as your mentor. Through this book, I will be with you, to guide you through the (sometimes) rocky path to financial independence.

Obstacle #3: I don't want to do it

Aha! This is the killer of all obstacles. It stems from not having a big enough *why*. You don't have a big enough reason to achieve financial independence. You've got to overcome this problem. You've got to ignite your passion for becoming financially independent.

As I write this, a few days ago, my younger daughter was learning how to ride a bicycle. Two of her friends were helping her. At first, she kept falling off. Then one of her friends told my daughter: "Imagine the whole world is lava. And there is a big giant standing there. And he is holding your family in his hands. If you fall off the bike, he will tip your family into the lava." My daughter sat on the bike and pedaled away—without falling off.

That's what it's about: something worth struggling for. Develop a passion for becoming financially independent. Then you will do whatever it takes to achieve it.

So why should you become financially independent? What benefits will you get? Think about it. Write down your answers. You have one minute, go!

I came up with one hundred and fifty answers (I did take more than one minute, though, and you can, too). Here are ten things I thought of:

1. Less stress.

2. More money.

3. Freedom.

4. Control over your life.

5. Feel better about yourself and your life.

6. Better health as have time to spend exercising and playing active sports.

7. Can hire somebody to do basic paperwork.

8. Can hire somebody to do manual labour (e.g. cleaning the yard, cooking).

9. Better family life as have more time to spend with family.

10. Better feeling of contribution to the world as can teach your knowledge to others.

Obstacle #4: I don't have enough time

Everybody has the same amount of time. We all have exactly twenty-four hours in a day. Then why is it that some people get ahead and some people don't? It's really quite simple. The ones that get ahead have worked out how to be ruthless with their time. They understand three things about time:

1. Time is the only thing we cannot make more of. Once it's gone, it's gone. So use your time wisely.

2. There is an opportunity cost to time. If you spend your time on one thing, then it can't be spent on another. So you can't be working on just anything. You must first figure out your goals in life, and then only do the things that take you towards those goals.

3. Utilise the concept of block time as opposed to multitasking. That is, if you are working on an important task, make sure you work on that task until it's finished. To accomplish this you need to block off the time to get the task done. That means blocking off hours, days or weeks where nothing else can be done. That is one of the important secrets of highly productive people.

Obstacle #5: I don't have enough money

If you are a ninety-nine percenter, of course you don't. The good news is that very few self-made millionaires did when they first started out. Only those who inherit wealth do. But that is a negligible number of people. The vast majority of self-made millionaires started out from scratch. As I told you a few pages back, I started out my journey from scratch. Neither my clients nor I am extraordinary in any way. Some of my clients did not even finish high school. What we all had in common, though, was a burning desire to get rich. A passion for it. Because of what wealth can do for us and our loved ones.

Therefore, if you don't have any money, don't worry; that shouldn't stop you from eventually having it. If anything, it should light a fire in your belly enabling you to move towards your goal of financial abundance.

If you are a one-percenter, be careful about this. Be vigilant about the money in your pocket. Having money in your pocket today is no guarantee that you will have it in your pocket tomorrow. You have to take care of it. Or else you could lose. You certainly don't want to lose your wealth after having been rich. I spend more time on this topic in Chapter 25 (*One-percenters*).

Warning

As we move forward on our journey through the *Route to Financial Success*, a word of warning: This is not a get rich quick scheme. It's for people who want to approach this from the point of view of mastery. Learning the art of building and retaining wealth, so that they can be financially secure no matter what the economy or life throws at them. This is for people who want to be in this for the long haul. And who want to serve others while building and retaining wealth.

Part II: Acquiring Financial Independence

Chapter 4: The Four Steps Millionaire Formula

So what were my rich clients doing to get rich anyway? Well, here it is. I call it the "Four Steps Millionaire Formula." It is everything you need to know about how the rich get rich. This is the most important chapter in this book. You need to understand it well. Read it carefully, and perhaps revisit it. However, after having reread the chapter once or twice, if you still don't get it, don't worry, you will by the time you finish reading the book.

The Four Steps Millionaire Formula consists of four steps. In this chapter we will explore the steps from a high-level perspective; then we will get into the nitty-gritty in chapters 5–8.

Step 1: Make money.
This is the starting point. You need to make money.

What? Make money?

"I knew it," you're thinking. "It takes money to make money. Oh, no! I don't have any money. That's it, I'm out of here."

Stop. Let's discuss that. Yes, you need to make money. But guess what? Most millionaires start out with nothing. Very few of my clients were born rich; only a small minority inherited their wealth. So in the game of wealth, we all essentially start out the same way—with nothing. It's a level playing field.

The real question then is: How do you make money?

It's a lot easier than you think. And we'll deal with that in Chapter 5 (*How to make money*). For now, let's just get an overview of the Four Steps Millionaire Formula. I want to give you the big picture, so you can see how it all comes together. Then, once you see how simple the path to wealth really is, I hope you'll be motivated to say to yourself: "I can do that." And follow up by taking the actions needed to make it happen for you.

Step 2: Save

Yes, once you make money you need to hang on to it. This is what the rich man I spoke of in the *Introduction* was telling me about. You need to save your money.

Saving is a very important pursuit, and many a great wealth story got derailed just about here.

Ever heard of Mike Tyson? He is purported to have made upwards of 400 million dollars in his career. In 2004, he filed for bankruptcy.[14] Ever heard of MC Hammer? He filed for bankruptcy in 1996.[15] The list of former millionaires goes on and on. But you don't want to be on that list. (Please note that I wish the aforementioned gentlemen well; we all make mistakes).

We will take a detailed look at how to save money in Chapter 6 (*How to Save Money*).

Step 3: Invest in Cash Flowing Investments

The next step is to invest in Cash Flowing Investments (CFI).

This is a key strategy. Once you have sufficient savings, the juice for your financial independence cocktail, you are ready for the next step: How to invest the savings. Again, this is where people end up making the worst possible mistakes.

The most common mistake people make is to invest in mutual funds, bought through their financial advisors.

I've been there, done that. I was a financial advisor for fifteen years. And I sold mutual funds. I found out the hard way that investing in mutual funds is not investing at all. It's gambling. You should not be buying these Weapons of Financial Destruction (WFD). If you want to become financially independent, once we go through the Four Steps Millionaire Formula, you'll see that the Four Steps Millionaire Formula is far superior to investing in mutual funds.

Let's see how the CFI step works. You need to find a suitable CFI. A CFI could be any of the following:

1. A business,

2. A property, or

3. A bond.

The easiest example for me to use to illustrate this strategy is to use property.

What kind of property? Essentially, property can be grouped into two categories—commercial or residential. Examples of commercial properties are office buildings, warehouses, movie studios, etc. Examples of residential properties are houses, apartment buildings, townhouses, etc.

For the purpose of our example, let's use residential property, and within that category, let's use a house. A house is a great place to start investing in property. Why? Because people need a place to live; it's a necessity of life. Therefore, a house is a good asset to own, whether for yourself to live in, or as an investment.

However, the key thing is that in the beginning of your journey to financial independence, you should not buy a house for yourself to live in. It should be one that you intend to rent out. That is one of the biggest mistakes I made in my financial career. When I had accumulated some savings, I bought a large house to live in, one that I would have to pay off by the dint of my own efforts. Nope, that's not what you want to do. You want your *tenant* to pay off your loan. This strategy is known as using leverge. Meaning that you use the bank's money to buy the house, and you use your tenant's money to pay off the loan. How smart is that? It's plenty smart.

Except when it goes wrong. There are plenty of things that can go wrong, which you must avoid. I will cover these later in Chapter 7 (*How to Invest Money*). For now, let's just wrap our heads around the CFI strategy and see why it's an essential part of the Four Steps Millionaire Formula.

Let's say you own a house as a property investment. Every month your tenant pays you rent. You take that rent and pay down your mortgage. We will assume that you are simultaneously making money from other sources, as well, for instance a job or a business. What you need to do with your savings from these other sources is to put it towards paying down the mortgage. You shouldn't use your savings to incur additional spending; that is, don't take your saving to go buy a flashy new car, or a bigger house to live in, or to go on a big vacation. No. *Focus* your efforts on paying down the mortgage on that investment property. Some years later you will have a paid-off house. Now you have some *passive income*. And that, dear reader, is your goal: Money that comes in without you having to actively work for it.

That's what you're gunning for.

Passive income.

You do not have to actively work for the rental income from the house that you bought with the bank's money, which your tenant helped you pay off. Your rent gets paid while you sleep, while you eat, or while you play.

Aha!

Capish?

Step 4: Generate Passive Income in excess of Living Expenses

Do you know what *Passive Income* (PI) is? We just saw it in the preceding step. Yes, it stands for money that comes in without you having to actively work for it.

To understand the rest of this step, you also need to understand the term *Living Expenses* (LE). These are expenses like food, rent, Internet, telephone, bus fare and automobile repairs. Basically, all the expenses you need to incur in order to live a moderate life. (No luxuries yet; they are to come. You can live the life of your dreams if you just follow this plan. It's how the rich do it.)

This step explains that once you have created your first bit of PI, you need to do it all over again. You buy another house and work on paying it off. And then another, and another, until ...

$$PI > LE$$

That is, until your passive income is in excess of your living expenses. I recommend that you keep repeating this plan until:

$$PI > 120 \text{ percent of LE}$$

Why? Let me explain. If your annual living expenses are $100,000 per annum (pa), then you need to keep repeating the above strategy until your rental income is greater than 120 percent of your living expenses. That is, you need to grow your passive income until your PI is more than $120,000.

Why do you need to grow your passive income to a level greater than your living expenses? Wouldn't it be fine if you grew it until it was equal to your living expenses? That is, if your passive income hit $100,000, wouldn't that be just fine?

No doubt, it would be a good job. How many people on this earth have passive income equivalent to their living expenses? My guess is very few, probably no more than one percent. So, yes, well done. But it's not enough. There are more roads on this journey. Here's what I mean:

1. Your living expenses increase each year because of inflation. I grant that it's not such a big problem because your rental income will also increase by the rate of inflation. I am just mentioning this point so that you are aware that there is such a thing as inflation and if you ignore it, it will hurt you.

2. You need to create some money buckets. Use the excess income (in this case $120,000 - $100,000 = $20,000) to allocate into several money buckets. You will need money for the following three buckets:

   a. One for emergencies. For example, your car may need emergency repairs. You don't want to be reaching into your annual living expense budget to pay for these expenses. The reason for this is that if the emergency expense is too big, it could force you to discontinue some essential expenditure, such as life insurance premiums. However, if you die, your family would not benefit from a life insurance pay-out. Remember, what life insurance salespeople say: The time to buy life insurance is before you need it. You do not want to discontinue your life insurance premium payments, no matter what.

b. One for additional CFIs. You may want to live a life of luxury. The sensible way to go about doing that is to acquire additional CFIs to pay for your luxuries; you should not be paying for them. For instance, say you want a bigger house. You invest in a CFI, for example, a house that you can rent out. You pay it down over time with money from your tenant's rent and your own earnings. Once that's done, then go and buy your bigger house. By all means take a loan to buy that bigger house. It's fine. Because you will use the rent from the CFI to pay for the loan payments on that big house.

c. One for opportunities. Here is the prize in the box of Cracker Jacks. If you've made it this far on your journey to financial independence, then you will likely be investment smart. You will be able to spot opportunities where others can't. And you will need money to go after those opportunities. If your investment in such a venture fails, then what's the problem? None. Your living expenses are taken care of by the passive income you've already built up. Your luxury house is taken care of by the CFI you bought for that particular purpose. You're fine. A little disappointed emotionally, but you'll get over that. But what if this new investment sky rockets and multiplies your money? Wow! Then you're playing in the big time.

You're done now.

Once you have completed step 4, you are there! You have arrived. You are financially independent. Congratulations. Now you can enjoy your life, help others, do whatever you want. Cheers!

The Four Steps Millionaire Formula can be composed into an acronym as follows:

M S I P (pronounced em-sip) where:

Step 1: M = **M**ake money.

Step 2: S = **S**ave

Step 3: I = Invest in cash Flowing **I**nvestments

Step 4: P = Generate **P**assive income in excess of Living Expenses

This is your checklist to remember the Four Steps Millionaire Formula—MSIP. Please commit it to memory.

Let me enhance your understanding of the Four Steps Millionaire Formula even further. Let me tell you a story of the rich man versus the poor man. It is a true story, and one that incorporates the above described formula for great wealth. It is a formula that has been successfully applied by rich men and women all over the world, time and time again, over millennia.

The rich man is one of my former financial advisory clients—let's call him John—and the poor man is me. The reason I am using myself as an example is that back then I had not learned what I want to teach here. It was a hard lesson to learn. You must avoid this mistake if you are going to get rich.

See Figure 1 below.

Figure 1: Rich Man vs. Poor Man

Rich Man

	Year 1	Year 5	Year 9	Year 12	Year 14
Income:	$100.00				
Expenses:	$60.00				
Savings:	$40.00	$200.00			

	Property 1			
Income:	$20.00	($200 x 10%)		
Savings:	$40.00	(From his business)		
Total Savings:	$60.00	$240.00	(4 years)	

	Property 2			
Income:	$24.00	($240 x 10%)		
Savings:	$60.00	(From $40 + $20)		
Total Savings:	$84.00	$252.00	(3 years)	

	Property 3			
Income:	$25.20	($252 x 10%)		
Savings:	$84.00	(From $40 + $20 +$24)		
Total Savings:	$109.20	$218.40	(2 years)	

Poor Man

				Property 4		
House:	$225.00			Income:	$21.84	($218.40 x 10%)
+ 9 Years				Income from Property Investments:	$69.20	($20 + $24 + 25.20)
House:	$225.00			Total Passive Income:	$91.04	
Savings:	$100.00					
Total Passive Income:	Nil			Total Passive Income (Adjusted for rental increases):	$100.00	

I will take you back in time. My client and I were both 35 years old. Both of us owned our own individual businesses. At the end of the first year of this comparison, our financial situations were exactly the same. For convenience, say we both earned $100, spent $60 in living expenses and taxes,[*]

and saved $40. You will see this illustrated in Figure 1. At the end of the next five years we had both accumulated $200 in savings. Again, you will see this illustrated in Figure 1. Please continue to refer to Figure 1.

At this point John bought his first investment property. He used up his entire $200 in savings to buy the investment property with cash. Let's assume that it gave him a 10 percent pa rental return. At that point, he had an additional ($200 × 10 percent) $20 every year from rental income, *over and above* his business earnings of $100 pa available to him. Therefore, every year he could save $40 from his business earnings and $20 from his rental income for a total of $60 pa.

This meant that, after an additional four years, he had another ($60 × 4) $240 saved up. So he went out and bought another rental property.

Let's assume that it gave him a 10 percent return or ($240 × 10 percent) $24 pa. Now he was saving ($40 + $20 + $24) $84 pa. In another three years he had saved up an additional ($84 × 3) $252. And off he went to buy another rental property, which again, let's assume, gave him a 10 percent annual rental return or $25.20 pa.

At that point John was saving ($40 + $20+ $24+ $25.20) $109.20. Two years later he repeated the process. He bought a property for ($109.20 × 2) $218.40, with a 10 percent pa rental return or ($218.40 × 10 percent) $21.84 pa.

Now let's see the magic. His total *passive income* from his rental investments is ($20 + $24 + $25.20 + $21.84) $91.04 pa. A total of (5 + 4 + 3 + 2) fourteen years have elapsed since he started this plan. He is now 49 years old. Let's just say that with rental increases earned over the years his passive income is $100 up from the $91 we previously calculated, which is the equivalent of what he is earning from his business. Therefore, if he quits going to work, he will be just fine because the passive income is sufficient to pay for all of his living expenses.

Financially, this puts John into a fine position. He can then take the next bit of savings from his business income, that is $40, and buy a bigger house, add to his emergency fund, or go for broke on an exciting new venture. Let's say he decides to hold off on the house and after adding to his emergency fund, decides to invest in an exciting new venture, and the new venture explodes upwards 10 times. He now has an additional $400 to play with. And he may not even have had any taxes to pay on those gains. The tax code is created to encourage people to get rich. Because rich people create jobs in the economy, build houses and do charitable work. The government loves rich people, and so should we.

Right, now let's look at me. Remember, this is a true story. Faiz saved $200 in the first five years and then decided to buy a magnificent house worth $225. It was a beautiful house and still is; Faiz still lives in it. But it was a big financial mistake. One of the biggest financial mistakes Faiz will ever make. You'll soon find out how.

Immediately after Faiz bought his big house, he had a small mortgage to pay off, equivalent to ($225 − $200) $25. Plus his living expenses had gone up; the costs of maintaining a larger house are greater. A larger house comes with additional expenses from property taxes, gardeners' bills, fees for pool maintenance and so forth. Jump forward nine years; Faiz has managed to pay off the mortgage and accumulated a small amount of savings, $100.

Let's compare the two scenarios. Faiz has a large house, but no passive income. His client has a small house but sufficient passive income. Faiz still has to go to work to earn a living. His client does not.

The key lesson to note is that while Faiz had been focusing on consumption, his client had been focusing on creating passive income. Faiz was building a lifestyle while his client was building wealth.

Aha! That's it! That's the difference between the rich man and the poor man. The rich man builds wealth while the poor man builds a lifestyle.

That's why the rich man is FREE early in his life and the poor man is a SLAVE all of his life.

Accordingly, I've been there, done that. I have been on the road to financial loss—I have made the mistake of putting my lifestyle expenditures ahead of my wealth-building expenditures. I don't want that for you. That's why I will continue to state: "Build your financial ark as fast as possible."

Good financial moves will get you there faster. Bad financial moves will not only delay you, but potentially may cause you never to get there. You may die along the way from poverty. That's why I am adamant that anything that gets in your way must be stopped.

In this chapter you have learned the formula for great wealth. This is how most of my clients got rich. Even those who inherited their wealth had been groomed by their parents to understand that this is the system used to maintain or grow inherited wealth. Otherwise, wealth can be lost all too easily. This is also how I went from practically zero to half a million dollars in thirteen years. Not by buying retirement accounts and mutual funds. I would probably have reached that milestone a lot faster had I known about the Four Steps Millionaire Formula from the start.

In his book, *The Pirates of Manhattan*, Barry Dyke has a chapter entitled: "Never met a man who made his millions in Mutual Funds."[16] I never did either. As I mentioned above, I did not become a self-made "half-millionaire" by buying mutual funds. Nor did any of my former clients.

But adverts by the mutual fund industry claim that buying mutual funds is the way to wealth. The siren call of misleading financial information put out by the mutual fund companies must be stopped. By whom? First, by people like Barry Dyke and me. We are financial professionals; we have the experience to look under the rocks and find what you may not be able to see. We need to use our voices to educate you, the masses.

Second, by the masses, that is, by people like you, the naïve consumer who has been perhaps misled by the financial services industry for long enough. How can you end this possible fraud? It's pretty simple. All you have to do is raise your hands and say:

> "No! No more 'investing' in these WFD (Weapons of Financial Destruction). I will follow the Four Steps Millionaire Formula like countless rich people before me and become financially independent the proven way. I will invest in products that make me rich, not in products that make me poor while making the financial services industry rich."

Now let's look at the Four Steps Millionaire Formula in more detail. This is covered in Chapters 5 through 7.

Chapter 5: How to make money

As we saw in the previous chapter, the first step on the way to millions is to make money, or in other words, to generate income. Please understand that your income plays the biggest role in your financial success. The higher your income the greater your opportunity to create wealth. Therefore, figure out how to maximise your income.

How can you create income? There are essentially two ways to do so:

1. First, through a job, or

2. Second, through entrepreneurship.

Obviously, I am partial to the latter, since that is the way of the future. For reasons that we covered in Chapter 1 (*The New World*), jobs are going to become scarcer. However, many of you will need to start off in a job, or are currently in a job, and it is certainly possible to become financially independent through a job, but it will take longer than if you go down the entrepreneurship route. In a job you cannot control how fast your income grows. Nevertheless, even if you hold down a job for your entire working life, if you diligently follow the Four Steps Millionaire Formula, you will make it.

If you are interested in going down this route, then you must also be knowledgeable on the following two topics:

1. How to get a job and

2. How to keep increasing your income at your job.

Both of these topics are discussed further in Chapter 15 (*New Graduate*).

Start a business

What is the second way you can make money? Become an entrepreneur. There is nothing that will build your wealth faster than a well-run business. You can become financially independent on a modest income, but to get seriously rich, you will need to get into your own business.

Today there is no longer job security in the world. The job route is a lot more risky than the entrepreneurial one. However, because entrepreneurship seems to be shrouded in mystery, most people shy away from it.

However, I'm about to reveal the secret of becoming an entrepreneur. In fact, the best part about entrepreneurship is that it is a learnable skill. Very few people are born with the knowledge of how to run a successful business. If they were born with those skills, it is because they were born into rich families. Those families teach entrepreneurship to their children as the children grow up. That's fantastic. But it's only the very few that have access to such privilege. There are thousands of other businessmen who have had to learn the skill in other ways, either by studying it, or more likely by doing it. Failing. Then getting up and doing it again. Failing. Then doing it again until finally understanding how to run a successful business.

The purpose of this book is to save you from much of the *failure* parts of the above story. I can't save you from all of the *failure* parts because failure is not unusual when you get into business. But your job is to learn how to minimise the risk of failure and the incidents that might lead to it.

I am going to teach you how to start a successful business. In broad terms. Then you can figure out the details.

Startup Checklist:
Here is my startup checklist:

The first thing when it comes to starting a business is to complete a business plan. It sounds awfully boring. And it is. But a business plan is the difference between success and failure. If you don't do one, it is likely you will fail. Why? Simply because the process of thinking through the business plan will help you to identify whether there is an opportunity at all, or is it just a pie-in-the-sky idea (and if you find it's the latter, that's not the end of your business career). The initial business plan need not even be too formal. Just lots of thought and writing in a journal will do. You will also need to research your idea, down on the ground, out there in the real world. This is the toughest part of your business planning process. But you just have to do it.

As Steven Blank, startup guru and Stanford University Professor, explains, during the dot com boom of the late 1990s, many a hi-tech startup decided that customer research was unwarranted, that it knew exactly what the customer wanted, and that there was no need to do the research in the real world. The product could be built sitting in an office, marketed based on information in the office, and that customers would beat a path to buy the product. That's why, he continues to explain, many a hi-tech startup went bust in the subsequent dot com bust, losing billions of dollars of investor's good, hard-earned money.[17]

What a waste of money, time and effort, I say. The work of the business plan just has to be done. Look nobody said that getting into business is easy. If it were, everybody on earth would be a businessman and rich. Because it's hard, therein lies the opportunity. What makes it hard?

Simply, a word that nobody likes—WORK. If you don't want to work, then forget about it. Close this book. Resign yourself to mediocrity, financial lack, worries, stress and unfulfilled dreams.

But if you are willing to work then the world is your oyster. A life of plenty, happiness, joys and fulfillment can be yours.

Million Dollar Tip: The key to becoming an entrepreneur is to have the mindset of an entrepreneur. What entrepreneurship educators most often teach are the tools and methodology of entrepreneurship: how to do a business plan, how to segment a market, how to raise money. But those are just tools and methodology; theory that you can learn and, then, go nowhere with. As a practicing entrepreneur, I can tell you that what really matters is whether or not you have the mindset of an entrepreneur. If you do, everything else will fall into place.

Again, the good news is that the mindset of an entrepreneur is something you can learn how to adopt. Once you know what it is, you can adopt it. And the moment you do, you are instantly a *certified entrepreneur*.

Let me show you what it takes to become an entrepreneur. Based on my research and in working with entrepreneurs for fifteen years I have come to realise that there are essentially three differences between an entrepreneur and an employee. I call these the *Entrepreneur Traits*. These are:

1. An entrepreneur is self-reliant. He believes that it's up to him. He is responsible for the outcomes in his life.[18]

2. An entrepreneur believes that he is not entitled to any compensation unless he produces—that is, he puts out something of value to the world.[19]

3. An entrepreneur does not worry about guaranteed outcomes. He lives with the risk of the unknown future as being part and parcel of the entrepreneurship strategy.[20]

Let's compact these Entrepreneur Traits into an acronym as follows:

S P O (pronounced "Spo").

Where:

> S = an entrepreneur is Self-reliant. He believes that it's up to him. He is responsible for the outcomes in his life.
>
> P = an entrepreneur believes that he is not entitled to any compensation unless he Produces—that is, puts out something of value in the world.
>
> O = an entrepreneur does not worry about guaranteed Outcomes. He lives with the risk of the unknown future as being part and parcel of the entrepreneurship strategy.

These are extremely powerful concepts. They represent the mindset of an entrepreneur. An entrepreneur only comes into existence once he embraces these three Entrepreneur Traits.

The Entrepreneur Traits are the foundation of becoming an entrepreneur. First, once a person decides to become self-reliant, he immediately acquires freedom. Freedom from a boss and from a ceiling to his income. A successful entrepreneur client of mine once told me that the reason he decided to quit his job and go into business, was because, when he was a child, a businessman friend of his father's had told him: "When you get a job, you are writing a cheque to God that you want exactly such and such an amount of money in your lifetime and no more; you limit your income. If you don't want a limit to your income, then never get a job." Recalling those fateful words, he quit his job, and said to himself, "No matter what happens to me financially, I am not going to get a job again." As they say, the rest is history. The man is hugely successful today.

Second, once a person has decided to become self-reliant, he has to come up with a way to serve other people. The more he serves other people, the more likely he is to acquire money for himself. Producing—that is, putting forth value into the world is how people get rich. No value-add, no business. That's the reason a lot of businesses go under. They are not putting forth value into the world.

Third, he accepts that the eventual outcome of his endeavours is unknown. He does not fall into depression and quit working when the going gets tough. Once he has done his homework, then it's full steam ahead. That's how an entrepreneur should work; namely, do the steps to minimise your risk, but know that if the research is saying "Go, man, go!" at some point you'll just have to say to yourself "Jump, dude! Get in the game!"

If you want to become an entrepreneur, it's as simple as embracing the three Entrepreneur Traits: SPO. Then you have become a *certified entrepreneur*. If you don't have the mindset, the methodology and the tools are of no use whatsoever. If you've decided to become an entrepreneur, good luck to you. May you be the next Bill Gates, or at least, the richest man or woman on your street.

As I said, the first step in starting a business is doing a business plan. It is not the purpose of this book to show you how to compile a business plan. You should take a course on how to do one. However, in what follows, I have covered the elements of a simple one. Basically, all you have to do is come up with the answers to this list of points and you will have a functioning business plan.

1. Establish the need:

Clearly identify the customer need.

Think through the following: What problem does your product solve or how does it make a person's life better? What are people hungry for?

After exiting my financial advisory practice, I had the notion of doing camping shows for television. I am a camping enthusiast and I thought that I could make a living out of my hobby (a big mistake startups make, as I explain here). I even got my show approved for broadcast by Botswana Television and went on the road to find sponsors for the show.

When I got out into the market to find sponsors (*customers*), I was promptly turned down by all of the major players. I did find a few small sponsors, but it would not have made me enough money. I immediately saw that there wasn't sufficient interest in the project, and shelved it. (Hence, hobbies do not necessarily make for a good business idea!)

How do you find out if there is a need for your product or service? Quite simply, you go out and ask your potential customers. You don't try to read their minds sitting in your office. You actually have to hit the streets and ask *them*: What do you want?

This is called market research. For this purpose you will need to do a survey, which will consist of a questionnaire. In coming up with questions, you will need to think about what you want to learn. For example, you may want to learn if there is a need for your product, or whether the current solutions in the marketplace are sufficient, or whether people want any improvements. Ask people: What are you looking for? What do you want? What do you use right now? Will you buy this product? What price will you be willing to pay? Where do you currently shop for such products? The questions simply depend on what you want to know.

Another important point in conducting the survey is to ensure that you find the right people to survey. Make sure that you know who your target market is. That is, what are their demographics?

- Who are they?

- Men or women?

- Age range?

- Income level? etc.

Once you know your potential customers, those are the people you want to direct your questions to. If you ask your questions to the wrong people, you will get useless information. For example, if you want to sell golf clubs, don't go to the cricket ground to ask the cricketers. You need to find out where people who buy golf clubs hang out, and go there to talk to them. Perhaps the local golf club. If you are selling an automotive part, then go to the local auto parts shops, and ask the managers or the customers who frequent the auto parts shops.

2. The Product/Service

You need to be able to explain your product or service in a simple way. If you are intending to sell a physical product then you must be prepared to answer a lot of questions about it: How will it be manufactured? How will it be delivered to the market place?

If you are providing a service you need to clearly articulate the answer to this very important question: *What do you do?* You will often be asked this question, and you don't want to be tongue-tied when it comes your way. For this purpose, I would suggest that you come up with an *elevator pitch*, which answers the question clearly and succinctly. An elevator pitch is a short statement that describes what you do and how it can benefit people. To craft an elevator pitch, I suggest that entrepreneurs come up with a statement that answers the following two questions:

a) I/We do Y (describe what you do),

b) So that Z (how this product/service solves their problem—the benefit)

For example, using this system, I have come up with the following elevator pitch for my financial education business:

Q: "So Faiz, what do you do?"

A: Faiz: "I help people understand matters of personal finance so that they can live a life free of money worries."

Let me break that down for you:

a) I/We do Y (describe what you do)—I help people understand matters of personal finance.

b) So that Z (they can solve their problem—the benefit)—so that they can live a life free of money worries.

Now test it on a few people. Tweak it if necessary. Once it's done, then memorise it and deliver it with enthusiasm.

3. How will you differentiate yourself?

Note a critical point here. When coming up with a business idea, you do not necessarily have to come up with a brand new idea. On the contrary, your best bet is to focus on an existing product or service, just do it in a superior way. The reasoning behind this is that if a market already exists for the business idea, then people are already buying the product. The market demand is proven. It is not just a pie in the sky idea.

Can you crack into such a space? Sure you can. Google was not the first search engine. Facebook was not the first social media site. But now they dominate their space, *simply because what they offer is superior to the competition's solution.*

Even in the ho-hum industry of grocery retail, a new company can appear out of nowhere and be a success. For instance, a supermarket chain called Choppies sprang up in Gaborone in the early 2000s. Previous to that, the group had just two stores for many years, but then expanded into a multi-store chain, seemingly overnight. In a matter of a few years they became a market leader. Why? Because they offered products at cheap prices, but in an upper class shopping environment—clean, well-lit, fully stocked and spacious stores. Middle and upper income customers were happy to migrate from other vendors because the value proposition was superior: Get cheaper groceries without lessening the shopping experience. Lower income customers loved it. It became their choice of where to shop for groceries. The supermarket space is crowded the world over, but an imaginative and innovative company came in and seized 30 percent of the market share in just a few years.

Subsequently, the company went public and made the owners multi-millionaires, many times over. The point is that if you want to go into business there is no particular need for you to come up with a brand new idea.

But you do need to be clear on why your product or service will succeed. Why would customers choose your product or service over that of the competition? The way you do this is to study the competition. Start a spreadsheet and list some of the major competitors in your line of business. Then start listing the key information for the competition. For example, their price points, the products they offer, the customer experience, the customer service. Then see if what you are offering is different in some way. The object is to figure out how you can differentiate yourself. Remember, in business: if you do your homework you win.

Earlier, we said the second Entrepreneur Trait is that an entrepreneur is one who has figured out that it's his job to produce, or add value. Well now is your moment to think hard about how you can add superior value to your customers.

You must try to go beyond the call of duty. Your job as value-creator is not just to satisfy the needs of your customer. That is sine qua non. But your goal should be to go beyond that; you also want to satisfy your customer's aspirations. Let's take Apple as an example. Apple products are not cheap. But they are superior. Everything from the packaging to the look and feel of the actual product is superior to the competing products. Hence, Apple can charge a higher price. People will pay a higher price for higher value. Make your product or service world class! *That's lifelong income security.*

Other than existing markets, where else can you look to come up with ideas for a business? Ideas are everywhere. You just need to listen to the complaints of people. What problems do they need solved? Then think through the idea in the format of doing a business plan. Is there a successful business lurking in the shadows that you can latch onto and bring to light?

4. Analyse the Opportunity:

a. How large is the targeted customer base:

How many people are there in your targeted customer base? For example, if you are planning to open a store in a particular neighbourhood, how many people live there? Or if your store will be in a shopping mall, what is the foot count per month? You need to know those figures to estimate how many sales you will make. If you plan to sell on the Internet, then your customer base opens up to a global one. But selling on the Internet requires specialised knowledge of Internet marketing. It's not just about throwing up a website. Anybody can do that. You should get a book on Internet marketing to get you started on learning about this important and evolving method of marketing.

You also need to figure out the total dollars that customers in this market space spend on your type of product or service. If the total number of customers or the total number of dollars is small, it may not be worth your while to get into this business.

b. Is the market growing?

You want to be in a growing market. If the market is stagnant or declining, it will be harder and harder for you to make money.

c. Competitive analysis:

We spoke about this in point number 3 (study the competition). You need to understand your competition, in detail. Please follow the spreadsheet approach that I talked to you about. Add any information that you think will help you to see where the competition is falling down and where you can do a different or better job. That's your point of differentiation.

5. How will the business generate revenue (money)

How will you make money from your product or service? Are you going to sell physical products or web (that is, digital) products, or both? How will you deliver the product or service?

And how will you get paid?

The issue of getting paid seems to be such a scary topic for entrepreneurs that they just skip it, hoping that it will take care of itself. Wrong approach. Do not ignore it. You need to know the answer to this question. If there are no sales, then revenue will lag and a financial crisis will loom.

6. Who is on your Team?

Most entrepreneurs think they can do it all by themselves. And yes, that's how most will start. A startup is usually a lean, mean machine. As it needs to be in the beginning. Even Google started in someone's garage. But a startup soon hits a ceiling. It cannot grow because the founding entrepreneur has simply run out of time. Then the entrepreneur finds out that business is not a solo sport. You need people around you who can do the things that you are not good at so you can focus on what you're good at. At a minimum, you will need the people listed below in your business life. In the beginning, it is very likely that you will outsource the work to these people, and they will not even be on your payroll:

> a. An accountant. A very important person this, but it's also very tricky to find the right person. Your accountant is supposed to keep your financial records in order, provide you with good tax advice and submit your tax filings on time. Be careful though. Not all accountants are created equal. Some are good at what they do, and some are not. You will find out by trial and error if your accountant is doing a good job for you. You must not trust him blindly. You need to watch him like a hawk. It seems that you actually need an accountant to watch your accountant.

> The way to minimise a potentially bad experience with your accountant is to get him to do up an engagement letter. This should clearly spell out his responsibilities.

And on this point, as an entrepreneur, you are simply going to have to get used to reading legal documents, line by line. And worse, you will have to get used to reading the small print on documents. Whoever it is that came up with the phrase "the fine print from hell" sure knew what he was talking about.

b. This brings us to the next professional in your team: a lawyer. If you are not comfortable reading the small print, make sure you run your legal documents through your trusted attorney, and have him explain it to you. Again, just like having to watch your accountant, you will have to watch your attorney just as closely. In time, you will find people that you can trust. But before you trust any professional wait until you have had sufficient experience with them. Never allow yourself to trust blindly. Always trust cautiously. This is a million dollar piece of advice.

c. An assistant: Get one as soon as you can afford to. You can't handle everything by yourself, and you need someone that you can delegate the administrative work to. Just be sure you learn to hire intelligently. Having run a business that, at its peak, employed eight people other than myself, the four most important criteria I can give you for staffing are:

i. Never hire a staff member until you absolutely need to. A staff member adds complexity and costs to your business. When you do have to build a team, keep it lean. Having more people does not necessarily equate to a more profitable business nor a happier one.

ii. When you hire, hire a smart person. Check their academic records. Check their references. A dull person is of no use to you. You will end-up re-doing all his work, and eventually firing him.

iii. If he's good, pay him as well as you can. This person is making you money. So pay him accordingly. This is important advice. Help him to fulfill his financial objectives. Consider giving him bonuses or a percentage of gross revenue/commissions. But do not offer profit sharing as then you will be answerable to your employee for the costs incurred in the business. Variable pay is the only way you will keep him for the long run.

Also help him to fulfill his personal career growth objectives. If you can afford it, help him to learn what he wants to, either through on the job training with you or through educational courses offered by external training providers.

7. Risk assessment:

What could go wrong? Ask yourself this question. Brainstorm the answers and make sure you have thought about how to prevent these problems. It is a fact of life that you will not always know the answers to all problems in advance. How can you? It's the first time you are going down this road. It would sure help if you had a roadmap that you could follow. As a minimum, though, you should be aware that problems will arise. Expect them in advance and make an allowance for them. Meaning that you need to set aside money and time for cleanups, emergencies or other exigencies that will surely arise.

For example, make sure that you are backing up all of your computer data. This is a must. In my financial advisory business, in the old days, we were cheerfully carrying on our business without computer backups. Then the inevitable happened. Of course, it was a disaster just waiting to happen. After a thunderstorm, our server failed, and we lost some data. Luckily, we were still "old-timers" back then, and had a hard copy of our data. So the process of rebuilding the data was not impossible, just painful, unnecessary, and time consuming.

In another instance, I was talking with a venerable friend of mine who wanted to start a farming business rearing cattle. The gentleman was in the profession of construction, but he had the notion to quit his construction business and rear cattle. I asked him if he had any experience in such a business. "A little," he replied. "I grew up on a farm when I was a kid."

"Okay," I said. "Do you know that, in Botswana, raising cattle is a risky business? They often contract diseases and die."

"Really?" he exclaimed.

After some further discussions he was more inclined to look into building a few houses and renting them out. That was what he knew how to do well.

I walked away, nonchalantly dusted my hands off and cockily remarked to myself, "Another soul I saved." A few moments later, I added, "Er, thank you, God!"

If all the steps we've talked about so far sound daunting to you, well, they are. For beginners in entrepreneurship, at least. But, tell me, do you remember the first time you tried to ride a bicycle? Was it difficult? Probably it was. Likely you fell off your bike a few times. But, then, after a few attempts it became easier, then gradually, a cinch. It's the same thing with business. You have to *do* to become any good at it.

8. Business Strategies:

  a. Operations:

    Who is on the operations team? These are the people who
    bring in the money: the value-creators, the idea people, and

the sales and marketing people. Probably, it will be just you in the beginning. But think one, two and five years out. What would your ideal operations team look like in each of those years?

b. Administration:

These are the people who work in the background, but are equally important. These are the people who make sure the bills of the company are paid, that customers are served once they've bought your product, and that the office reception is looking neat and tidy. Again, it could be that you are the whole administration department in the beginning. But soon, you must start to hire in this area. Look one, two and five years out. What would your ideal administrative team look like in each of those years?

c. What is your long-term goal:

This is a serious issue. Because this seems like a good time to discuss this, I am going to digress into a really important topic—"Four Ways to making money from a business." Then we'll come back and continue the discussion.

FOUR WAYS TO MAKING MONEY FROM A BUSINESS

If you intend to become an entrepreneur, or are already an entrepreneur, this concept will blow your mind. So listen up. There are only four ways that a business makes you money. And it is a progression of steps. From steps one to step four. Here's how it works:

Figure 2

Step 1:	Step 2:	Step 3:	Step 4:
Salary and Dividends	Buy investments with your savings to give you more passive income	Convert the business into a passive income stream	Sell the business

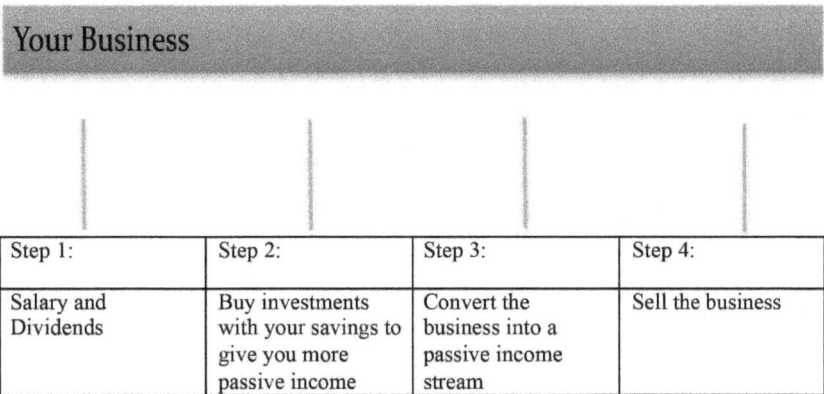

This is such an important idea. In order to help you remember it, we'll call it the "Four Ways Business Formula" for short.

Step 1: Salary or Dividends:

As your business starts to make money you will start to draw a salary. At the end of the financial year you may even have a profit. Let's say your Income Statement looks like this at the end of a particular year:

Income Statement

Sales		$ 100,000
Expenses		
	Accounting fees	$ 5,000
	Rent	$ 12,000
	Salaries	$ 50,000
Total expenses		$ 67,000
Net Profit		$ 33,000

Also, let's say included in the "Salaries" figure (that is, the total staff salaries figure of $50,000) is a salary for you and let's say you earned a salary of $30,000.

Let's also say you decided to take $7,000 as dividends. A dividend comes out of the profit figure of $33,000. Don't worry too much about the mechanics of it. Your accountant will take care of that. For our purposes it means that you received a cheque for $7,000 *over and above* your salary. You now have an additional $7,000 to spend.

The key question is next. What are you going to spend these monies on? First, let's assume that you managed to save 15 percent from your salary of $30,000. My advice to employees is that they should save at least 15 percent from their paycheques. So, in total, let's say that you have the following cash in your hands at the end of the year:

Savings from salary (15% of $30,000; ignore payroll taxes for the purposes of this illustration)	$4,500.00
Dividend cheque	$7,000.00
Total cash in your hand	$11,500.00

Now back to the key question: What are you going to spend this money on? Hmm? A new car? A vacation to a gorgeous Malaysian island? How about dinner at the local Chinese restaurant? I am willing to give you only the last one. If you've been following along up till now, then you know that what you should be doing is building your passive income. As fast as possible.

Step 2: Buy investments with your savings to give you passive income
This means that you should channel all of your savings into Four Ways Business Formula Step 2. Buy cash-flowing investments, which will eventually make you passive income *in excess of your living expenses.*

In a nutshell, you are building your company for the purpose of buying assets.

Folks, you have just witnessed the holy grail of making money from a business. Make money in your business, save furiously, and invest the savings to make passive income. If you invest the money in this way, then in due course, say fifteen to twenty years, you will be financially free. Then one day, no matter how passionate you are about your business, when the time comes that you are tired—you want to work less, or maybe not at all—well, if you have built up sufficient passive income, you will have the freedom to choose whether to keep on working, work less or retire.

This strategy applies to many different types of businesses and even non-business careers.

Even for employees. It's the same principle. Make the money in your job, save like mad and invest in cash flowing investments. Then, one day, you can retire.

Wait a minute. Haven't we seen this strategy before? Sure we have—it's the Four Steps Millionaire Formula.

Just the Four Steps Millionaire Formula, folks; it's just the Four Steps Millionaire Formula. It applies to doctors. It applies to celebrities and sports athletes. (Later in the book I will expound on how the Four Steps Millionaire Formula applies to doctors, celebrities and sports athletes.)

I mentioned above that you have just witnessed the holy grail of making money using a business. Actually, it's *the* holy grail of making money, period. This is how most of my wealthy clients became self-made millionaires. It's how people over millennia have become self-made millionaires.

Step 3: Convert the business into a passive income stream
Step 3 is a great option. But it's not *a necessary* part of the millionaire equation.

Steps 1 and 2 are imperative. Step 3 and step 4 are totally optional, meaning once you have accomplished step 2, you can just close down the business, liquidate (sell) the assets (such as office equipment, vehicles and the like) and live off your income from step 2. If you want to accomplish step 3 and 4, then consider them a kind of bonus prize.

Now if you opt for steps 3 and 4, you will have to plan well in advance to achieve a successful outcome. In the case of step 3, the idea is for you to spend less and less time in the business. You will have to put a management team in place that will allow the business to depend less and less on you. It's a very risky proposition. Lots can go wrong and much of the hard work that you have done over the years can be undone if you don't plan for this one properly. For example, if you have not separated your personal assets from that of the business and the business blows up, meaning it goes bankrupt, then there go your hard won personal assets along with the business. I know of people who own their personal homes inside their operating companies. Bad move. We will talk more about wealth protection scenarios later in this book.

Here's the checklist for step 3:

1) Separate all personal assets from that of the business. Make sure that, if, unfortunately, something does go wrong with the business, then your personal assets cannot be attacked by anyone claiming money from the business. (Your accountant will know how to do the paperwork for this).

2) Move away from operations and into administration. Meaning it is not your job to provide any goods or services to your customers. Let the customers know about this shift. You'll have to handle this change carefully. Many of your customers will be used to dealing with you. It must be a gradual process, where you participate in the operations role less and less. Take a year or so to complete this move.

3) Then reduce your administrative responsibilities, although you will not be able to do away with all your administrative responsibilities. Expect to be involved to some degree in the day to day running of the business. Your goal should be to reduce this to about 15 percent of your work time. Therefore, if formerly you spent 50 hours a week on the business, it will be reduced to 7.5 hours per week, which is probably one half day in the office, and one half day at home working on business matters.

4) The way you will engender steps 2 and 3 is to institute proper controls for the tasks that you used to do, but now want to delegate. Some steps that may be handled in this way include lead generation, cheque signing and purchasing. You will need an expert on business controls such as a Chartered Accountant to guide you in this area.[21]

5) Have an external accountant do up the monthly financial statements (or if you already have an internal accountant, and if you can afford it, get an annual audit). Then check them. Let your staff know that the external accountant must have access to anything and everything, whether it has to do with financial accounting or not, for instance, the human resources filing cabinet where he may browse employee files. This man is your eyes and ears where you cannot be. Pay him well.

6) Do not let your staff sign any legal documents. If the staff has been authorized to do so, beware lest they sign a document that might bind you. If you haven't read it, you do not have the full knowledge of it. One of the Golden Rules of business is to know the terms of any agreement you enter into.

7) Watch the bank account like a hawk. You know the trends in your business. If cash balances are stable or growing quarter on quarter, you're okay. If not, there could be trouble brewing.

Step 4: Sell the business

Basically, the idea here is that the business owner sells the business, walks away with the proceeds, and then depending on how financially well-off he is, he either invests it per step 2, or enjoys the money.

Here's the secret. If you want to sell your business, you must try to make it look as much like the business of step 3 as you can. Pretty it up for sale. And you do that by increasing its passivity. That is, it should depend less and less on you. Then it will sell at a higher *multiple*.[22] Let me explain (see Figure 3).

Figure 3. Valuation Multiples

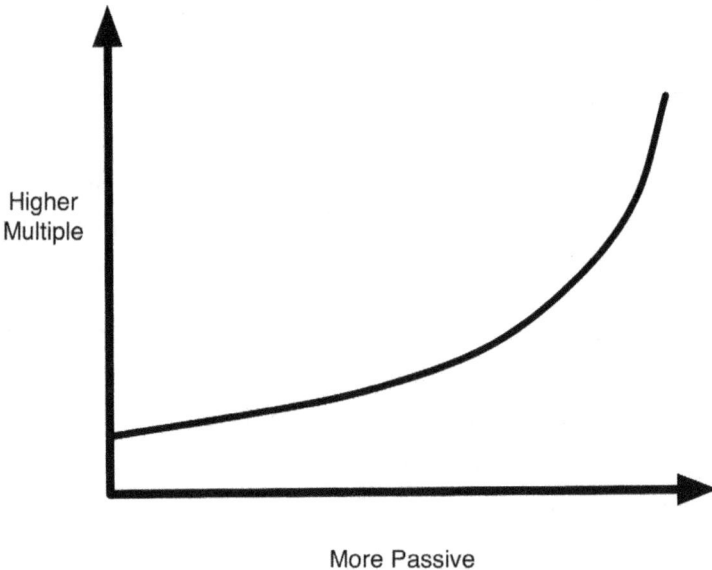

Let's say the net income of your business is $50,000 pa. If the business is such that it cannot run without you, then, you might get two times the net income, which would work out to ($50,000 × 2) $100,000. In this case, we would say *the multiple is 2*. However, if this same business could operate without substantial input from you, then it could sell for a much higher price, say five times the net earnings, or ($50,000 × 5) $250,000. In this case we would say *the multiple is 5*.

Because the valuation methodology of companies varies from industry to industry, your accountant will work out the exact valuation for your company. However, what is constant is that the level of *passivity* of the business plays a key role in determining its price. The more you need to be involved, the less it will sell for, and the less you need to be involved the more it will sell for. Therefore, if you want to sell, take your time to setup systems so that you become irrelevant to the business.

Before you sell your business, give some thought to the influence of tax on the capital that you will receive. As a general proposition, you will be taxed less on the sale of shares than on the sale of the business assets, because in the latter case, in order to realize your capital, you will have to declare an after tax dividend to yourself and suffer the accompanying taxes. The sale of shares would attract either income tax or capital gains tax once off, but no subsequent dividend tax.

Question: The last bit ... uh ... come again, please?

Answer: The sale of your company shares will attract tax. Unless the selling of shares is your business the funds realized will be capital in nature. Note that there are two ways to dispose of your business. The first method is simply to sell the shares to the new owner. You will receive cash for your shares and walk away after paying capital gains tax. The second method of disposing of your business is to sell the assets out of the company. You retain the shares. The business assets will belong to its new owner and your company will now consist not of business assets, but will be full of cash. You now have a choice as to whether to purchase assets in the name of your company or to take the cash and wind the company down. If you take the cash, you will pay possible income tax in the company as well as withholding tax as the receipt of the funds may constitute a dividend.

Note also, that when business assets are sold there will be an element of VAT (Value Added Tax) to take into account. When shares are sold there is no VAT because a company's shares are VAT exempt.

How to get Über-Rich:

The astute reader will have recognised by now that steps one and two of Four Ways Business Formula are actually just the same as the Four Steps Millionaire Formula. So let's start to call Four Ways Business Formula the extension of Four Steps Millionaire Formula. Actually the Four Ways Business Formula steps numbers three and four are the extension, but for the sake of convenience, let's just say Four Ways Business Formula is the extension of Four Steps Millionaire Formula. And the reason that this connection is relevant is that while Four Steps Millionaire Formula will make you rich, Four Ways Business Formula will take you to the next level and make you über-rich. If you want that, you have to master the Four Ways Business Formula. If you just want to be comfortably rich, then the knowledge and implementation of Four Steps Millionaire Formula is sufficient.

So let's assign an alphabet to Four Ways Business Formula steps 3 and 4:

Step 3: P = **P**retty up the business

Step 4: S = **S**ell the business

If we combine the Four Steps Millionaire Formula and Four Ways Business Formula we have another useful acronym for the strategy to get über-rich:

M S I P P S (pronounced em-sips)

Where:

Step 1 (from Four Steps Millionaire Formula): **M** = **M**ake money

Step 2 (from Four Steps Millionaire Formula): **S** = **S**ave

Step 3 (from Four Steps Millionaire Formula): **I** = Invest in Cash Flowing **I**nvestment

Step 4 (from Four Steps Millionaire Formula): **P** = Generate **P**assive income in excess of Living Expenses

Step 3 (from Four Ways Business Formula): P = **P**retty up the business

Step 4 (from Four Ways Business Formula): S = **S**ell the business

We can come back from the digression, which we started several pages back. As you'll see in a moment, it is relevant to completing the discussion we were having earlier on, which was: 8(c) "What is your long-term goal?"

So, what is your long-term goal? Consider a goal that is ten years out. You should try to get a handle on this goal right now, even before you start your business. You now know there are only four ways that your business can make you money, so how do you want to go about making money from your business?

That is, do you want to go only as far as step 2 and just keep building your passive income until someday you decide to exit the business by closing it down?

Or do you want to go on to Four Ways Business Formula step 3 and keep the business as a passive income producing entity? Perhaps you want to work less as discussed above; or perhaps you are planning a succession to your heirs, employees or a trusted manager?

Or do you want to go on to Four Ways Business Formula step 4, where you will sell the business and exit that way?

Someday you will have to leave your business. You need to think through your *exit strategy* today so that you can build a business accordingly. There is nothing wrong with exiting at step 2. That is called a lifestyle business. It made you enough money to retire on. But once the purpose of the business is served, you quit. It can't be turned into a passive income stream or sold because you didn't put those steps into place. If you do go down the Four Ways Business Formula step 3 or step 4 routes, then you need to plan for those outcomes.

The reason you need to think through these options in advance, or at least know that they exist, is that if you decide to build a lifestyle business rather than a saleable business, then you need to make sure that you focus on building on steps 1 and 2 really well. If these are weak, you will never be able to achieve financial independence. If, however, you want to go all the way to a saleable business, then you need to incorporate setting up systems that maximise the proceeds from the sale of your business.

This is important stuff. I hope you got it.

8. Business Strategies (continued):

> d. What are other goals of the business: 90 days, 180 days, one year, three and five years out:

> You need to think through the goals for your business in terms of product creation, revenue generation, cash reserves and premises for each of these periods of time for the next five years. Thereafter, you will think about these for the next five years, and so on.

9. Marketing:

How will you get someone to buy from you? How will you reach out to him? Will it be an on-line or an off-line strategy, or both? On-line includes websites and direct sales strategies (email marketing). Off-line includes print advertising and flyers. You will likely need a combination of both on-line and off-line marketing strategies. These days, some of the most effective marketing is done by employing direct sales strategies, for example, email marketing. This is a specialised marketing technique and a deep discussion of this is beyond the scope of this book. Please get a book on this topic.

Along with knowing some marketing you should also know how to sell. That is also a topic where a deep discussion is beyond the scope of this book, but let me get you started. I started a financial planning business twice on two continents and both times grew them to reasonable figures. The first time was in Canada where I was managing approximately twenty-five million Canadian dollars on behalf of investors, and the second time was in Botswana where I was managing approximately thirty million U.S. dollars on behalf of investors. So I have had to learn how to sell. Let me give you some tips:

i) The first thing is to get inside your customer's mind. Don't try to sell him something that does not address *his* self-interest. Find out what he needs. Do not try to sell what you want to sell him, but sell him what he wants. How do you find this out? You get out on the street, find your potential customer and ask him some questions about the product or service you would like to offer. Does the prospect actually have the problem that you think he has?

ii) Be a great listener. When you land in front of a potential customer, understand the problem he needs solving. Listen intently. Repeat back to the customer what he said. That way you will be certain that what you think you heard is actually what the prospect said. In addition, the customer will feel like you understand his needs. Once the customer feels you understand his needs, he will be inclined to buy from you. Of course, you don't just sell him anything. You match your product or service to his needs.

iii) Hang up a sign. That is, open an office, or a shop, or put up a web site. Tell people what you do and where they can buy your product or service.

iv) Never be shy about charging the appropriate price. Clients pay according to the value they get. So do not try to undercut your price to get a sale. Explain the benefits of your product or service, and if the client doesn't see the value, then go back to the drawing board and do your homework. Maybe you need to offer more value so that you can charge the price that you want. Of course, if you are selling a commodity, for instance, chewing gum, you can't charge a big price. But if what you are selling is knowledge or expertise, it can be very valuable, so don't undercharge for it.

v) Always ask for the order. A lot of salespeople are great at presenting their wares and then forget to ask the customer, "Are you ready to go ahead?" You must ask this question. Without this call to action the customer does not know what the next step is in the buying process. Don't forget about it.

10. Financing your business:

How much money do you need to start your business? Where is it going to come from? My recommendation is that you should *over-estimate* what you will need in order to set up the business and what it will cost you to operate the business until the business starts to bring in cash flow.

Where are you going to get the money? There are several options:

a. Your own savings. I highly recommend this option. Simply because the agenda is your agenda. If you take other people's money then your agenda is no longer your own, it's your investors' agenda. If the money is yours, you don't have anybody to answer to both in the startup stage and thereafter. And if things go awry, then at least you don't have angry investors breathing down your neck.

Warning: Just because you have the money doesn't mean that you should start the business you're thinking of starting. Make sure you have proven the business case before investing a lot of money in it.

b. Friends and family. Avoid this as much as possible. Money is a sensitive issue, and if things turn out badly then it will spoil your friendships and family relations. If you have no choice but to go down this route, then spell out everything in writing, including how the investors can get their money back and how they can lose it. At least, in this way, nobody should complain later that they were not fully informed by you about all the risk and reward aspects the business venture carried with it.

c. A bank. It is very hard to get a loan from a bank for a startup venture, unless you can put up collateral. If you have to offer your personal house as collateral ... ouch ... I'd be very careful! You might consider waiting until you have enough personal savings, and use those rather than put your house on the line.

d. Outside investors. Again, it is very difficult to get monies for a startup from outside investors, such as Venture Capitalists. Usually, your business would have to be a fully functioning business for you to raise capital (capital means money, see FAQ). In addition, consider the fact that you would have to relinquish at least some control of your company. You can try this route, but it is a tough one. Outside investors have just one goal in mind: to make money. On the other hand, your goal may not be to make money at all costs. You may have a conscience, and hence, you could lose control of your venture, your mind, and your soul. Risky approach, this, for starting a new business.

11. Projected Financial Statements:

The term *projected financial statements* refers to financial numbers in the future—numbers that you hope to achieve. You need to be careful with these projections. The numbers can be pulled out of thin air and mean nothing, or you could put a lot of thought into the numbers based on your research. During my fifteen years practicing as a financial advisor, I did financial projections for each subsequent year. At the end of that subsequent year I'd compare the actual results with the projections, and they'd be very close. So if you can do projections with as realistic a view as possible, it will guide you over the next twelve months. You will know if you are on-course or off-course. Without financial projections you are flying blind, and you will not know if you have met your goals. If you realise that you are off-course then you can do whatever is needed to correct course.

For a startup you need to prepare five years of projections. You need to estimate when it is that you will become profitable. Realistically, these numbers are just fluff. No one can see that far ahead with any degree of accuracy. But that's what people recommend for business plans. I say do it, but be conservative in your numbers, until the business actually gets going. Then you have some real life basis on which to make the projections.

Some additional points:

I list below three more points to consider when completing your business plan. Some business plan courses will put these at the beginning of the process of preparing a business plan, but I put them at the end, simply because these are the foundational aspects of your business. How can you possibly formulate these unless you have thought through and worked on the preceding eleven points? However, when presenting your business plan to anyone put these three points first.

12. Mission:

What is the emotional *rason d'etre* for your business? What goal are you trying to achieve? For instance, for me it's to *save lives through financial and entrepreneurship education.*

You need to have a big goal like this for your business. If the goal of your business is just to make you money, then sure, it may do so, but it is likely to stumble and fall when the going gets tough.

As we've spoken about before, you need a really big *why* to be in business. The *why* has to be something that will both encourage and provoke you into carrying on even when the going gets tough. Why are you in this world? It's a big question. You need to answer it. The big *why* for my financial education business is passing on this knowledge to my children and saving the world from the bad financial advice out there in the world today. I know that if I don't teach my children what I know about personal finance and entrepreneurship then I will leave them severely handicapped with respect to achieving financial success in their life. Similarly, if I allow the bad financial advice out in the world today to continue unchecked, then thousands of lives will be lost. These are big *whys*. Some mornings I wake up thinking, 'Why am I putting myself through all this?' Writing a book is no joke. Moreover, maybe nobody will like it. Why don't I just stop all this—putting myself out on a limb?

Then I think to myself, "What about my kids? Who's going to teach them all this information? Information they need to know to become financially independent. And who's going to teach this information to the world? People may die if they continue to spend money on buying trinkets, bigger houses than they can afford, and investing in mutual funds."

When those thoughts cross my mind, it's no problem for me to swing out of bed and hit the computer with a vengeance.

13. Vision:

Where do you see your business being over the long-term? How big will it grow? How many people will it serve?

14. Values:

What do you and your company stand for? For example: Honesty? Courage? Reliability?

These are the components of a business plan.

Who should write your business plan? Your business plan is a very valuable tool. Maybe you need it for external purposes, for example, to raise money. But just as importantly, it's an internal document that confirms or negates your business case and in the case of confirming your business case, it guides your actions going forward. So don't outsource your business plan. Do it yourself. Of course, you may need to get assistance on the technical aspects of the business plan. But make sure you direct all the content that goes into it.

I want *you* to think through all the sections, all the questions. There should be smoke coming out of your ears when you're working on your business plan. It's not an easy document to put together, but the benefit of your doing it yourself is enormously valuable. It forces you to look at your business in a way that ensures you understand your business thoroughly. At the end of such a process, you may realise that you were not on the right track. Great! It saves you from having to put more sweat equity and money into a venture that would likely have failed anyway.

But if that happens—that is, if you realise that you were not on the right track—it doesn't mean it's the end of your career as a businessman.

Instead, maybe what you need to do is—PIVOT. That is, go back into the market research phase to figure out what other product or service will work for you. For example, after I abandoned my camping project, I started to think about what else I could do? And the spark of inspiration was not long in coming. Shortly thereafter, I had the opportunity to discuss personal finance with some young people in their teens and early twenties. I taught them the Four Steps Millionaire Formula. They were fascinated by the concept, and started to discuss how they could bring it into their lives—in a hurry.

That's when the light bulb came on. I realised that youngsters needed financial education, which they could't get from universities. Maybe this was my real mission in life: To help people understand how to become financially successful. The more I thought about it, the more I felt comfortable with the idea. As I write this book one of those youngsters has purchased his first investment property. That's terribly exciting for both of us.

As an entrepreneur you will get a lot out of your business plan if you do it yourself, as long as you realise that it is a living document. That is, it will change many times, even after you have launched a successful business. Hence you must keep updating it.

That's it for my discussion on the business plan. It's your starting point. It does not need to be a formally prepared document. If it's for your internal use, just notes in a computer document accompanied with spreadsheets for the financials and the analysis of the competition is sufficient. If you need a formal document, for instance, to raise funds, then too, it needs to be no more complicated than what we've discussed. In fact, keep it simple. When approaching financiers, remember that they are essentially financing you, not the project. Keep the business plan simple, and make sure you are building up your reputation in the market place. For example, be known as a person who is trustworthy. How would you accomplish that? For example: be known as a person who keeps appointments and pays people on time. If your reputation is solid, you will be in the top one percent of the world's population in terms of your chance for entrepreneurial success.

Let's look at a few other points in your startup checklist:

Licenses and permits: If you're serious about setting up a business you'll need to sort out the relevant licenses and permits. You'll want to contact a business consultant to find out about any licenses or permits you may need to make your business legal.

Corporate Structure: Very important topic. If you are going to get into your own business, by no means should you do it as a sole proprietor. Being a *sole proprietor* means that your business is conducted in your personal name, not through a company. I am surprised how many people get into business as a sole proprietor. This is very risky because, should you get sued for any of your business activities, you risk losing all of your personal assets as well.

For instance, let's say you are a plumber and that you operate as a sole proprietor. This is not an appropriate corporate structure strategy. Let me explain.

Let's say that you ran into an unexpected problem while fixing the geyser of a rather fancy house. The geyser exploded and the house burned down. The owners of the house sue you for one million dollars. Now, if you don't have a million dollars in the bank to give them, then they can go after your personal house. Let's say your personal house is worth $500,000. That's still not a million dollars. Now they can go after your investment property. Let's say that's worth $200,000. Add both properties up and it's still not a million. It's $700,000. So now they can go after your car, and your work tools, your computer, etc. That one mishap could wipe you out. You and your family could be on the street.

On the other hand, suppose you had incorporated the business. Meaning you owned a company and did all your plumbing work through the company. Further, let's say you read this book and learned that your *company should own no assets (other than operational income and debtors)*. Most of your assets are owned outside of the business. Then even if the plumbing company gets sued and goes belly up, you get to keep all those assets: your personal house, your investment property, your car, your work tools and your computer. You may be out of pocket some legal fees, but you can start up a new plumbing business again—appropriately incorporated—all because you were not operating the business under your personal name.

This is called an "Asset Protection Strategy."

And it's huge.

I happened to be attending a meeting at a government institution … somewhere in the world. The meeting was intended to inform the attendees about the particulars of a government *tender* that was on offer. A *tender* means that the government needed work done and had put out an advertisement in the public media to request vendors to apply for the job. To apply for the *tender* a vendor was required to use a particular form as supplied by the government officials. As I glanced through the form I noticed that it asked the vendor to fill out different sections depending on whether the vendor was a sole proprietor or a company.

"Yikes!" it struck me. What that government should have been doing is educating the attendees that "Hey! Please *do not* do business with us as a sole proprietor. Make sure you are incorporated before you fill out this form." Instead, the government form blithely allowed the vendors to make the potentially lethal mistake of doing business with them as a sole proprietor.

I once read a story in the papers of a man who was a builder. He won a large contract. He was contracted to build some two hundred homes for a certain institutional customer. After the builder had built one hundred homes, somehow, his contract was terminated and he was replaced. The contractor suffered major losses as his profits were based on his completing the entire project. Not only that, he owed his suppliers money. The suppliers sued him for everything he owned including his personal house. He ended up homeless and penniless.

I suppose he must have been operating as a sole proprietor.

You get the idea. Do not operate as a sole proprietor. You want to do business? Then you must set up a corporation.

Question: What is a corporation, again?

Answer: Because this topic is so important, and even though I may be at the risk of sounding repetitious, I'm going to explain it again.

A corporation is simply an entity that is separate from you. When you want to start a business, it is important to set up a corporation. You will own it, but it's separate from you.

A corporation is not just a name. It's like a separate box from you. You own it, but you will put your business into that box and your business will operate from the box.

To understand a corporation better, let's contrast it with a sole proprietorship. Basically a business that operates as a sole proprietorship is just the same as you operating the business; there is no separation between you and the business.

The big difference between the two entities is that if Joe Smith Corporation gets sued for anything, Joe Smith's personal assets are protected from the lawsuit. The corporation is separate from Joe Smith. However, if Joe Smith, sole proprietor, gets sued for anything, his personal assets can also be lost (if he loses the lawsuit).

So, if you're planning to get into business, the first thing you want to do is go to your accountant and set up a corporation.

However, it should be noted that the protection that a corporation affords will not apply in the event that "the corporate veil is pierced"—that is, when a court holds the shareholders personally liable for business debts. This is usually when shareholders are proven to be negligent or to have a willful intent to harm the company.

Once you have set up a corporation, make sure that any contract you sign is in the name of the corporation, not you personally.

If you sign a rental agreement, it should read: This Lease agreement, between the Landlord and "Sample Corporation" (that is, your corporation). You may represent your corporation as the signing authority for the rental agreement, but the rental agreement is between the Landlord and Sample Corporation, not between the Landlord and John Doe (you).

Ditto for any other contract you sign. It must be between your corporation and the vendor or customer.

Beware of signing a personal surety with respect to your corporation debts. A personal surety will strip away the protection that a corporation affords.

Regarding operations as a sole proprietor, at some point a sole proprietor will have to register as a VAT (Value Added Tax) vendor. It may be impossible to deregister as a VAT vendor, and if problems arise with tax authorities, those problems will be very personal.

Trusts

Another type of asset protection strategy that you need to be aware of is a *trust*. A trust allows you to distance yourself from your personal assets. So, if you ever get sued for anything personally, you cannot lose the assets sitting in the trust. Smart entrepreneurs use trusts to protect their personal assets.

For example, how does one live in a home, but not personally own it? In many jurisdictions around the world, this process is accomplished by establishing a trust and having the trust own the house (or own the company that owns the house). This is a complex legal process. It is time-consuming to set up and very costly. But if you have any intention of getting rich, then the time to start this process is early on in the game. From an asset protection perspective, you are much safer going on your financial independence journey without owning any assets in your personal name. If you are an entrepreneur, then, as we discussed earlier, you are a producer. This means you are doing things, sometimes not necessarily knowing all the issues that lie ahead. You can't. Otherwise you would not be an entrepreneur. If you were obsessed with being one hundred percent perfect, you'd be stuck in analysis paralysis and you would never actually get moving with any live projects.

As a producer, you may have a few problems along the way. For example, say your customers do not pay you on time. This might then cause cash flow problems that lead to insolvency (bankruptcy) of the business (that's why I tell you a little later on to take a 50% deposit up-front for your product or services). If you have signed personal sureties for credit, the creditors could come after your personal assets. However, when your personal assets are placed in a trust, then the creditors cannot touch them. Hence, the assets in the trust are free from the risks associated with operating a business. If you have built up a trust estate, it will give you great peace of mind, and encourage you to take entrepreneurial risk.

The point of this discussion has been to encourage you to look into and consider forming a trust in due course. Find a competent trust attorney to guide you through the intricacies of how to set up a trust.

Cash Reserves vs. Greed: Just know that any money that comes in from your customers is not your money that you can spend on personal items. A whole host of your business partners need to be paid before you get paid. Yes, you will need to take a salary, but, again, make sure that your salary is minimal, so that the other people that you do business with are being paid before you pay yourself. If you are a bad bill payer, word will get around and key partners that you need in your business will desert you.

Be patient. Your time to make big money from your business will come. But you must let your business breathe until it gets there. And one of the most important ways you can make it breathe is not to bleed it dry of cash reserves, which means unused cash piled up in the bank. Let the cash reserves grow inside your business for the first two to three years. Thereafter, if you have a healthy business, all you have to do is follow Four Ways Business Formula (MSIPPS). And you will be rich. But get greedy and you will not make it.

Let me share with you a wonderful saying we have in the financial services business with respect to investing in stocks. When you buy a stock that seems to be going up and up, the appropriate strategy is that you have to be willing to get out of the stock at some point and crystallise your winnings. If you wait too long the stock may come crashing down, and you could lose all your winnings. Don't get greedy.

This applies to other types of investments, as well. In my travels overseas during 2012, I met Ravi, a gentleman who had bought some properties in India in 2009. The properties had appreciated significantly by 2012. Ravi had bought the properties using leverage (he borrowed the money; it was on loan) and asked my advice about whether or not to hold onto the properties. His theory was that the Indian property market would continue to rise. On the other hand, he was aware that properties in the USA, where he lived, appeared to be at rock bottom prices. I told him to encash the Indian properties. "Don't get too greedy," I told him. "If you've made a good buck, get out. Especially since you have no intention of holding the properties forever."

I haven't met Ravi since. But I've been following the USA property market, and from that time in 2012 to the time of writing this book, the property prices in the USA have gone up. In Ravi's case he was interested in holding his USA property investments for a long time, focusing on earning cash flow rather than capital gains (price appreciation of the investment—in this case the property), if he followed my advice, he ought to be happy today. He would have crystallised the profits from his Indian property investments and invested them in the USA at a time when he was able to get monumental yields of twenty percent. (For a definition of *yield*, see Chapter 7 (*How to Invest Money*).

Just one more point to add here. Another option that the aforementioned gentleman had been thinking about was to use the proceeds of his Indian property investments to buy a bigger house in the USA for himself. Here's the clash: On the one hand, if he used the proceeds from his Indian properties to buy investment properties in the USA and then rent them out, the cash flow would be sufficient to allow him to retire. Let's call this plan A. On the other hand, if he bought a personal house for himself to live in, it would use up all of his money, and he would have had to start the investment process from scratch. And he would have had to continue depending on his paycheque from his job to earn a living. Let's call this plan B.

The answer, I told him, is that it all depended on his wife. If she was willing to continue to live in a small house, then, financially speaking, plan A was superior to plan B. If she wanted the bigger house, "Well, then you're stuck. You'll have to go for plan B, but you will have to continue working for many years to come before you can retire."

That's when Ravi gave me the good news. He said, "Actually it's my wife who wants me to buy the investment properties and not move into the bigger house. She is a working woman, too. If we buy the investment properties she'll be able to retire. That's what she wants."

I breathed a sigh of relief. "You are a lucky man," I told him. "You have a smart wife."

Additionally, with respect to cash reserves, do not become a profitable company on paper with no cash in the bank. Do not make sales on credit.

Avoid this if you can. At a minimum ask for 50 percent deposit from your customers before starting the work or supplying the goods. There is no point in being a profitable company ... on paper ... and then going bankrupt because your customers failed to pay you on time. Avoid this if you can. Ask for the deposit. This is a million dollar idea.

Dear budding entrepreneur, you now have enough. You're never going to know it all. That's the difference between a failure and a successful person. A failure is easy to predict. He just never gets going. On the other hand a successful person says, 'I don't know how all of this works, but let me go ahead anyway.' I would much rather bet on the latter; those are better odds. Get out there and start your business. If you already have a business make it soar to new heights. You can do it. The only thing that can stop you now is your own fear. What will get you over your fear is your *why*. When the going gets tough, or the doubts start appearing in your mind, or you're feeling lazy, the only thing that will move you forward is your *why*. If your *why* is big enough, you will overcome any obstacle in your way.

Do your homework, and then go for it. What's the worst that can happen? You might fail? So what? Successful businessmen fail many times in their business careers. Whenever I asked a former client whether or not he had ever failed, he would enthusiastically respond, "Many times! You go up, then you go down, then you go up, then you go down."

But when saying this, there was always a light in their eyes, a passion in their voice. Nobody likes to fail, but entrepreneurs just take it in their stride. If they fail, they get up, they try again until someday, they get it right. They don't look at failure as *rejection*. I often asked my entrepreneur clients how many correct decisions have they made in their life. In almost every case the reply was "50 percent." And yet they were successful. This is an important insight. If you are only going to get half your decisions right and still be successful, the odds of being successful are within anybody's reach.

The most important strategy when going into business is to *get in the game*. There will be much learning that will occur along the way, which you could not have anticipated no matter how much you prepared. Preparation is important, no doubt, but you will have to know when to stop preparing, and when to get going.

If you do the business startup homework described in this chapter, you're ready to start a business. Don't delay. Don't worry about failure. It can happen, but you've done a lot of work to mitigate the downside risks.

As an entrepreneur you are a gift to mankind. Your product or service could help someone. It could change a life; or it could save a life. Do not delay!

Go for it!

Money-making ideas

The best way to come up with a money-making idea is to be on the lookout for problems that people are trying to solve. Solve any of those problems and you could have a profitable business on your hands.

To generate new business ideas you should start a journal. Create a brain bank. Whenever a new idea hits you write it down. If you don't write it down, you will lose it.

To kick-start your efforts let me give you some money-making ideas:

1. Consulting: Consider providing a consulting service using your current expertise. You could start with providing consulting services to your existing employer and then expand to other companies in your industry.

2. Manufacturing: Can you make something that the market needs? Even preparing and delivering food to local businesses

or the residences of working housewives can fall into this category.

3. Distribution: How can you help a current business get its products out into the market place?

4. Marketing: Do you know something about Internet market-ing? You could help companies promote their goods and ser-vices using online channels.

5. Retail*: This ranges from bakery products to supermarkets to computer equipment.

6. Training: Do you have a skill that other people will pay to learn? For instance, computer software such as Microsoft Word or Excel? Or Apple's OS X? Consider providing one-on-one tutoring or do a workshop.

7. Construction: Are you any good at fixing-up houses? Somebody needs your help.

8. Tourism: Can you set up a bed and breakfast establishment?

9. Government: Government is a huge purchaser of goods and services. What can you offer to the government that it needs?

Chapter 6: How to Save Money

To acquire financial independence you must follow the Four Steps Millionaire Formula to a "T." After you have started to generate income, the next step is to make sure that you are not blowing your money; instead, you must ensure that you are saving as much as you can. My recommendation is that you save at least 15 percent of your salary (and *all* of your "found money," as well, such as bonuses).

Let's look at this in more detail. Let's say that your income is $3,000 per month. After taxes, that amount may be reduced to $2,700. How you go about spending this amount is entirely in your own hands. There are three ways that you can spend this money.

First, you may end up spending more than what you earn. How could you do that? Well, in addition to spending the $2,700 you end up charging amounts to your credit card. Let's say that you charge $500 to your credit card each month over and above the $2,700 that you spend in cash. And you don't pay off the credit card the following month. Meaning you keep building up the outstanding balance on your credit card. Well, let me tell you, you are heading straight for a financial crash.

I have been there, done that. When I graduated from university, I was immediately inundated with credit card offers. I applied for all of the credit card offers and soon had a stash of these plastic "bombs," or WFD

(Weapons of Financial Destruction). In this way, I think the universities do a great disservice. Students who have just graduated have no idea how to handle debt. Universities get a payment for allowing credit card companies to recruit customers from their campuses in this way.[23] This is shameful behaviour by universities. We trust them, and this is what they do to us. You'll find out more and more as you read this book that there are many institutions that we've been trained to trust, that we just shouldn't.

Of course, such bad behaviour by the very institutions that we trust is the reason for my book. As I mentioned in the beginning, bad financial advice is causing havoc among human beings today. And it's part of my mission to protect people from the scourge of bad financial advice.

Credit cards are very useful, but quite dangerous if not used correctly. Soon after I acquired several, I found myself in a pile of credit card debt. Five thousand dollars worth, on which I was only able to make the minimum payments.

But I got lucky. I married the right woman. My new wife helped me get out of debt. First, she was horrified to learn that "we" were in debt. Thereafter, she forced me to make a plan to pay off the debt as soon as possible. We lived lean for two years, putting every spare penny into the credit card debt.

Let me say that we lived lean, but we had fun. G. Ross Lord Park in Toronto was our favourite haunt. It was free. Walking about in downtown Toronto was another favourite. It was free. Lake Simcoe, about forty-five minutes to the north of Toronto, in the summertime; it was not free, but the cost was minimal. A movie was only allowed on a special occasion. We were young birds in love and didn't need any of the props of luxury to feel that we were in love. This is a theme I'm going to drive home time and again. That to be happy nobody needs the trappings of luxury, or "peer pressure," like the big house, the big car, expensive vacations, trinkets, that the sneaky marketing machine of Big Bad Business would have you be-lieve. All the happiness you need is right within you; no need to go outside chasing around for it.

My wife and I are still married. It's been nineteen years. Three children along the way. We are still in love (God Bless). Even when money is tight, as it has been on many an occasion over the years, we still enjoy life to the fullest. Just sharing a smile, a kind word, a walk in nature. That's all we need to be happy. Compare that to a couple that has every material good. Big house, big cars, trinkets, and are still miserable and depressed. You have to learn to say "no" to the Big Marketing Machine. Instead learn to say "yes" to the simple pleasures of life—having food on the table, a loving family, good health, and some cash in the bank.

A respected friend of mine once told me that to be depressed is a sin. If you have shelter above your head, clothes on your back and food in your stomach, then you are luckier than 80 percent of the world's population. They are missing at least one of those.

You get the idea.

Since my first encounter with credit card debt, I am very careful how I use it. I only use it as a convenience, for example to make a purchase on the Internet. I only spend what I can pay off when the bill comes in. In other words, I try to use it as a convenience, and not as a "bank" to provide me with loans, so that I can spend the money on consumptive goods such as clothes, movies and shoes. If I have the money I buy, if I don't have the money, I don't.

So the moral of the story is: Be very wary of credit cards. They are WFD. They will allow you to easily spend more money than you earn. Then once you start carrying a balance on the credit cards, the danger is that the bal-ance becomes a perpetual one; it grows over time and you cannot pay it off. Then one day, you lose your job and you may have to file for bank-ruptcy. Not good!

The second way you could spend this money is to spend exactly what you earn. So if you make $2,700 after tax then you spend exactly $2,700. This is also a problem. You will not move ahead financially.

You need to consider the third way to spend your money, which is that you save some money for yourself immediately as you get paid, and live on the rest. This is an important concept.

The first point in this concept is the idea of *paying yourself first*. Think about that. When you pay money for groceries or electricity or clothes, you are making *other* people rich. If you are in the business of making other people rich, go right ahead. I can't stop you. But when you are in financial trouble, I won't be coming to help you, either.

That may be a bit harsh. The mere fact that you have this book in your hands says that you want to get smarter financially. Even if you were formerly in the business of making other people rich, you are now thinking that it may not be such a good idea. Maybe it's time for you to be in the business of receiving money rather than in the business of just sending it. So, great! Congratulations! Welcome aboard the ship "Wealth Builder." She's the ship you're on now.

So pay yourself first. As I mentioned earlier, I recommend you pay yourself 15 percent of your income to start off, and build it up from there. In our example it means you will save approximately $400 every month. And live on the rest. You are not going to touch these savings. They are there for a very special purpose, a life saving and a life giving purpose, both of which we will tackle shortly.

The second point in this concept is the idea of living on less. We all like to live large and enjoy the great luxuries of life: a big house, a big car, a big vacation, a big wedding. Nothing wrong with that. The problem, though, lies in that we have been trained by the sneaky marketing machine of Big Bad Business to have all these goodies ... NOW! Yes, it's easy. Just charge it. Or get a personal loan from your friendly neighbourhood banker. Therein lies the fallacy. Therein lies the myth.

You cannot enjoy the luxuries of life unless you've paid for them. Do not go for the instant fix—meaning buy now, pay later. If you do, you're toast. Done. Finito. This is the single biggest reason that people are not rich.

To be financially successful in life, you need to be able to take the *long-term view* (LTV). This means you need to be able to cultivate the ability to endure short-term pain for a greater delayed gratification.

People who take the long term view, those that are willing to put in the hard work now and delay their personal gratification, generally reap greater rewards over the long term. Taking shortcuts in life generally doesn't cut it. For example, take the case of a doctor. He spends many years training at his craft. Because of that training he brings great value to the lives of his patients. As a result his patients are willing to pay him a high fee for his services. Whereas, if you take the case of a high school dropout, his chance of earning a high wage is limited.

The high school dropout could become an entrepreneur, though, as I will talk about shortly. But that, too, requires *long term view* thinking, manifested as hard work and persistence. With the proceeds of that business correctly invested to earn him a passive income even this kid can make it. So in no way am I discounting the high school dropout. He, too, can make it, if he gets back on track; meaning that he gets into a profession or a business and realigns with LTV thinking.

The point is that any way you look at it, there is no short cut in life.

Above all, understand that your real goal—a life without monetary worries—is beyond your reach if you keep indulging in instant gratification— buying stuff you don't need.

Get this into your head.

Since you've already had a bird's eye view of the entire Four Steps Millionaire Formula strategy, let's integrate this knowledge with LTV. The client of mine that I spoke about in Chapter 4 *The Four Steps Millionaire Formula*, the one who bought investment properties while I spent my money buying a bigger house, had LTV. He focused on allocating his savings to create passive income instead of spending his savings on instant gratification. I, on the other hand, spent the money on instant gratification, i.e., I bought myself a bigger house. As a result, fourteen years down the road, he was financially independent, whereas I was still behind.

Do you get it? *Long-term view*. What a dynamite concept. It's everything when it comes to saving money and, hence, achieving financial independence.

The Psychology of Saving Money

Before we go further on the topic of saving money, I want to touch on the *psychology* of saving money. Unless you can master the psychology of saving money, no amount of *savings techniques* will help you to save money.

The biggest *obstacles* to saving are *peer pressure* and the feeling of being *deprived*[24]. Both emotions are the inventions of Big Bad Business. But that's not the fault of Big Bad Business. They are just doing their job—selling you whatever it is that they are trying to sell you. It's up to you to think before you buy. I cover these topics in more detail in Chapter 12 (*Trap #4: Your friends*), Chapter 13 (*Trap # 5: Big Business*), and in Chapter 15 (*New Graduate*). After you read these chapters, make sure that you become immune to the siren call of bad advertising, the deadly chains of peer pressure, and the fatal allure of luxury goods. None of these "pleasures" will move you towards your goal of financial security.

The Techniques of Saving Money

Moving on to the techniques of saving money, we have already dealt with the most important way to save. It's by paying yourself first. Let that be the main tool that you use to save money.

However, if you want to have an advanced grasp of how to save effectively, then there is another tool, which you may find useful.

Here it is. What I am referring to is a *budget*.

A budget is simply a spreadsheet where you put down how much you spend during the course of the year. On the following page is an example, which I've named: "Living Expenses Schedule."

The expenses section is subdivided into five major headings:

1. Housing

2. Living

3. Auto and Transportation

4. Extracurricular and Entertainment

5. Miscellaneous

Under each heading is a list of expenses. You can enter the monthly expense or an annual figure. It doesn't really matter which one. Enter an estimate of the one that you are most easily able to estimate. There are a few trick items that I have intentionally put on the worksheet to trip you up. For instance there is a line item for "Mortgage or Rent" and one for "Rates/Property taxes." Hah! These are trick items. If you come up with an amount that you think you should be putting into these boxes, then—buzzer sound—you're in trouble. If we were playing the game of Monopoly, I'd say to you: "Go to jail, do not collect $200 and miss a turn."

Figure 4: Living Expenses Schedule

Name: John Doe

Date Prepared: 21-Feb-13

Expenses	Annually $	Monthly $	Expenses	Annually $	Monthly $
Housing			**Auto and Transportation**		
Mortgage or Rent			Car Insurance		50.00
Condominium Dues			Car Lease Payments		50.00
Rates/Property taxes			Fuel		25.00
Property Insurance	437.50		Auto repairs and service		25.00
Telephone			Bus fare		
Internet			Other		
Heat			**Total**	0	150.00
Water					
Electricity			**Extracurricular and Entertainment**		
Home Repairs	250.00		Camping		
TV subscription		75.00	Club Membership		
Other		62.50	Gym	150.00	
Total	687.50	137.50	Vacations/Travel	625.00	
			Books & Magazines		12.50
Living			Dining Out		62.50
Food & Groceries		437.50	Children's activities		
Doctor & Dental		62.50	Sporting Events		
Education for Adults			Movies/Hobbies		
Education for Children	12,375.00		Other		
Clothing & Footwear	600.00		**Total**	775.00	75.00
Hair & Personal Care		125.00			
Lunch & Pocket Money		125.00	**Miscellaneous**		
Pool & Garden Chemicals		50.00	Credit Card		
Gardener		125.00	Life insurance premium		62.50
Maid			Gifts	62.50	
Home Improvements & Painting			Donations		
Pet Care		62.50	Income Tax	375.00	
Other			Other	25.00	
Total	12,975.00	987.50	**Total**	462.50	62.50

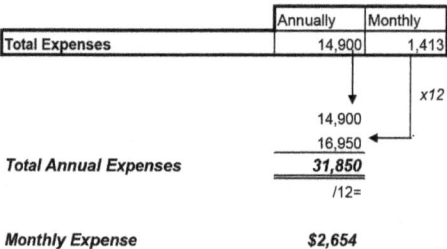

	Annually	Monthly
Total Expenses	14,900	1,413

                    ↓   x12

                    14,900
                    16,950 ←

Total Annual Expenses   31,850
                    /12=

Monthly Expense $2,654

Why?

Because you do not want to have such an expense on your list of *personal* expenses. That is, as we discussed earlier, you should not own a home in your personal name (if you are paying Rates/Property taxes it means the house is in your name; if you are paying a mortgage, same thing; paying rent from your personal expenses is fine). Ideally, you should always distance yourself from your personal assets.

Once you've put in the figures in the top portion of the budget spreadsheet, then you need to look at the last line at the bottom—Monthly Expense. In this case it's $2,654 per month. Because people invariably underestimate their expenses, add 20 percent to that figure. So in this case, your monthly expenses are:

$$\$2,654 \times 1.2 = \$3,184.$$

Compare this last figure, $3,184, to your income. If your income is higher than this amount then you should be able to save money. And the right way to do that is to put that savings away first thing every month as your paycheque comes in. If, at the end of the year, you get a bonus cheque, or a dividend if you are in business, make sure that that amount also gets saved. After that follow the Four Steps Millionaire Formula, and if you wish, the Four Ways Business Formula steps 3 and 4. And you're done.

If your income is lower than your expenses, then you are in big trouble. You need to find a way to lower your expenses or increase your income. The first objective should be to see where you could lower your expenses. This is where the budget comes in handy. Go over each *line item* (accounting speak for *each item*) and see what expense you can reduce or cut out entirely.

For instance, TV expense. When I was hunkering down to get through the process of writing this first book of mine, I knew that I would have to go through a certain period of time without earning a regular income. The first thing I cut from my expenses was the monthly TV subscription. That turned out to be a wise move. Not only did I save a lot of money, because the Internet provides almost everything that we wanted to watch, we also discovered that we didn't miss TV. As a family, we got to spend more time together. Now, when one of the kids has some free time, he or she will wander over to Mom (never Dad for some odd reason ...) and sit and talk. Not so when there was a TV channel that was available in the house 24/7.

I also cut out numerous other little items like buying soft drinks and potato chips every other day. That has helped us to eat healthier, as well.

It's not that I am taking the moral high ground and telling you to live a Spartan lifestyle. What I am saying is that if you can live cheaply then it gives you the guts to take tough decisions like quitting a dead-end job and starting up a business. If you can think like that then your options open up.

Now think about the income side. What can you do to increase your income? A second job is usually not a good idea. Trading your time for dollars is a dead end road. If you opt for a second job, at some point you will get burned out and will have no more hours to sell. Better you invest your spare time in learning a skill or trade that you can turn into a business.

Needs vs. Wants

I was listening once to a Maulana (a Muslim priest) give a talk at the Masjid in Gaborone. The topic was Islamic Finance, and one item he spoke about was: Know the difference between a want and a need. This matter is a huge stumbling block in the lives of humans. It is absolutely key that you discipline yourself to understand the difference between a want and a need. Let me borrow an example from the Maulana's speech. He told the story of a wise man of yesteryear who would say to his pupils:

"When you need something *then* go to the bazaar to buy it. Don't go to the bazaar to go looking for your needs."

On my way home after the speech, I stopped at a grocery store with the intention of buying a bottle of diet cola. I walked out of the grocery store with the diet cola and two more bottles of cola, five bags of chips, five ice cream cones, and a bag of peanuts. As I reached my car, I was hit with the realisation that I had just done exactly the opposite of what I had learned in the Islamic Finance seminar.

Saving money is no easy task. You will have to work hard at it if you want to be financially independent.

Chapter 7: How to Invest Money

If you've come this far in the book, I would like to congratulate you. I know some of the reading has been pretty heavy, especially if the topic of making money is new to you. I hope that in real life, too, you will have managed to arrive at this stage of the wealth-building process. What you need to learn now is how to invest your money.

The rules of the game for this step are a little complicated. It will take me a bit of time to explain the whole story, but it's imperative that you get this step right. Please consider the following issues:

1. Avoid mutual funds like the plague.

2. Invest for cash flow.

Section 1: Avoid mutual funds like the plague

A lot of people think they can build wealth by investing their hard earned savings into mutual funds. This notion is as a result of poor advice from the financial services industry. Poor advice has spawned a worldwide culture of people investing in mutual funds. If you are a 99-percenter, you mustn't even think of doing such a thing. If you are a one-percenter, you may do so, but be warned, you don't need to. However, Mr. One-percenter, if you are determined to invest in mutual funds, I have specific advice for you towards the end of this chapter.

Investing in mutual funds is a technical topic. But it is very important that all of you, 99-percenters and one-percenters alike, get a basic understanding of it. To get to the bottom of the mystery, we need to understand a few things. Let's start with understanding the overall structure of a *mutual fund*. Then we will drill deeper to get a look at what's really going on—the part that mutual fund investors know little about. See below for a diagram that will help you understand mutual funds.

Figure 5. Picture of a Mutual Fund

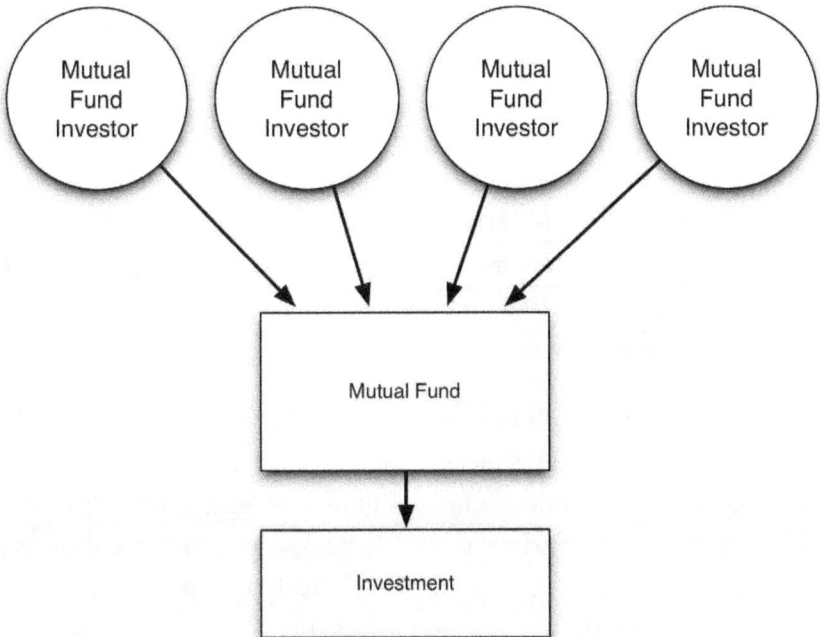

Mutual fund investors pool their money into a fund, which then buys investments on their behalf. There are different types of investments including:

1. Cash*

2. Bonds*

3. Stocks

    * See FAQ.

Another popular name for mutual funds is *unit trusts*. For all intents and purposes, they are exactly the same thing. Mutual funds became popular over the last twenty years or so. They originally came about to solve a problem for investors; investors may have had savings, but if they did not have the expertise to invest the money themselves, they could not benefit from the returns of investments such as those listed above (Cash, Bonds and Stocks).

A mutual fund is supposed to be a secure way for small investors to invest in such instruments and make money. In some instances people have benefitted from mutual funds, for example, those people who wouldn't have saved money anyway. They are better off because some form of saving is better than none at all. However, in my experience, mutual funds are not a secure way to make money.

To understand this we will need to dig deeper. We will need to get to the level of the underlying investment. One popular mutual fund investment is stocks. Let's say a particular mutual fund invests in stocks. What is a stock (the term *share* is synonymous)? It represents part ownership of a company. If you hold one share of Sample Cola, you hold a very small piece. It is the equivalent of one share divided by however many shares of Sample Cola are in issue (for example, ten million). This is your interest in the company. If there are 100 shareholders who each own one share, you own one one-hundredth of the company. Let's say you think you're *Stockmarket Wunderkind's* cousin, and since you heard that *Stockmarket Wunderkind* made a lot of money investing in Sample Cola shares in the past, you think this must be a surefire way to make money. Therefore, you invest your entire hard-earned savings of $10,000 into shares of Sample Cola. But will you make money? Let's discuss this.

Of course, Sample Cola is just an imaginary company. You could just as easily have invested your money into the shares of any company that trades on any *stock exchange* on the face of this earth. Such a company, that is, one that trades on a stock exchange, is referred to as a *public company*.

And a stock exchange is a place where shares are bought and sold. Just like the grocery store, for example, is where milk is bought (by you the customer) and sold (by the grocery store).

Why did you invest in shares of Sample Cola in the first place? To make money of course! You want your $10,000 to grow. You desire to get back more money than you put in sometime in the future. How? Either through dividends or through capital gains, or both.

How do you earn dividends? In exactly the same way we learned in the Four Ways Business Formula discussion in chapter 5 (*How to Make Money*). After retaining some money for its own needs, the company will pay some out to the shareholders.

The second way an investor makes money is through capital gains, that is, appreciation of the share price. This will occur if the company's earnings have grown.

The problem is that in real life there are many obstacles for these two scenarios to actually work out in your favour. It's not worth the trouble. Hence, you should avoid investing in shares altogether.

Here are just a few of the obstacles:

Obstacle (1): You have no control over the forces that affect your underlying mutual fund investments. Now that we have used the terms Cash, Bonds and Stocks, we will refer to these collectively as stock market investments. Some may wish to call these a *Portfolio*. One of the biggest problems with investing in a portfolio is that you have no control over your underlying investment. For example, in your portfolio you may own shares of Sample Cola, but you have no say in the day-to-day operations of Sample Cola. If you have no control, then your strategy of earning a return from your investment is a 'hope and pray' strategy, which is not an investment strategy at all. It's just foolish. Even God is probably having a laugh at you.

Obstacle (2): You also have no control over the stock market. And, usually, it must go up for you to make money. Does it go up on a regular basis sufficiently for you to trust that your money will go up and not down? Let's look at this. Financial advisors often say that the stock market *averages* returns of "X" percent per year. The figure changes with the times. These days, say, it's "eight" percent per year, implying that you can get eight percent per year steady returns. This is a huge myth. I have to trash it because it is a myth that can kill people in real life when they find their investment returns have vaporised, contrary to the beautiful *projections* that the financial advisor showed them on paper.

See, many financial advisors only talk about portfolio *growth*. The reality is that portfolios can go up, down, and sideways. The down and the sideways movement can give you *losses* of such magnitude that the portfolio becomes irreparable. So if you were relying on an investment portfolio to provide for your retirement, you may be in for a shock. Instead of achieving a comfortable retirement you may end up in financial destitution.

Let's take the case of the DOW. This is a stock market index of 30 large, publicly owned companies in the USA. It's the simplest way for me to demonstrate the immense riskiness of a paper assets portfolio. The point: You should avoid having your money in one of these investment vehicles.

Consider the following graph:

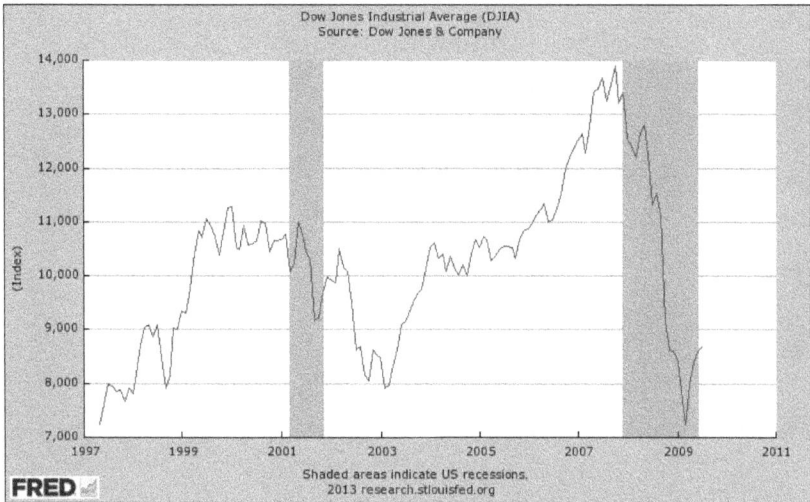

Reprinted with permission (see Copyright page)

Note the following: In 1997 the DOW was approximately 7000 points. In 2009,_twelve_years later it was still at approximately 7000 points. During the course of that period, the DOW had hit a high of approximately 14,000 points. That was around October 2007.

Now let's see what kind of damage an investment in the stock market can potentially do to an investor:

i) Let's assume that an investor had put $100,000 into a portfolio tracking the DOW in 1997 and took it out in 2009. Let's ignore portfolio fees for a moment. First, after twelve years the investor had no more money than he had at his original investment. Even though it may not be obvious, this investor lost a great deal because of inflation. Briefly, inflation is the loss in value of what your money can buy. So if you could buy a new car in 1997 for $20,000, and the same car cost you $30,000 in 2009 you lost half your money. So just getting your money back in 2009 could be a horrible result. Let's use some actual data. During 1997 to 2009 U.S. inflation averaged approximately 2.8 percent pa. Therefore, your money lost (12 years × 2.8%) or 33.6 percent in value. That's a 33.6 percent loss! A real life loss! How do you feel about just getting your money back? Not so hot, huh? The big problem here is that financial advisors dish out this mantra about long term investing, meaning that you must invest for the long-term and you will be fine. That's just a load of gobbledygook. If you follow that advice, not only could you lose your money, you could lose your life (because you could run out of money). That's what I'm really worried about.

ii) How about the guy who invested at the peak, in October 2007, when the DOW was approximately 14,000. By 2009 he had lost (7000–14000) 7000; then if we divide the 7000 loss by the original investment at 14,000 we get a minus factor of 50 percent. Factor in two years worth of inflation, and you add approximately a further 5.6 percent, bringing the total loss to 55.6 percent. If this guy is depending on his stock portfolio for his retirement expenses he will want to jump out of the window.

iii) We have not even factored in portfolio fees yet. Fees are largely ignored in returns calculations. But fees are a killer. In this particular example, because the portfolio was higher between the beginning point (1997) and the end point (2009), the portfolio fees during this period would have been taken care of by the growth in the value of the portfolio. So the negative impact of fees is not easily seen.

However, please note that during sideways and down markets, portfolio fees can be a drain on your capital.

For instance, let's look at down markets. If we assume portfolio fees of three percent pa, then in example two above, the total loss would be (55.6% + 6% for fees) 61.6 percent. Not good, my friend, not good at all.

iv) At this point, some people reading this will say "Hey, not fair, you cherry-picked the time frame to suit you." My response is: This is real life; this book is about real life, not academic theories. I didn't pick these numbers from my mind. This is actually what happened out there in real life. And that's the biggest problem with mutual funds. The people who sell them have been trained how to sell mutual funds, and while they believe in what they are selling, in my experience, there is a disconnect in their sales *spiel* from "real life."

"Can't be," you say?

I would like to ask the financial advisor community out there: Where is the value you are adding? Is it in the financial plans, which you produce for your clients? Faiz Versey's Answer, "If you produce a financial plan, then, 'Yes.' There is value there. However, how do you get paid for producing a financial plan? Is it from fees you charge the client directly or from subsequently selling the client a financial product? If it's a financial product that you sell, for example, a mutual fund, then I think you are going into sham territory." Let me explain.

Earlier, I told you that one of the entrepreneur traits is "P" of
"SPO"—that is, someone who does not expect to get paid unless he is producing, or *adding value* to the world. Financial
advisors, you are mostly entrepreneurs. So what is the "value-
add" that a client is looking for from you? In the case of savings plans, it's that you can make him more money than he
can make on his own. A client can simply put his money in a
bank account and earn cash returns, that is, the interest the
bank pays you when you put money into the bank. An advisor is competing with this. A client does not want to make
less than the bank. The client is not interested in the financial advisor's mantra: "We lost less than the benchmark."
Quite simply what he wants is to make more than the bank
and not to lose any money.[25]

That is the result the client is looking for. When that financial advisor loses his money instead, that's a *non-result*. A
failure.

Therefore, I ask the financial advisor community the following question: "In selling mutual funds to your clients are you
adding value to them?"

Here's what I mean. If a mutual fund portfolio has a negative
return in any year, you will not get paid. You only get paid
during the years that the portfolio produced a positive return
on investments. Also, as an advisor you'd have to personally
guarantee the client's capital. If the capital is ever lost, then
you pay from your pocket. Are you willing to do this?

When mutual funds drop in value, financial advisors have
all the excuses in the world to explain that it wasn't their
fault. "It was the market, Mr. Client, and you didn't lose as
much as the benchmark. Lucky you!" These could be quite

genuine excuses in the sense that the financial advisor didn't intentionally lose the money. But still, the client lost money ... and sleep. So, Mr. Financial Advisor, I am going to ask again, "In selling mutual funds to your clients did you add value?" Providing a negative return or a loss of capital is not *adding value*. Financial advisors should stop misleading people. Stop mis-selling. Stop playing with other peoples' money. Do something that adds real value to people's lives.

After having been a financial advisor for fifteen years, I don't have much respect for the financial advisory profession anymore. But I do have respect for financial advisors. I was one. And I encourage financial advisors to get out of the business.

Financial advisors could also turn to the segment of the financial advisory business that does good work in the world, like the sale of life insurance and annuities. The investment product business, for example, sales of mutual funds, is fraught with undue risk for clients. A whole decade can go by and a client might not make any money. Factor in inflation and fees and a client faces a magnificent loss. Financial advisors could also do what I'm doing by becoming a financial educator, for the right side of the equation, of course. This is my heartfelt advice for you.

v) If you are already convinced that you shouldn't be investing in mutual funds, you can skip ahead to the next section, where I show you how to build wealth the rich man's way; the section is titled *Invest for Cash Flow*. But if you are curious about learning more about mutual funds, then let's continue. It is a bit technical, but you may learn a few more things about stock markets and mutual funds.

As I said earlier, most mutual fund sales people will show you a projection of how much your money will grow to over a period of time using steady growth rates. See Figure 6 next page.

This is false marketing. Stock markets do not go up in a straight line. Sometimes they go up, sometimes they go down, and sometimes they go sideways, for years on end. If you are caught in one of the down draughts, or one of the sideways cycles, you could be in trouble. The downward markets are easy to understand. If stocks go down you lose money. Period. This ignores shorting and option strategies, which are not included in this book. The sideways markets are not so easy to understand. But let me tell you that in point number three above I showed you an example of a period in the stock markets that, to some degree, resembled a sideways market. You started at 7000 points on the DOW and ended up twelve years later at the same level, that is, 7000 points, and yet lost 33.6 percent of your money. Sideways markets can have a devastating effect on your savings. Examples of such periods for the DOW are: 1900-1920, 1938-1948, 1964-1982.[26]

Figure 6. Projected Value of Assets Using a Steady Growth Rate

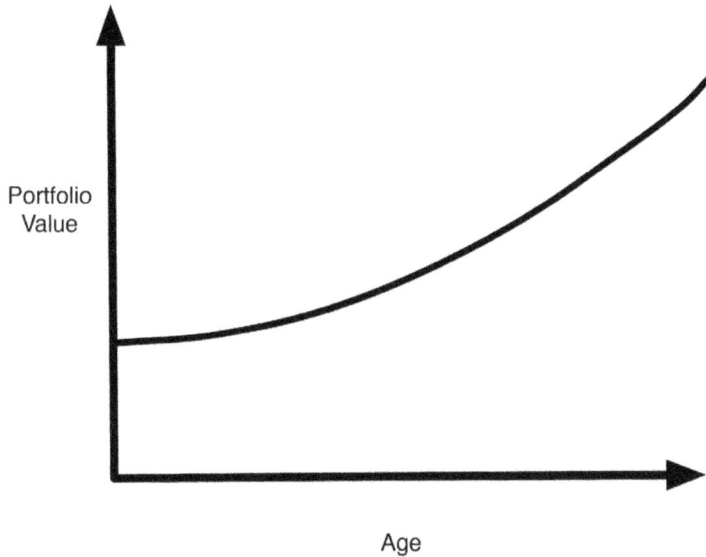

Portfolio Value

Age

vi) Some of you may complain and then think, 'Nobody in-vests in just a stock portfolio. Financial advisors recommend that people *diversify* and use a *Balanced Mutual Fund*, which spreads its investments into both stocks and bonds. Surely, such *diversification* will *smooth* out the volatility of returns and I'll enjoy fairly smooth returns of eight percent pa as my fi-nancial advisor predicts.'

Not in my experience. I'll grant that balanced portfolios are somewhat less volatile than purely stock portfolios, but not by much. Diversification is based on the theory of *correlation between securities*. In my experience when markets go down, balanced funds go down. And they can go down a lot, which is a problem. Remember a big truth about investing in the stock market. If your fund loses 50 percent it has to make back 100 percent just to break even. That is not easy. It could take years to just get back to break-even, if it ever does. So, losing money in a mutual fund is not a good thing. Factor in fees and inflation and the total negative effects on your wealth could be devastating.

Jim Otar has done credible work on the topic of diversification. In his book *Unveiling the Retirement Myth*, Otar explains that diversification does not necessarily prevent losses.[27]

This has been my experience during the fifteen years I spent as a financial advisor. For the most part, in difficult market conditions, when the markets go down, mutual funds tend to go down in unison. Even money market funds go down. Which are the ones you'd least expect to be negatively affected by market downturns. In the 2008 crisis when Lehman Brothers went under, money market funds holding a particular Lehman Brothers asset lost money. There is no mutual fund that is immune to the vagaries of the market.

The conclusion: Balanced Portfolios are almost as volatile as pure stock portfolios. The possibility that you will earn a *smooth* eight percent pa return is practically nil. It is a myth.

Obstacle (3): You have no (or, at best, limited access to) leverage (the ability to take a loan from a bank). This is the biggest reason for you to never invest in mutual funds. Almost none of my rich clients got rich without using leverage.

For example, say you purchased $10,000 of a mutual fund and it moved up by 10 percent in a particular year. If you encashed it, you would then have $11,000 in your pocket.

Alternately, you put a $10,000 down payment on a house worth $100,000. That means you had a loan of $90,000. As mentioned above, this loan is referred to as *leverage*. Let's say that the house value increased by 10 percent. It is now worth $110,000. If you encashed it and paid off the original loan of $90,000 then you now have $20,000 in your pocket.

Question: Which is more: $11,000 or $ 20,000? Which sum would you prefer to have in your pocket?

This is an important matter. Without leverage your chances of accumulating serious wealth are greatly reduced. Without leverage you will not be able to access the investments that make people rich. Very few banks will lend you money to buy mutual funds. And if they do, the amount of the loan as a percentage of your mutual fund holding will rarely exceed 50 percent. Therefore, in the above case, if you had a $10,000 mutual fund investment it is unlikely you would get a loan of more than $5,000.00. But if buying a house the loan can be multiples of your down payment, in the above case nine times ($90,000/$10,000).

In fact, you should never take a loan to buy mutual funds. Yes, people do take loans to fund retirement accounts, like RRSPs in Canada, and that is also a bad strategy. Taking loans to buy mutual funds is not a good strategy simply because you have no control over the mutual fund investment. If it blows up, you are in debt for the loan amount.

For a house to blow up is rare. But even when buying a house, leverage is a double-edged sword, and if you don't manage it with the utmost care it could hurt you. So that you may avoid them, we will talk about the pitfalls of investing in real estate shortly.

Obstacle (4): If you are already invested in mutual funds, then here's something to consider: The world stock markets have had an excellent run since approximately March 2009. At the time of writing this book in 2013, the DOW has gone even higher than its previous peak in October 2007 of approximately 14,000. It may go higher from here. I am not in the business of making forecasts. I want to suggest that if you do not want to encash your stock market investments altogether—and do something sensible with the money like start your own business or just leave it in cash—then at least do this: convert 50 percent of all volatile investments (stock funds, balanced funds, bond funds) into cash funds. And don't ever put any more of your money into volatile mutual funds.

This is because the returns in volatile mutual funds are not permanent. They could vaporise at anytime. With 50 percent of your money in cash funds, at least half of your *investment* is safe, notwithstanding the loss in money market investments noted earlier. It's still your *safest* investment inside a retirement account.

More on this note. If you watch financial channels on TV, the market gurus often come up with the refrain that because fixed income returns are zero, and people want returns, they should put their money into the stock market. This is the game: Entice people into the stock market. Brokers make a lot of money on the way up. The sellers of financial securities make a lot of money on the way up. And then kaboom! The stock market comes plunging down. Brokers make a lot of money on the way down. The early sellers of financial securities are already out of the market. The house wins on the way up and the way down, but ordinary people lose. People, return *of* your money is much more important than return *on* your money. It's your *hard earned* money that we are talking about. What you should be doing in-stead is investing in cash flowing investments. If you can't find such, leave the money in cash. That's the best investment strategy.

Do not be drawn into the game of *pyramid*. The stock market even has a name for this game called the *Greater Fool Theory*. This means that when you buy a share you are holding onto it in the expectation that a greater fool will come along and buy it from you at an even higher price. There's no real value being created, just greater fools. Someday the supply of greater fools will stop, and if you are still in the game you will be left holding the bag, which will have nothing in it. That's how the pyramid scheme works. This is also the way a *Ponzi scheme* works. Do not get enticed into anything that appears to be a Ponzi or a pyramid scheme, or something that appears to be too good to be true.

Consider this: Make money and put it in the bank. Then go out and make more money—through your job or ownership of busi-nesses or property. Leave the stock market alone.

Obstacle (5): Stop putting money into *retirement accounts*, which, for the most part, allow you to invest only in mutual funds. The mutual fund companies win and you lose. The mutual fund companies foist all the risk onto you, the investor. If the mutual fund loses value, you bear the loss, not the fund manager.

This is a massive point.

In the old days, employers used to provide *defined benefit* pension schemes. In such cases, the employer provided the employee with the promised pension payment upon retirement. However, in recent times, employers have decided to shed this responsibil-ity and a new type of pension scheme has come about, the *retirement account.* If you own a retirement account, the risk of the investment plan rests entirely on your shoulders. If the investment plan has performed badly it is too bad. Nobody is responsible but you.[28]

Understand that no one cares more about your money than you do. Self-directing your retirement plan puts YOU in control versus mutual fund companies and the financial system. So invest your assets into what you know and can control for the best long-term returns. Don't put your fate into the hands of others. Of course, that's what mutual fund companies and the financial system hopes you'll continue to do with your savings.

Let's get back to a topic we started some ways back: What happened to your $10,000 investment in the shares of Sample Cola? From the aforementioned discussion, you'll realise that there is no way for you to know whether you made money or lost money. You have no control over the direction of the shares, nor do you know if the company will be around in the long run. There is too much uncertainty. Leave this type of investment alone and put your money in the bank. We will soon discuss how the rich invest, which is by buying cash flowing investments.

Question: How will I ever know what the difference is between a mutual fund, cash, a bond, or a stock?

Answer: The financial product will say so. If the financial product says "xyz fund"–for example, balanced fund, equity fund, bond fund, etc., you don't want to own it. If it says cash, bank account, fixed deposit, money market fund (a good type of mutual fund), you can own it. If it says "xyz bond"–for example, XYZ Company Bond–stay away. If it says "xyz share"–for example, XYZ Company share–stay away.

Now, 99 percenters—do not read further. Skip to the next section.

Just kidding! Feel free to read on, but don't implement the advice. You already have your marching orders as per above (that is, follow the Four Steps Millionaire Formula; if you are in business then you can follow the Four Ways Business Formula and move on to steps 3 and 4 should you so choose).

If you are a one-percenter, you don't need to be in a portfolio at all. You have enough new cash coming in each year from your passive income. Why lose sleep on those nights when the markets are gyrating? Why complicate your life even further. To become a one-percenter you already have a pretty complicated setup. So don't get deeper into an administrative matter, which won't give you any significant upside. You don't need the hassle. Just enjoy your cash flows.

In my financial advisory days, I once tried to convince one of my wealthy clients to invest his cash into an investment product, which I was selling. He told me: "You know me. I'd much rather have money in the bank depreciating (for an explanation of how money in the bank can depreciate see FAQ) rather than take a chance investing it." Today, having looked under the hood of the financial services industry, I can confidently say this is the best strategy for one-percenters.

However, despite my warnings about investing in mutual funds, if you still insist on going down the mutual fund route, then get a financial advisor. This is one of the few instances when you will need a financial advisor.

Ask your financial advisor for his advice. I'd go with whatever he recommends. In the end all these portfolios are likely going to lose you money. I am just trying to give you the best *hope* of success. Just stay away from anything that says *offshore investment* as I will explain in a section later in this book. Only invest in funds or investment policies that are domiciled, that is, registered where you live. If you are an expat, only consider investments that are domiciled in your home country. That said, I would consider certain reputable offshore centres, but for the uninitiated, I'd say better to play it safe and avoid offshore investments altogether.

If you don't trust your financial advisor's expertise sufficiently to go with his investment recommendations, then use what I suggest below. Ask your financial advisor to split up your investment portfolio as follows:

i) One quarter into a *Cautious Fund*. A *Cautious Fund* is essentially a fund with 70 percent fixed income and 30 percent equities. A money market fund will do just as well.

ii) One quarter into a *Managed Fund*. A *Managed Fund* is essentially a fund with 50 percent fixed income and 50 percent equities; another common name for a *Managed Fund* is a *Balanced Fund*.

iii) One quarter into an *Aggressive Fund*. An *Aggressive Fund* is essentially a fund with 30 percent fixed income and 70 percent equities. A pure equities fund will do fine, as well.

iv) One quarter into a market-timing fund.*

And that's it. Leave it on autopilot and look at it in ten years.

The first three are easy to find. The last one is difficult to find. But you need it because the markets go up and down. If you can avoid the downturns, you'll do fine. The problem is that such a fund isn't easy to come by. It usually exists in the hedge fund world, a topic way too advanced for this book.

In the meantime, tell your financial advisor to study market-timing techniques and do his best to replicate the strategy with a quarter of your portfolio. If he can't do it, then just allocate the money, in equal proportions, to the first three strategies. Don't look for a financial advisor who can do market-timing. You'd be looking for a needle in a haystack. So don't waste your time; just allocate your entire portfolio to the first three strategies. If you are lucky, you'll make some money. If at any time you decide this is too much bother, then happily shut down the portfolio. Put the money in a bank account. And focus on living your life.

Advanced Information: If you want to hold individual stocks instead of mutual funds, buy the *dogs of the Dow* strategy, and change your stock holdings in January of every year according to the dictates of that strategy. Any stockbroker can set up the *dogs of the Dow* strategy for you. In addition, for international investors, you could also hold five to ten individual stocks on your local bourse. You will have to do your own research. Mr. One per-center, make sure you are not putting a lot of money into any of the *investment* strategies noted above. Keep the rest of your investable money as cash and, as I said above, focus on living your life.

Section 2: Invest for cash flow

Let me show you how to invest the way the rich invest. They invest for cash flow. That is their goal. Furthermore, they want to make enough cash flow from their investments so that their passive income exceeds their living expenses; by a margin, as explained in Chapter 4 (*The Four Steps*

Millionaire Formula). Let's say that margin is twenty percent. Then the man is rich, and he's free.

Rich people don't worry about capital gains; they do not hunt for price appreciation. Capital gains are a bonus. Chasing capital gains is like chasing dreams. The rich know very well that snake oil salesmen can spin fancy tails of wealth that exists somewhere in the sky, but in the end it takes a real dollar bill to buy bread, a real dollar bill to buy petrol, and a real dollar bill to pay for the children's school fees.

So their goal is simple. Find the investment that can pay me back a cash flow. "I must see the money coming in," they say. "Not earn some hypothetical return on some *paper investment*" account.

Speaking of *paper investments*, I have also discovered that the rich are extremely wary of paper investments. An example of a paper investment is a mutual fund. If the rich can't touch it and feel it, they don't want it. "Bricks and mortar," they often cry. That is their favourite type of investment.

Question: What is a paper investment?

Answer: An example of a paper investment is a mutual fund. Contrast this with a property. The property is bricks and mortar. You can feel it. But you can't actually touch the investments in your mutual fund. You only see your mutual fund on a paper statement, which you get from the investment company. Hence, the term *paper investment*.

Question: So is a paper investment a good thing or a bad thing?

Answer: For the most part, it's a bad thing. For example, a mutual fund is a paper investment, and as we have discussed previously it's not good for you.

Rich people also like stock in the warehouse, meaning their inventory of goods. That's another favourite. Why? In this way, they totally control the returns on the stock investment. If a retailer turns over his stock once per quarter, and he makes 25 percent markup, he can generate a 25 percent return per quarter. Most stock market investments do not generate anywhere near this return.

They also believe in leveraging, as little as necessary. They work hard in primary businesses earning as big a paycheque as possible, saving furiously in order to minimise the amount needed to borrow from the bank.

Not only is saving emphasized, children of the rich are taught to ensure that their spending does not increase along with their income. This is an important concept.

Further, once they start making money, the children are taught that the first investment that they should buy is *Revenue Producing Property* (*RPP*). Not bare land, although that is a possibility down the road because bare land is not worth much unless there is a building on it.

What types of property constitute RPP?

1. A house or other residential dwelling (for example, an apartment building) that can be rented out.

2. An office or other commercial premises (for example, a warehouse) that can be rented out.

This is what you must aim for as soon as you start to save money. The key word here is "aim." If you aim at something you will eventually hit it. In the beginning your goal may seem far, far away. But if you chip away at the problem, you will eventually get there, and you will achieve your prize.

When I turned 40, I decided to put my blood through a number of tests. At some time or another in years past, I had read that when one turns 40, it's time to get a full medical checkup.

The results, unfortunately, were a little startling. High cholesterol and sugar. But luckily for me the damage was not permanent. As my dad, a medical doctor, explained to me, with a proper diet and exercise plan I could reverse the situation.

The point I want to make here is that after I discovered my bad health situation, and I started to exercise in earnest, at first, I couldn't touch my toes. On the contrary, my toes seemed as far away as the moon.

On July 31, 2013, eight years later, I finally touched my toes.

I had been *aiming* for that result. Accordingly, I put in the stretching exercises, which I needed to accomplish that goal. It sure took a long time, but eventually I got there.

Similarly, in your life you need to aim at your goals. If you expend your precious time and energy without aiming at anything, you will dissipate those valuable resources and end up God knows where. It may not be a happy place. And you will wonder what happened. You can easily lose sight of your purpose if you do not focus your time and energy on specific goals.

But sometimes you just don't know what to aim at. That's where this book will help. Once you are aware of the *route to financial success*—all you have to do is aim for the end of the road. Along the way there are some milestones. Continually aim for the next milestone on your journey. Eventually you will get to your destination.

Compare that strategy to just driving along on the road of life without any direction. You'll eventually get lost.

Unfortunately, that's what happens to millions of people. They either wander around in circles totally unaware that they have to become financially independent, or they are aware that they need to become financially independent but they just don't know how. Either path will lead to financial destitution. I have met so many people during my financial planning career who were old and poor. They wanted me to do some magic for them to make them rich. But, of course, I am not a magician, and unfortunately, these people will probably endure a difficult end to their life.

It's sad, but true: 99 percent versus one percent.

I hope that you are reading this book early enough in your life to change course towards financial independence. If you are, and you find this book helpful, please share it with others. I am firmly of the opinion that this book needs to get into the hands of every person on this planet. Today, that's seven billion strong. I can't reach them just by myself. But you can help me to get my message out even further than I can. Let people know about the book's website: www.RouteToFinancialSuccess.com. Then they can decide whether or not the book is for them.

Let's buy a property:
This is book is intended to be a primer on financial success. I plan to offer an overview of the most important things to consider when buying residential or commercial property.

Before I go ahead, though, I'd like to bend a rule from the Four Steps Millionaire Formula, just a little. It's in regards to buying a personal home for yourself to live in.

First, let's revisit the recommended strategy per the Four Steps Millionaire Formula. This system recommends that you don't buy a home for yourself until your passive income is in excess of your living expenses. That is, as you start your journey to financial independence, consider living in a rented home, while working on building up passive income. Live this way until such time that you can use your passive income to buy a house for personal use.

Let's also use the Four Steps Millionaire Formula to come up with a definition of the term *rich*. From studying the strategy, we have learned that your financial goal should be to achieve a situation where your passive income exceeds your living expenses. Essentially, then, my take on the definition of rich is this: it's the point in your life when your passive income exceeds your living expenses.

For example, say your passive income is $120,000 and your living expenses are $100,000. By the definition above, you are now rich.

Great! Coming back to the issue of buying a personal home for yourself to live in, once you are rich, you have a lot of financial wiggle room to buy it. You can allocate the rent that you currently pay plus an additional amount from the excess of passive income over living expenses to buy your home. If your rent was $2,000 per month, you could take another $1,000 per month ($12,000) *from* the excess of passive income over living expenses ($120,000–$100,000) 20,000. You could then afford a home that would cost the amount that you are currently paying in rent, $2,000, plus the additional $1,000, for a total of $3,000, in monthly loan payments.

Of course, your living expenses have gone up by ($1,000 × 12) $12,000 to $112,000. But that's fine. You can afford it. In summary, note that now your passive income is $120,000 and living expenses are $112,000.

If you have the patience to wait until you are in this type of financial situation, great. Good for you. Just know that it could take you fifteen to twenty years to accomplish this.

Indeed, that's how some of my rich clients did it. They lived in rented quarters for a good quarter of a century, building up their primary businesses and their passive incomes, until they were able to afford their dream homes. Today, many are financially stable; the income from their Four Steps Millionaire Formula activities, and from their Four Ways Business Formula, step 3 businesses, pays for their living expenses, their house, and then some. They spend several months travelling or spending time with their family or being involved with hobbies they love. Fantastic!

However, there is some leeway here. If you do not want to wait that long—fifteen to twenty years—to own your own home, then do it a little earlier. But, and here is the big warning, do not buy your *dream home* early. Buy a starter home. Live in it until you have accomplished the Four Steps Millionaire Formula strategy. Then you can buy a more lavish home, or even your dream home.

As I've mentioned to you earlier, my buying a *big house* long before I was financially secure, was one of the biggest financial mistakes of my life. It set me back at least half a dozen years. Prior to buying the *big house*, I owned a tiny starter home. It served me well for the first six years of my career in Gaborone. With a growing family, however, the space became very tight and I had to move into a larger space. I could easily have upgraded to a slightly bigger home for half the price that I paid for the big house. I could have invested the other half into another residential property, an office building or a warehouse, each of which would have more or less tripled in value by today. In addition, the rental income would have doubled, at least. At that point, I could have properly afforded to move into the big house.

However, at the time, I was financially uneducated about what I am teaching you here.

So please avoid such a mistake. Do not buy your dream home until you can afford it. In other words, wait until your passive income can buy it for you.

> **Question:** Can't I just buy my dream home straight away? I won't have to pay rent and that reduces my expenses.
>
> **Answer:** No. You must go step by step. You may not be paying rent when you buy your dream home, but you are still making a loan

repayment. That's money leaving your pocket, with nothing coming in. If you had bought a smaller home, and then also bought a second home (or a warehouse or an office building) to rent out, you would be in the following position: Some monies would be leaving your pocket as a loan repayment on your house, which you live in, and some monies would be coming in from your investment property and paying off the loan on that investment property. Therefore, you are building up passive income.

That way, some years down the road, when you have bought more investment properties, you can take all the passive income from those properties and buy your dream home. After a few more years, you'll have paid down your dream home *and* paid down your investment properties. Then you'll have your dream home and your passive income, too.

Question: If passive income is greater than expenses is it possible for the situation to turn around at any given time?

Answer: Sure! That's exactly what you have to guard against. Your situation can turn around if you increase your lifestyle expenses and start living beyond your means. This is one of the biggest lessons that rich people teach to their children; when your income grows, make sure that your expenses don't grow with it. Keep increasing the margin between your income and your expenses. In other words, always keep your expenses in check. Income can rise and fall; and you don't want to be caught off-guard living beyond your means when the economy crashes.

Big American Dream

In 2012, on a flight within the United States, from Salt Lake City, Utah, to Atlanta, Georgia, I found myself sitting next to a Mexican-American woman. She told me the story of both her financial success and her financial woe. In the mid-2000s she and her husband had started a retail business in the San Francisco area. They grew their business from zero stores to several stores in four years. The stores were doing a roaring business. People were buying their wares. Then the great recession of 2008 hit, and people stopped buying as much. People had lost their jobs and had no money.

"When we were making money, we looked rich. We had a big house, big cars, but all were bought on big mortgages," she told me. "But look at the people in Mexico—small house, but no mortgage." she said.

"So ours was the Big American Dream and it was wrong financially."

"We were reinvesting in our business, thinking it would go on forever, and then Bang! When the recession hit, we came down!" she exclaimed. "We took our last twenty odd thousand dollars and also reinvested it, and we lost it all."

"If we had diversified, and not put all our eggs in one basket, we would have been better off today," she continued. "We should have bought a small house, cash, a small car, cash. Without debt we would have survived the financial crisis."

She smiled and said: "That's why people in Mexico are better off: they have small houses, but no mortgage."

"But at least I'm smiling today," she said. "The past is the past. You must learn from it and let it go."

Wow! I was amazed and inspired. Amazed at how the same financial mistakes occur around the world. This lady in the USA, and me in Botswana. Same problem. Chasing the Big American Dream: big house, big car, too much bad debt. I was also inspired by the resilience of the lady and her husband, starting all over again after having lost it all.

The Big American Dream can be summarised as follows: Live a debt-ridden, consumption-crazy, heady lifestyle.

Moral of the story: DON'T CHASE THE BIG AMERICAN DREAM. This applies to Americans, Batswana (the people of Botswana are called Batswana), Pakistanis and everybody else in the world. You can comfortably substitute "American" in "DON'T CHASE THE BIG *AMERICAN* DREAM," for Motswana (singular for Batswana) or Pakistani or XYZ citizenry. It's the same everywhere. Bottom line: DON'T CHASE THE BIG "DEBT-RIDDEN, CONSUMPTION-CRAZY, HEADY LIFESTYLE" DREAM.

Let's get back to buying property. Here is some key advice.

Residential Property
Why buy residential property? For a very simple reason. People need a place to live. It is a necessity. Therefore, it's potentially a safe investment. But there could be pitfalls, as well.

Your goal in buying a residential property is to earn a cash flow from it. You also want to enjoy rising rental returns from rental increments over the years. You must have a minimum ten-year time horizon when buying such a property. It's better to have an unlimited time horizon. Many of the rich people I know will just not sell their properties. They just keep adding to their properties, so that over a period of time they have a "portfolio" of properties. Some of those properties will be performing well and some not so well. But overall, the cash flow will be healthy and growing.

Some people do not want to invest in real estate because it's risky. "It's just not for me," they say. If you don't know what you are doing anything is risky. But consider two things. First, we all have a connection to real estate. Basically, if you live on this earth you have a connection to real estate

Second, let me remind you of the Law of Cause and Effect. If you know of other people who have been successful at investing in real estate, then if you want the same result all you have to do is work backwards to the causes of that result. If you can figure out those causes and implement them yourself, is there any reason that you too could not have the same result? It is not guaranteed, but at least you have a good chance of getting the same result. Good odds are all you need as an entrepreneur. It should give you great confidence.

Accumulating a portfolio of residential properties will be a slow process at the beginning. After ten years you can go faster, because, first, you will have so much more cash flow available to invest in new properties; second, you will have more experience at selecting good properties (ones that cash flow early); third, you will be visible in the market place so that property brokers will call *you* about deals; and, finally, the banks will be happier to lend to you on short notice. Everything in life gets easier as you go along, but you've got to stick with it for a while.

There are two types of residential property to consider. One is an already built-up and well-maintained home, and the other a *fixer-upper*. There is more upside in the fixer-upper. You can buy it cheaply, fix it up and rent it out, or simply sell it. However, if you make a profit, you shouldn't spend it on personal consumption. Rather, the profit should be reinvested in a similar project. This is crucial. Remember: do not leak your savings until your passive income exceeds your living expenses. Either route—renting or selling—is good. However, instead of selling the property, I prefer the buy-and-keep-and-rent-forever approach.

When looking to buy a residential property, you will need to do your homework. Here are the steps to consider:

1. Location is a major issue. You have to buy in a town or a country where jobs and population are growing. If you cannot

see a growth trend in the jobs or population in a particular location, move on to another location.

2. When you first start out on this journey, buy close to where you live. You know the area well, and you can manage the property with relative ease. When you are first getting your toes wet in the property game, hands-on management works best. Once you have a portfolio of properties you could consider hiring a property management company to look after it for you.

However, property management companies are not necessarily good managers. If you don't remember anything else in this book, remember one thing: Nobody cares about your money more than you do. Not your property management company, not your financial advisor, not your CPA, nobody. Therefore, having someone else look after your money is not recommended, unless it is done with proper systems and controls, as discussed in Four Ways Business Formula, step 3.

Of course, if there is no job and population growth where you live, then you are in a difficult situation. Stay away from property investments and focus on increasing your money-making potential in your own business or job. Save your money, in cash, until you can find a way to invest in property in another location. For a fuller discussion on long-distance property investing, please refer to chapter 23 (Expats).

In addition, think through the impact of the microchip on property investments. What I mean is that, because of the microchip, more and more people are being able to work from home. Companies no longer need to rent large office space. This has been the global trend for the last twenty years or so and will continue for the foreseeable future.

So for those of you, who find opportunities to invest in property close to where you live, let's carry on.

3. Another important skill you need is learning how to negotiate This applies not just to real estate, but also to any other situation in life. The key to is to be comfortable with being able to walk away if your conditions are not met. If you are selling something, know that if you have to say "Sorry, no deal," that you can do it. Never appear desperate, even if you are desperate. You must never let your desperation become apparent.

It is the same thing if you are buying something. Your attitude, whether selling or buying should be: I'm interested, but not desperate.

In addition, never let your weak point be known to the other party. But keep probing for the other party's weak point, and when you know it, exploit it in the negotiation.

4. Know the total all-in cost of the purchase. The purchase price is usually the largest figure, but by no means the only cost that you will incur in purchasing the property. Other costs include:

1) Transfer tax. Most countries will apply a transfer tax. The attorney helping you with the purchase will know the cost.

2) Commissions. If there is a real estate agent involved, there may be a commission to pay. Usually, the seller pays the real estate agent's commission.

3) Cost of renovations. How much will you have to spend to make the house inhabitable?

Make sure you take all of these into account when figuring out the affordability of the property.

5. Before making an offer, do a full due diligence of the house (in some jurisdictions this is done after the offer is accepted, but before the purchase agreement is signed). This involves property inspection and clearing various matters pertaining to the house so that you are not left holding a dummy. It is best to engage the services of a real estate agent to do this for you. If you want to do it by yourself, here are the minimum areas of inspection that you must cover:

i) Approved plans: the seller must be able to provide you with building plans approved by the city council. If the structure is not approved by the city council, the council could, conceivably, tear down the building.

ii) Building permit: Was the construction of the house authorised by the city council? If not, again, they could come in and tear it down.

iii) Services reticulation (sewage and waste water infrastructure): Someday you may find that the gutters are overflowing. You need to know where the manholes are located so that you can identify where the blockage is happening.

iv) Occupation Permit: Is the house legal to live in?

v) Rates/Property Tax clearance certificate. The transfer will get delayed without this.

vi) There should not be any outstanding amounts on the utilities—water, electricity and telephone—bills. The onus to pay these usually falls on the landlord. So if the previous owner hasn't paid them, they could become your problem.

vi) Are sewerage and power properly connected?

viii) Service manuals for the house—e.g. how to use the air conditioning units, kitchen fittings, light switches around the house. For instance, after we bought our house we found a light bulb in the middle of the garden. But we had no idea how to switch it on. It took me four years to figure that out. The switch was obscured behind a bush near the swimming pool!

ix) Maintenance records—is there any major appliance that needs to be regularly maintained? If possible, obtain the maintenance records.

x) Swimming pool—has it been properly maintained? Are there any major renovations looming, which could come back to haunt you?

xi) The latest property valuation should be less than six months old, or else your bank may not accept it for the purpose of granting you a loan.

6. How do you know what price to offer? I will explain this below, but first, let's look at a hypothetical example:

Total cost of the house you are interested to buy:	$110,000
Expected rental:	$800 per month or ($800 × 12) $9,600 per annum
From expected rental deduct: an allowance for repairs and maintenance of the property:	A good rule of thumb is to use eight percent of the annual rentals, which in this case is ($9,600 × 8%) $768 per annum
Therefore, Net Rent is:	($9,600 minus $768) $8,832 per annum

Now if you take the Net Rent figure and divide it by the Total Cost of the House you get:

$8,832/$110,000 = 8.0%

This is your current expected rate of return on the house, or rental yield.

This figure is key. You've got to assess whether it's good enough. The way to assess it is to compare it with two figures. The first is simply the interest rate on a bank savings account. But with interest rates at zero in many countries around the world, that doesn't help too much. Any return above zero sounds good, so zero is not a good yardstick against which to measure your potential rental return.

The other figure that you could use to assess the rate of return on your particular property is to figure out what rate of return other similar properties are selling for? This is usually the domain of a real estate agent. If you know an agent, call and ask for the *cap rate* (short for capitalisation rate) for a residential house in the locality you are considering.

If you don't have access to a real estate agent, then another way you can estimate the cap rate is to find out the interest rate on a ten-year government bond. Use five percent as an example. Since a property is not an investment that is guaranteed by government, your required rate of return could be higher (but not necessarily—since a government bond will pay the same amount every year for the next ten years. As rentals usually increase over time, you may not want to factor in additional risk premium for the purposes of your calculation). In this case let's just say we decide that it should be higher by ten percent. In this case consider your estimated cap rate is (5% × 1.1=) 5.5 percent.

If the rate of return you calculated were higher than this, I'd put in an offer. So, for example, earlier we calculated that on a purchase price of $110,000 our net yield would be 8 percent. This is higher than the cap rate of 5.5 percent. If you invested in the property, compared to the cap rate, you'd get a higher return. It's a good deal. I'd put in an offer.

The highest you are willing to pay for this property is:

$8,832/5.5% = $160,582 (all costs in).

I'd make an offer, but I'd also know in advance how high I'm willing to go. I'd start off on a low-ball bid, maybe at $ 90,000 (let's say that the additional costs will be 5 percent so the total all-in cost in this case would be $90,000 × 1.05 = 94,500). It would be a good place to start, allowing you room to move up.

If it's a buyer's market (meaning there are a lot of unsold houses on the market), start off with a low-ball bid. Have the attitude that if you don't get the property, no big deal. You'll find another.

However, if the market is hot, and people are buying properties, then you'll have to be cautious about the extent of your bargain hunting. It all depends on the market conditions. If it's a seller's market (meaning there are few properties for sale on the market), then it's best not to drive too hard a bargain. You could lose out on the deal. That's why it's so important to complete the above calculations before you make an offer. That way you'll know what you are willing to pay for the property. But draw a line and know your limits. Do not get drawn into a bidding war where you may end up paying more than your limit.

This is why I want you to think twice before *selling* your property. It is no small task to buy a property. Then you have to spend time to fix it up. Then you have to spend time to find tenants. Then you have to spend time creating leases. If you are offered a higher price for the house, factor in all of the hours that you have put into buying the property, fixing it up, finding tenants, preparing the leases. It should be apparent that it's better to hang on to it and keep enjoying the rental income.

Of course, if there is a major catastrophe in your life and you do have to sell, then sell. That's one of the purposes that the property is there for, to provide you with a cushion against financial disasters.

Buying a house to live in:
When it comes to buying a house for you to live in, the aforementioned calculations may not be entirely relevant. If your wife likes the house, then you may have to ante up whatever you have to in order to buy the house. In the above example I had said that the upper limit to your purchase cost figure is $160,582. However, if the house is for you and your family, you may be willing to pay even more than that. There is no problem with that. A house is a woman's castle. It's also her office. So there's both an emotional and a logical side to it. If she is going to be happy there, just buy it. From the woman's perspective, the home is her *office*. If she's got the office that she needs, she'll be happy. That means that she's got the kitchen space to store the groceries and her pots and pans. She's got the cupboard space to store your children's clothes. She's organised. So she'll be in a good mood more often, and be more of your partner in life than your adversary. This is the type of understanding a couple needs to move ahead in life financially.

I would like to re-emphasize the information about buying a *starter home* rather than your dream home when you are *early* in your journey to financial independence. Don't forget this one. Figure out a budget and stick to it. Don't do what I did. My budget was a certain amount, but just because I could afford it at the time, I went and bought a house for more than the budgeted price. Remember, at that time, my wife and I had not known the Four Steps Millionaire Formula. If we had, my wife and I would have been happy purchasing a smaller house, knowing full well that the real prize we were going after was much bigger—FREEDOM.

Commercial Property

When it comes to buying commercial property, the procedures and calculations you need to make are exactly the same as the ones we did above for buying a residential property. After you are satisfied that the property is in a good location, that there will be rental demand for it, and the due diligence report is negative (meaning there are no problems with the property), then you calculate the offer price.

As discussed earlier under *Residential Property–step* 6, the steps to calculate the offer price are as follows:

1. First, calculate the total all-in cost ($110,000 as per the example under *Residential Property–step* 6),

2. Second, calculate the Net Rent ($8,832 as per the example under *Residential Property–step* 6).

3. Third, calculate the rental yield (8.0 percent as per the example under *Residential Property–step* 6).

4. Fourth, compare the answer for step 3 with the cap rate for similar properties in that area (5.5 percent as per the example under

Residential Property–step 6). Again a real estate agent will be of great help here. But if you've been working on this project for a little while, you'll come to know of the applicable cap rate.

Once you have the figures, you can put in an offer, knowing how high you'll go before you walk away.

Other property information

After your offer has been accepted, what comes next? First, I'll assume that you have already engaged an attorney to draft the offer letter. Do not do it yourself. Engage an attorney, who will know the correct *offer* clauses to put in a letter, including the appropriate *out* clauses, in case your offer runs into trouble. For example, you will need the *out* clause if your bank does not approve your loan amount. Your attorney will have put in the appropriate clause, which allows you *out* without suffering a penalty.

If all goes well, then what? At that point your attorney will draft the Sale Agreement. If you are the *seller* ensure that there is a clause that says *Voetstoots*, which essentially means that the buyer is buying the property with all faults, latent and patent, so he cannot come back to you with any complaints once the property is transferred. Thereafter, it's his problem. If you are the buyer, ensure that before buying the property you do your due diligence as discussed earlier. Then you should be fine.

At that point you will own the property. If it's an investment property, you want to get it renovated and rented out as soon as possible. Once you have a prospective tenant, do not accept the tenant until you have done a background check on him, especially to determine if he pays his rent on time. You can do this by talking to his previous landlord.

Do not prepare the rental agreement (also known as lease agreement) yourself. Get an attorney knowledgeable in property rentals to do it. Even so, you could still find that your attorney may have forgotten to put in an essential clause, and it comes back to haunt you. Therefore, in Appendix I, there is an example of a lease agreement. Please note therein some key clauses that are not usually included in "standard" leases, such as "EXCLUSION OF LESSOR'S LIABILITY" and "NEW TENANTS AND PURCHASERS." If applicable, you'll have to get your attorney to insert them.

Also, do not let your tenant move in before the lease is signed. If you do, and subsequently you want to evict him, but there is no signed lease in place, you could have a problem. Once the lease is signed, everything is clear. The law can help the aggrieved party.

Hence, I can't emphasize how important your lease document is. You must read it line by line before you are satisfied with it. If anything doesn't seem right to you, query it with your attorney. Another problem, in fact, the biggest problem that I've come across is that key clauses have been left out. This would be difficult for you to know. You are not a property attorney.

In this regard, Appendix I will help you. Also, you will learn with experience, sometimes the hard way. Often, you learn as you go. However, when trouble happens, don't get miffed. You are allowed to be nasty, angry, depressed for five minutes, but no more. Learn the lesson and move on. You are in great company. All great wealth is built in this very same way. Nobody got it right the first time. Most importantly don't waste your most valuable resource—time—dwelling on messes that you can't do anything about. Just don't let them happen again.

Don't overcharge for your rental property.[29] Keep it affordable and the tenant turnover will be low. This is good for you because it will mean fewer months during the year when the property is without a tenant and your incoming cash flow will continue.

What's next after your tenant moves in? This is important. If your project is slightly underwater, it is not a huge problem. By *underwater* I mean that the rent is not completely covering the loan repayments (conversely, if the rent is covering the loan repayments, as well as the other expenses associated with the property, and you are left with a positive cash flow, then the property is said to be *cash flowing*). You are putting in some money from your own pocket. But that's not a huge problem.

What's happening at that point is that your tenant is helping you to pay off the house. With rental increases in the subsequent years, the cash flow will improve. And if the cash flow was underwater the first year, it should right itself in the next year or two.

You also need to do your part. That is, put most of your future savings into the property. Pay it off as soon as possible. Your goal is to have unencumbered (loan-free) cash flow from the property. In that way, you can do it all over again. If you need to be reminded how this strategy works, please reread Chapter 4, which includes a practical application of this scenario by describing how one of my former clients became financially independent in fourteen years.

Other Cash Flowing Investments

What other cash flowing investments could you use to achieve this same effect? For all practical purposes, none. Theoretically, we could consider ownership of other businesses, but that is too risky. I do not recommend you do this until you have attained financial freedom. Thereafter, investing in other businesses is a great way to become richer even faster. Basically, as was discussed in Chapter 4 (*The Four Steps Millionaire Formula*) once your PI> LE, you are in a position to try to achieve greater wealth. You could make a lot of money or lose a lot; but losing is not a problem, as long as it doesn't affect the basic foundation of passive income that you've built.

You could also consider investing in dividend paying shares or bonds. This is feasible, but it is a really slow way to get rich. You cannot obtain leverage—a bank would not easily lend you money to invest in these instruments. You'd have to use your own money. We looked at this point earlier in the chapter when discussing the *avoid mutual funds like the plague* topic: "Obstacle (3): You have no (or, at best, limited access to) leverage (that is, the ability to take a loan from a bank)."

Another key to investing in property is to have a sufficient cushion of spare cash lying around. The reason people lose money in property is that they do not anticipate the bad times. These are the times when there will be no tenant in your building, and you will have to pay the loan repayments from your own pocket. You must have an allowance for this type of event. You must be able to make at least three months of loan repayments from your own pocket.

If you can't make the loan repayments, your property will be repossessed by the bank and sold off to repay the mortgage (in other words, if you can't make the loan repayments then the bank has the right to sell your property and collect the amount owed to it; this process is known as foreclosure). If there is still a shortfall on the amount owed to the bank, you could be on the hook for even more money. Foreclosure is one of the biggest risks to investing in property. To guard against it, ensure that you are not too heavily indebted to the bank in the first place (a minimum of 20 percent down payment is suggested), pay off your loan as fast as possible, and have a slush fund stashed away to be able to make loan repayments, even if the property is temporarily untenanted.

Another big reason that people lose money investing in real estate is that they invest with the idea of making money from price appreciation. This tactic is called *flipping.** I discuss it in more detail in Chapter 10 (*Enemy #2: Your Bank*) under the "Good Debt versus Bad Debt" section. If you only invest in property for the cash flow and not for capital gains, then you will avoid this problem.

Some of you may be thinking "Hey, investing in property is easy for you, but what about me? I don't know a thing about investing in property."

When I first started fifteen years ago, neither did I, but just by having read the above, you are already more knowledgeable than probably 80 percent of the population.

That's really all you need. Nobody has a 100 percent advantage. That's like saying I want a guarantee. Well, no entrepreneur asks for guarantees, just a favourable probability. How do you create a favourable probability? Simply by *education*. Get the education you need. That will give you a leg up and you will be about 80 percent ahead of everybody else. From there you have to *do*. When you *do*, you'll get another 80 percent. You will get the 80 percent of the 20 percent you didn't know. Then you'll be at 96 percent perfection (80% plus 80% × 20% =16%; that is (80% + 16%) = 96%). That's an amazing place to be. Get there and you'll be on your way to financial abundance. But to get there you have to start.

That's how I have done a lot of things in my life. Get some education and then get in the game. And I've had fair success, even with property. Not all of my property deals have made me money. I've lost money, too. But I've learned from the losses, corrected course, and now with over fifteen years of experience investing in property, I can happily say that my gains significantly outweigh my losses.

Here's a question I get asked a lot: What if I can't find a property to buy at a good price? The answer is: Simply wait. Don't get nervous if your cash is lying in the bank "doing nothing." This term "doing nothing" is a favourite term of the financial services industry. It is used in order to make you feel like you're missing out on something good. It's a red herring. You'll end up putting your money into mutual funds.

Be patient. A property will eventually fall into your hands. If not, there is no harm with accumulating cash in the bank. Someday you could have sufficient cash to start your own business. The cash could potentially grow much faster and you may never need to get into property investments at all. Just holding the cash could be sufficient for you to become financially independent.

This is an important point. Let me explain.

Let's say that after having done my living expenses budget, I realised that I needed $100,000 per annum to live comfortably. I also figured that my life expectancy is 90 years, and the life expectancy of my wife, who is younger than me, is also 90. Using my own life expectancy, I will explain below.

My age today is 48. If I expect to live to age 90, that's another 42 years of life left. So if I had the following amount of money in the bank $4,200,000.00 (42 years × $100,000 pa), then I'm done. There is no need for further investment. Of course, I may live longer than 90, so it's best to have some amount greater than $4,200,000 in my bank account. The point is that to become financially independent you do not have to be invested in property, or bonds or other businesses, or anything else. If you have enough cash saved, you're sorted. Then you go out and enjoy life.

Think about this. It will make your life a whole lot less complicated.

To complete the analysis, let's say you had a property portfolio yielding a five percent net rental. At that point, all you would need is a property portfolio that's worth ($100,000/0.05) $2,000,000, which is much less than the $4,200,000 mentioned earlier. You could retire sooner as it will take you less time to accumulate a property portfolio worth $2,000,000, rather than cash in the bank of $4,200,000.

Also the capital graph would look very different in the two scenarios. See figures 7 and 8 on the following page.

Figure 7. Graph A

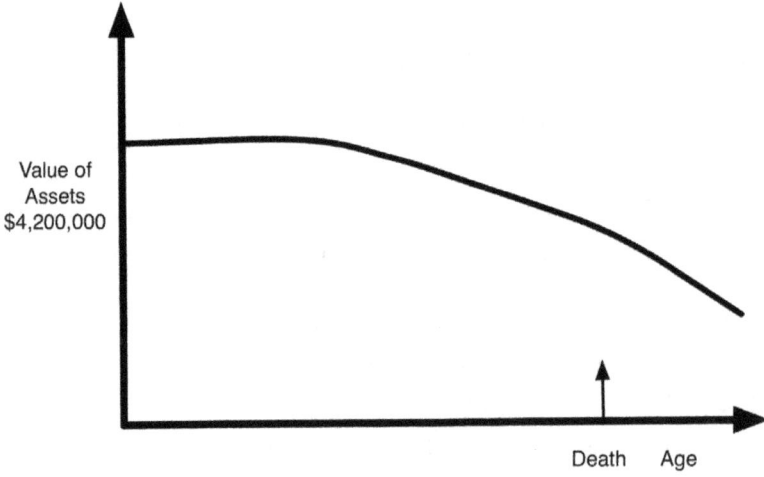

Figure 8. Graph B

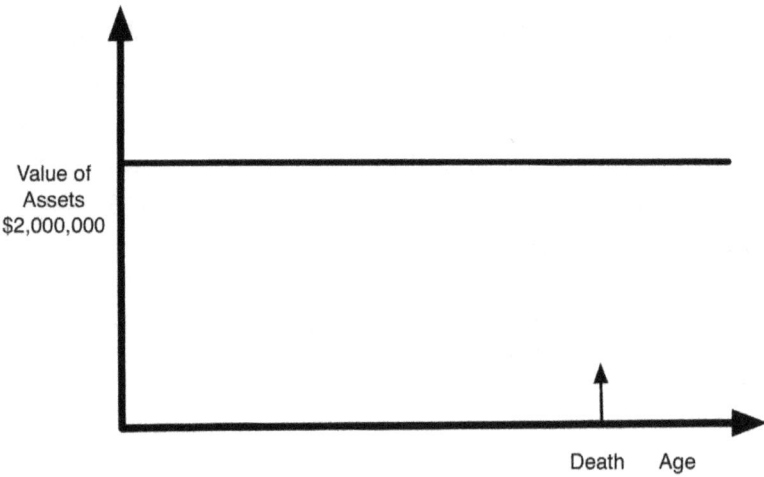

This is an important point. Graph A represents the case of having $4,200,000 in cash savings today and drawing it down at the rate of $100,000 pa over the next 42 years (as per the earlier example based on my age). You will eat into the capital, but your cash (that is, your capital) should last you for your lifetime. Graph B represents the situation of having a property portfolio worth $2,000,000, which creates a rental yield of $100,000 pa. In this case you do not eat into your capital; it stays intact throughout the next 42 years. You live off the yield (income) of $100,000. In scenario A you leave nothing behind for your heirs, in scenario B you leave behind $2,000,000 worth of property investments.

There is nothing wrong with the situation depicted in scenario A. Many retirees feel that they should leave something behind for their heirs. If you could, it's fine. But if you don't have enough to affect that, then think of yourself first. Let your heirs figure out how to secure their retirement. Please give them a copy of this book, they'll be fine.

> **Question:** Are you saying that if I have money in the bank, as I use it, it will decrease over time, but if the money is invested, and I use the income from the investment, the capital will remain constant?

> **Answer:** You are right. That's exactly what Graph A versus Graph B is depicting. In the Graph A scenario, the money is in a bank account. As you use it, it decreases over time versus the Graph B scenario. Here the money is invested in a property portfolio. The property portfolio throws off income, and that's what you use for your living expenses. The capital value of the money is preserved.

Let's carry on talking about property investing. It may take you a while to pay off your first property. It could take seven to ten years. But once that's done, then you have the income from your first property, plus your savings from your job or business to buy a second property and pay it off sooner than the first one. We assume that your property income and your personal savings are now bigger than when you started this process.

This is a realistic assumption because most peoples' incomes grow over time. The key question is whether or not they hold onto their greater income. If you remember in the *Introduction* I said that one of the richest men in Botswana told me that he takes care of his money. He was talking about holding onto your money, meaning hold onto the profits and excess cash that you earn as a result of your hard work. If you can't do that, no matter how much money you make, you'll always be poor. If you can't, no matter whether you make $50,000 pa or $500,000 pa, you'll always spend more than you make.

If you apply the Four Steps Millionaire Formula diligently over your lifetime, you will find that your cash flow snowballs; there's more money coming in automatically than you know what to do with. That's the whole idea. That's where you want to get to as soon as possible. That is also the only way to fight inflation: having more money coming in automatically than going out.

Buying trinkets instead of buying cash flowing assets will retard your growth. Don't let Big Bad Business kill you by fooling your brain into buying products that are bad for you—the expensive wedding dress, which you will only wear for one night, the big wedding, which you don't really need, the bigger car, which costs more to run, the bigger house, which would be lovely, but just be patient, and the luxurious vacation. These are all obstacles, which will trip you up on your road to financial independence. Intentionally planted there by Big Bad Business to make them rich and you poor. We've been brainwashed to spend our money without giving a thought to it. We've been trained to spend rather than save. DON'T play their game. Be smarter. Play so that *you win and they lose*. You get the idea.

The Key to Great Wealth

Here's the key to great wealth:

Invest for cash flow. If you do, it won't matter if the markets are going up or down. The cash keeps coming in. Invest primarily for cash flow, not capital gains. Acquire assets for their cash flow, and then use the cash flow to acquire more assets. Get away from transactional business, like buying and selling stocks, mutual funds and real estate.

Let's look at an example of why a cash flowing investment is better than a capital gains type investment.

Say you had one million dollars. If it were invested in a revenue producing property earning ten percent pa, you'd get $100,000 *every year*. If you spend the income, you still have your capital intact. And you'd have another $100,000 at the end of the next year as well as at the end of every year after that. However, if it were invested in a capital gains type investment, such as a mutual fund, it could be worth the same—one million dollars—or it could potentially be worth ten percent more. However, it could also be worth ten percent less at the end of the year. If it's worth ten percent more, you could withdraw $100,000 and you would be even. Your capital would still be intact. But if it's worth ten percent less *and* you withdraw $100,000, then your investment is worth (one million dollars less 10 percent = $900,000 − withdrawal of $100,000) $800,000. This could cause you great difficulty, so make sure you invest for cash flow first; when that's done, you can go for capital gains.

Financial Plan of the Rich

Before I move on to the next chapter let me blast through a common myth. The common financial advisor's refrain, pay yourself first, is great advice. But it stops there. What you mustn't do is put the money into a retirement account and buy mutual funds as financial advisors would suggest. Instead, fund a property down payment account. Judging from my clients' and my own experience this strategy should outdo a retirement account over time. See the following page for an example.

This diagram is saying that your objective in life is to take your personal efforts (salary) and keep buying assets (Asset #1, Asset #2, etc.).

Continue doing so until such time as PI (passive income), such as dividends are greater than 120 percent of LE (living expenses). Then you achieve FREEDOM!

The astute observer will also notice that the above is simply a rendition of the Four Steps Millionaire Formula, or MSIP.

Figure 9: Financial Plan of the Rich

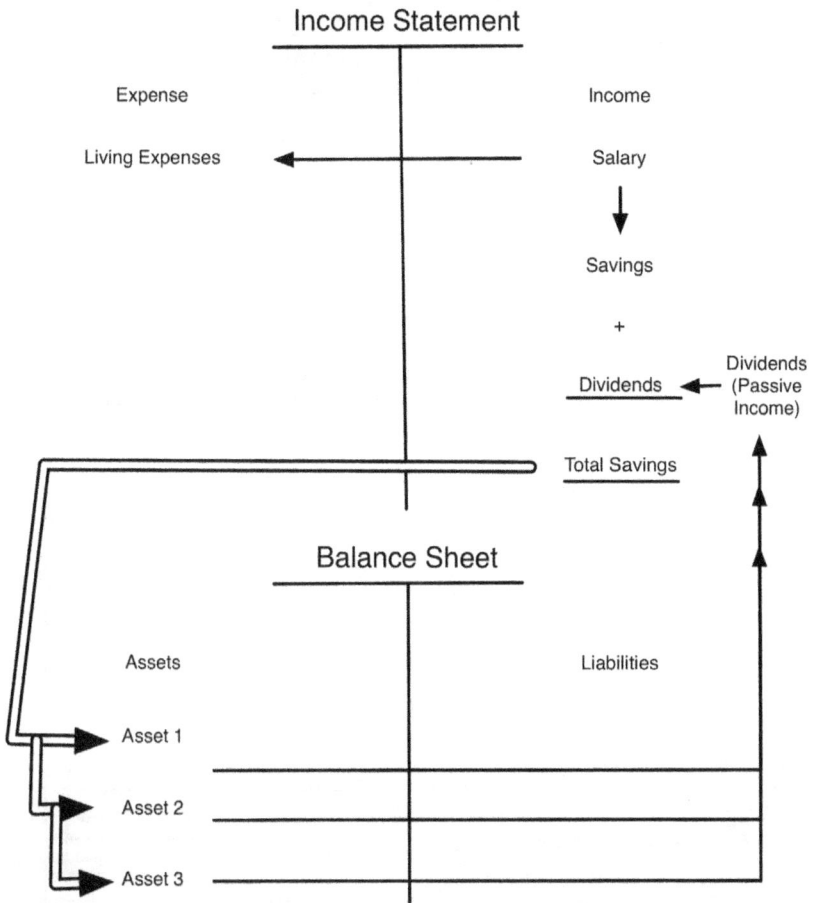

Income Statement

Expense	Income
Living Expenses ←	Salary
	↓
	Savings
	+
	Dividends ← Dividends (Passive Income)
	Total Savings

Balance Sheet

Assets	Liabilities
Asset 1	
Asset 2	
Asset 3	

To polish your understanding of the power of the Financial Plan of the Rich, let's compare it to the Financial Plan of the Poor. Please refer to figure 9.1.

Figure 9.1: Financial Plan of the Rich
vs. Financial Plan of the Poor

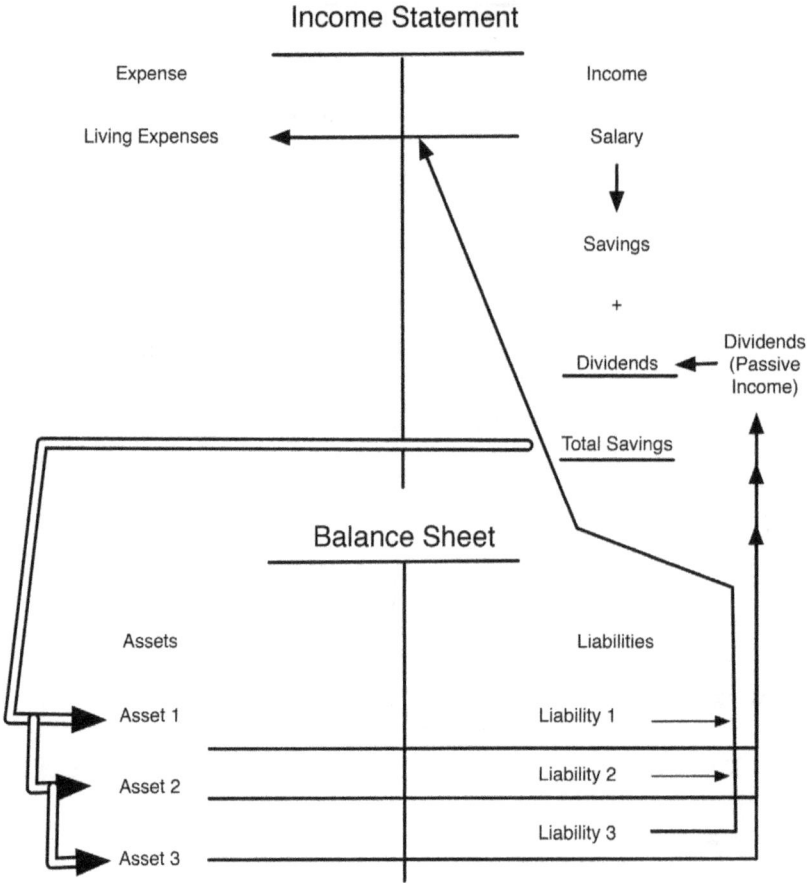

This diagram is saying that compared to the rich, what the poor do with their savings is buy liabilities (Liability #1, Liability #2, etc.). For example, a bigger house, a flashy car or a luxurious vacation. They pay for these goodies with credit, and then spend much of their lives paying off the credit. Instead of being retained, cash flow is leaving their pockets.

Hence, an excellent way to understand the difference between an Asset and a Liability is as follows:

An ASSET *produces* money, for example, rental income from a warehouse, or business income from a beauty parlour.

A LIABILITY *takes* your money, for example, paying for branded clothes.

Buying Assets leads to FREEDOM; buying liabilities leads to POVERTY.

If you have understood everything we discussed in this chapter, congratulations! In terms of financial literacy, you are now in the top one percent of the world's population. You deserve a celebration.

Chapter 8: How to Win Big

Understand that you have limited resources, for example, the resource of time. There are only 24 hours in a day. Subtract the sleeping, eating and ablution bits and you only have approximately ten hours of productive time left. These hours are the only time that you have to engage in activities that will lead you to the goals that you desire. Let's assume that one of your goals is financial independence. You can spend those productive hours in activities such as working at your job, learning a new skill or engaging in truly refreshing leisure. Or you could spend that time watching TV, playing video games or gossiping with your friends.

Which use of your time will move you toward your desired result of becoming financially independent faster? The first set of activities or the second?

I think you'll agree that the first set of activities has a better chance of moving you towards financial independence.

Consider a similar situation with one of your other major resources—money.

What will get you to your goal of financial independence faster? Leaking your money by spending on trinkets and then investing what's left it into a *hope and pray* mutual fund? Or, saying *no* to trinkets and frantically shoveling your money into a piggy bank, and then investing it in self-controlled, cash flowing investments? You decide.

The key to getting rich is to learn how to make good choices when it comes to the use of your resources. You must be efficient. Get the biggest bang for your buck. Most of us start out with the same resources. For example, we all have the same amount of time. So why is it that some people become financially independent and others are poor? The answer is simple: The rich know how to make good choices when it comes to the use of their resources. They are constantly moving resources from a lower level of productivity to a higher level of productivity. You need to do the same. It is how you win big.

That is also how nineteenth century French economist, J.B. Say, described entrepreneurs. It is a powerful thought—in fact, it is the gist of this book. It is the main lesson. Move your resources from a lower level of productivity to a higher level of productivity. For example, instead of spending your whole life at dead-end jobs, start a business. You ought to make more money with the same amount of time and effort. Instead of buying retirement accounts, use your savings to start a business or buy a property.

Those who move resources from a lower level of productivity to a higher level of productivity win big. *Finish and Klaar!* (South African lingo meaning ... *Really finished*)

Entrepreneur Roadmap

We now have the last piece of the puzzle; a huge mystery that mankind has been trying to solve for centuries—the mystery of how to become an entrepreneur. The answer is simple. Just follow **TAM**:

T: Embrace the Entrepreneurial Traits: You know them—*SPO*.

A: Know the winning **A**ttitude: It is—*How to Win Big.*

M: Master the **M**ethodology: Know how to do a Business Plan—covered in Chapter 5 (*How to Make Money*).

If you know the answer to this puzzle, this mystery—how to become an entrepreneur—and you implement it, what can stop you from achieving financial success?

Part III: Mind the Trap

Chapter 9: Trap #1: Yourself

Yes, it's you. Let me take you back to the first Entrepreneur Trait: An entrepreneur is a person who relies on himself. That's it. Nobody is going to make you rich. It's not going to fall into your lap. You have to decide to become rich. And once you decide to become rich, the next step is for you to figure out how it works. There's no use blaming the banks or the educational system. They will continue to do what they do. But it's your life, and if you want to be financially independent then you have to figure it out.

By making yourself responsible for the financial outcomes in your life, you will feel extremely liberated. You will no longer have to depend on anyone else. Nor will you have to waste your energy blaming anyone else. Say to yourself "I am responsible for my life." Those are not just words; that's your manifesto. It's how you're going to live your life. And you will live with all the consequences of that decision.

There is no reason for the consequences to be undesirable. Let's revisit the *Law of Cause and Effect*. If you want to be rich, simply follow what the rich do to become rich. And by reading this book, you now know how the rich get rich. It's the Four Steps Millionaire Formula as well as the Four Ways Business Formula, should you choose to use it. And that's it.

What can go wrong? Oh, just about a million things. And yes, you should worry about what can go wrong. But just enough to come up with a good plan; and then you have to jump! If you've done a certain amount of homework, you've eliminated a good number of pitfalls. The rest you will figure out as you go along.

Some of you may fail. If you do, you will figure out how to start again. There's no shame in failing. It's part of the process of becoming successful. Remember how you learned to ride a bike? You didn't get it right the first time. But eventually you were pedaling along just fine. Obviously, it's better if you can avoid failure, but it can happen.

The biggest obstacle to your financial independence is your lack of financial education. That is why you are reading this book. Whatever you feel needs further work, read up on it. There is plenty of information in this world. But you need someone to make sense of it for you. That's what I've done in this book. I've shown you the roadmap. Now you know which direction to go. You will fill in the details as it suits you. For example, your choice of career, you'll decide. For example, your choice of business, you'll decide. For example, your choice of investment, stay away from mutual funds and you'll do fine.

I look forward to hearing about your successes. Good Luck!

Chapter 10: Trap #2: Your bank

Your bank can be both your friend and your enemy. We'll cover the enemy part first then we'll look at how a bank can be your friend.

Good Debt vs. Bad Debt.

First, understand there is no such thing as good debt. Debt is bad, period. So try not to have any. But when you are early in the process of building your financial independence, if used wisely, it can help you to get a good start. This is where I have my biggest issue with bankers. They do not provide any education with respect to good debt and bad debt. They hand out loans to anyone who qualifies on the basis of his numbers (income, assets, etc.). Giving out loans to people who are not intimately familiar with the *good debt–bad debt* divide is like handing a loaded gun to a toddler. In essence, giving a loan to a person without proper education about how to use the loan is like handing a loaded gun to a toddler.

It is no wonder that we have huge problems in the world related to debt. The 2008 debt crisis is hardly over yet. And here's the amazing thing. During 2010 to 2012, banks in Botswana had started to promote *home equity extraction loans*. It was just a few years back that we had witnessed the massacre of people all over the world because of the subprime problem, and then banks in Botswana have the gall to promote the same thing all over again. Soon thereafter, the International Monetary Fund (in simple terms, the global central bank) came out with a warning for Botswana stating that the country needs to consider the increasing levels of individual debt.[30]

This is exactly what the book is preaching to you. Get smart, or be eaten alive by the Gruesome Trifecta: Government, Big Business and Financial Services. Their sneaky tricks will bankrupt you, so beware.

What is bad debt? Bad debt is any loan that you take out for consumption or for the wrong sort of investment. Let's look at a few examples.

> Credit cards. As previously discussed, credit cards are a poor move if used for consumption. See Chapter 6 (*How to Save Money*).

> Personal loans. When you take out such a loan, it is signaling one of two things: first, that you are not making enough money, or second, that you have no idea how to control your expenses. So forget about taking out a personal loan. Instead, learn how to make more money and/or control your expenses. Suggestions can be found in the sections on *Start a Business*, (Chapter 5) as well as in *How to Make More Money at your Job*, (Chapter 15) and *How to Save Money* (Chapter 6).

> Car loans are a genuine "Catch-22." It is so easy to justify a car loan. All you need to do is to convince yourself that you need a car to get to work in order to produce income. However, if you live in a city with a reasonable public transport system, that is a far cheaper way to get to work and back. If you do, in fact, *need* a car, the problem is that soon you start to convince yourself that you need a *nice* car because then you won't have to buy one again in the future. This is a big mistake. If you insist on buying a car, buy one; but buy the least expensive one, the one that gets your work done and that's it.

I would like to introduce you to my *car buying* mistake. Living in Botswana, I had gotten caught up in the "4x4 craze." Botswana is 4x4 country; and a 4x4 in Botswana is a very useful option because, as a developing nation, the tar often ends and you find yourself travelling on gravel. In addition, there are countless opportunities to travel into the wilderness. Having spent time in Botswana as a child, I had come to love the big wilderness and yearned to go camping in the wild. The flames of my budding desire were abundantly fanned by my reading 4x4 magazines and watching 4x4 *fundies* (South African lingo for *expert*) on TV describing their 4x4 adventures in the wild.

At just about that time, I also discovered loans. I found that my bank manager was very willing to give me loans, big loans. So off I went and bought a 4x4, a Toyota Land Cruiser 100 Station Wagon, 4.2 Turbo Diesel. It was slightly used—had only 9,000 km on the odometer when I bought it. It cost me $80,000. I happily spent another $15,000 to kit it out for the bush—roof rack, Old Man Emu suspension, VPS paint protection film, winch, the works.

I paid off the car in about four years. But, financially speaking, it was not a great idea. Today, about ten years later, I still have the car, but, at best, it's worth less than a third of what it cost me; it may be worth $ 30,000 today. Of course, I did not need such a lavish car. It has taken me on some amazing camping trips all over Botswana, but I did not need such an expensive car at that time in my financial journey. A $10,000 car would have done the job just as well. At the time, I could have bought a *house* for what the land cruiser cost me. That house today would have doubled in price, possibly to ($80,000+$15,000=$95,000 × 2)$190,000, and it would have been giving me a net rental return of a potential 20 percent on the *original* purchase price. In this case the rental would have been about ($95,000 × 20%) $19,000 pa.

But in financial terms, the Land Cruiser has caused me a whopping loss. Since I still have the car, let's calculate this *notional* loss as follows:

On Capital:

What the Land cruiser is worth today:	$30,000
What the property could be worth today:	$190,000
Difference:	$160,000

On Income:

What the Land cruiser provides in passive income:	$0
What the property could have provided in passive income:	$19,000
Difference:	$19,000

Total Loss as of this point in time:

Capital Loss:	$160,000
Income Loss (assuming I held the property for the past year):	$19,000
Total Loss:	$179,000

What does the above mean? It means that if I had bought the property instead of the Toyota Land Cruiser, today, I might have been enjoying an EXTRA $179,000 in my pocket, plus I could have owned a used Land Cruiser. To accomplish that it would have meant that I had sold the property for $190,000, and also pocketed a year's worth of rental income, which adds up to ($190,000 + $19,000) $209,000. Subtract the cost of a used Land Cruiser worth $30,000 = $179,000. This calculation assumes that I had purchased a used Land Cruiser worth $30,000,which I can easily obtain. So I would have had both the cash ($179,000) and the Land Cruiser. Instead, I just have the Land Cruiser, but not the $179,000.

This is similar to what we talked about in Chapter 8 (*How to Win Big*): the efficient allocation of your resources. I allocated $95,000 to an expensive car. As a result, I now own an expensive car, which has depreciated in value. Or I could have allocated the money to a property investment, and today I could have had both the car and more money in my bank account. I could do a great deal with an extra $179,000 today. This is an amount that could change your life.

But I made the wrong choice. I opted to take out a loan to fund my *consumption* (4x4 adventures), whereas I should have taken out a loan to fund my *cash flowing investments* (the property investment I never made). I had opted to build a lifestyle rather than build wealth. This was a huge loss for me.

This occurred because I did not know the difference between good debt and bad debt. Nor did I know the story of the Financial Plan of the Rich (Figure 9).

Obviously, the money is not coming back. I've lost it. If I had to do it all over again, of course I would not buy the Land Cruiser. That's the lesson: reduce how much car you buy. Cars depreciate. The moral of the story: Get rich first using debt to buy cash flowing investments. Then upgrade your car.

There you are. Loans can kill. Or they can make you rich. Be careful how you use them. Allocate your resources toward higher productive use.

How can you go bankrupt taking out loans? If I could not make the repayments on the car loan, the bank would repossess the car. If I still owed money on the loan after the bank auctioned it off and recouped some of the money, then they could come after me for more money. If I don't have it, then I might go bankrupt.

Borrowing to invest in mutual funds. Thou shalt not do this! As we have discussed previously, you have no control over the forces that impact the direction of the value of the mutual fund. If the mutual fund falls in value and the bank gets nervous and *calls* on the loan—meaning they want you to pay it back—and the value of the mutual fund is below the amount of the loan, you're in trouble. Unless you service the loan from other sources, meaning you put more good money in after bad, you're in trouble. This is not a smart strategy. Borrowing to invest in mutual funds is a bad idea; it is as bad as gambling. It's not the path to riches, but ruin.

These are some examples of bad debt. What is good debt? You have to be careful because there really is no such thing as good debt. You are better off not having any debt at all. As a global society, we have been brainwashed into thinking that having debt is acceptable. This is not true. Many of my rich clients had debt early in their careers, but now avoid it. Some always avoided it, choosing to bootstrap their way to financial success. They reinvested the profits of their businesses building their property assets slowly, rather than obtaining loans.

The loan approach can be very dangerous. But if you are educated about the risks and manage them very carefully, then there is money to be made from borrowing.

Here are examples of good debt:

Car Loans. We have discussed this one above. Just to reiterate, buy the least amount of vehicle possible. Used is better than new. However, if you have passive income, which is going to pay for the car rather than your active income, that's less of a problem.

House Loan: This is the same as the car loan. Buy as little house as you absolutely need. You will upgrade to a larger home later on when you have built up sufficient passive income.

Investment property. Good choice, but you still have to be careful. You must put as high a down payment as possible. Make sure that you have thought about vacancies. What if the rental income stops for three months? Will you be able to fund the loan repayments? You must have money allocated for this purpose. What about repairs and maintenance? Repairs and maintenance issues will happen. Make sure you have allocated money for this, as well. Keep money for a margin of error.

Here is the biggest mistake to avoid: Do not invest for capital growth. Do not count on the property increasing in value. This may never happen. In fact, the price may reverse. You simply want to pay off the property and enjoy the cash flow from rental income for the rest of your life. If you have selected the right location and the economy is on your side, the rental income should continue to increase because of rental escalations.

If the economy is not on your side and you have to lower your rental rate, then as long as you had not borrowed too heavily, you should be able to ride out the downturn.

The reason people went broke investing in property during the recent (2008) subprime mortgage crisis, which became a global problem, not just a U.S. problem, is that investors had adopted a *flipping* mentality. That is, the idea was to buy houses with no money down, and sell them twelve months later. The buyers assumed that the increase in property values would continue forever, and when they didn't, these *flippers* were in trouble. What followed was a financial blood bath, caused by a combination of a lack of financial education and greed.

But if you have invested for cash flow it really doesn't matter if the economy has gone bad, and the market value of your property has fallen. As long as you have tenants and there is cash flow coming in, you are making money. Of course, as mentioned above, if your property is mortgaged, you have to manage the downturn in the economy very carefully, or you could lose your property investment and the money you have invested in the property.

This point is so important that I need to illustrate it with an example.

Let's say you bought a property worth $200,000, And you put down 20 percent ($200,000 × 20%) or $40,000 on it. You are left with a loan for $160,000. This would be your original situation at the time of purchasing the property:

Total Cost of Purchase:	$200,000
Down payment:	$40,000
Bank Loan:	$160,000

Let's say that in the next year, the economy goes bad, and the market value of your property drops to $170,000. If you were forced to sell it you would have to repay the bank its $160,000 and you would be left with ($170,000-160,000) $10,000 for yourself. That's a 75 percent loss for you, calculated as follows:

Down payment:	$40,000
Net Sale proceeds (proceeds from sale of house less loan):	$10,000
Net Loss:	($30,000)
Percent Loss: (−30,000/40,000)	−75%

Obviously, that was not what you had in mind when you bought the property. This illustrates one of the ways you can lose money when you buy property. It is an important lesson. Heed it well.

However, if you are *not forced* to sell the property, and the property is fully rented, and the loan repayments are being met from the rent coming in from the tenants, there is no problem. It does not matter what happens to the market value of the property. If you have sufficient cash reserves, as we discussed earlier, then even if the property goes without a tenant for a short while there is no problem. If you had not geared up the property too much (meaning that the level of your borrowings were not too high), then even if you have to make the loan payments from your own pocket while you find new tenants there is no problem. Finally, let's assume that you have to lower the rent to get new tenants in the door. If you can sustain the difference in cash flow to make the loan payments from your own pocket, then again there is no problem.

Question: If I buy a property to rent it out, will the rental rate not be affected by the market value of the property? If the market value goes down will it adversely affect the rent? Does this still make buying the property with the objective of renting it better than buying the property with the objective of selling it?

Answer: If the market value of the property goes down because the economy is in a funk, then, yes, your property rentals could fall, as well. However, you have a lot of control over this. For example, you could divide your property up and let it out to multiple tenants so that your total rent is still the same as before the economy went bad. If you have chosen the location of the property well, then even if the market value of the property goes down, you should still be able to rent out the property. Meaning it still makes you money in the form of rent, or cash flow. If you sell it, you could be selling at a bad time. If you wait for a few years and the economy recovers, you may get a better price. Therefore, it usually works out better to buy with the objective of renting rather than selling.

Hence, it is imperative that you are aware of all of these scenarios when you buy property on loan. Leverage is a double-edged sword, it can make you money, but it can also lose you money. You have to be careful and consider all the downside effects of leverage before getting into such a situation.

On the flip side, do you see how this is a far superior investment as compared to investing in mutual funds? Mutual funds depend, for the most part, on capital gains. But capital gains are not in your control. Cash flowing investments are very much in your control. For instance, in the above example, you could not control that the price of the property had fallen to $170,000. But if you were not pressed to sell it, you'd just continue to let it out. Therefore, it would matter naught whether the value of the property was up or down. All that would matter was that the rental income was coming in. In addition, the price of the property would probably go up eventually because, as the rentals increase as a result of inflation, the price of the property would normally follow suit.

That's a far more sensible investment than putting your money into mutual funds and watching the money gyrate all over the place. If the fund is down, there is nothing you can do to give it a positive outcome. Not only could you lose money, you could lose things that are much more important in your life like peace of mind.

Your bank, your friend

How can your bank be your friend? In many ways. First, it is your friend when it lends you money, which you can use as good debt. Second, it is a place for you to keep your cash. Cash should not be saved in your home. Third, it helps you to keep track of all the transactions that your accountant will need to collate at the end of the year to do your books and tax returns.

It is important to have a separate bank account for your personal transactions from the bank account for your property or business transactions. Your accountant will love you for it, and you will also be pleased because you won't have to go through the mess of separating your personal transactions from your property or business transactions. Remember, as proponents of *How to Win Big*, we are into achieving maximum results with minimal effort. So a little bit of planning here will pay off when doing the books for your property or business.

There you have it. The *scoundrels* (bankers) actually do some good, as well. However, it is ultimately your responsibility to figure out what's good for you in life and what's not.

Chapter 11: Trap #3: The U.S. Fed

This is a difficult topic, but I will try to deal with it in as simple a manner as possible offering only the most necessary information you need to understand the huge impact it has on your life. For a more detailed analysis, books on the U.S, Fed are widely available; it has been closely studied in recent times following the great financial crisis of 2008 (also known as the subprime mortgage crisis, the credit crisis and the great recession).

One more point: this section is not intended as an indictment of the U.S. Fed. Many of the central banks around the world are doing exactly what the Fed is doing. Therefore, consider the Fed as a metaphor, which can help you understand the manipulation of money that is taking place around the globe and how it could impact your future financial security.

It is imperative that you understand the meaning of all this, which of course I'll come to as we go along.

Background:
In the past, humans transacted with each other by bartering. We exchanged goods and services, not money. If you were a chicken farmer, and I did your accounting, you paid me with a chicken. Now how many

chickens could I eat? The wife wanted me to bring home some mutton, as well. But you didn't have any goats.

Therefore, a more efficient medium of exchange was required, which encouraged the development and use of gold coins. You paid me in gold coins, which I could use to buy a goat. The wife was happy, and hence, so was I. The problem arose when occasionally I would have to travel to a far away town to buy some other type of animal for my wife, perhaps a cow. She kind of liked the creamy white liquid that came from cows, and I, being full of love for this beautiful woman, had to oblige. However, once, when I travelled to a distant town, I was waylaid by robbers. I was travelling on foot. I was a young accountant and couldn't yet afford a horse and I lost my gold coins to these thieves. "A curse on ye!" I screamed after they had disappeared over the nearby grassy knoll and were out of earshot. That was not a pleasant experience.

The next time I had accumulated enough gold coins to buy a cow, I went to my local goldsmith, a nice chap whose family I knew well. I asked him if he would keep my gold coins in his safe and give me a receipt for them. He obliged, and off I went to buy the cow.

I didn't meet the robbers again, but a new problem arose: When I went to purchase the cow, it was selling for six gold coins. The problem was that I had *one* receipt for a full ten gold coins. I had to return to my local goldsmith to ask him to give me ten individual receipts for the ten gold coins.

I paid for the cow with six receipts and kept four. The farmer who sold me the cow was just as happy. He knew he could collect on his six gold coins anytime. In fact, he didn't really need to do that. He could just use one of the receipts to buy a water canteen if he so wished.

Hence was born money.

All was well and good to that point.

However, problems soon started. My local goldsmith realised that I would never come back for the ten gold coins. In fact, every month I would come to him and deposit more gold coins for his safekeeping. In return, he issued me additional receipts. After a while I had placed one hundred gold coins in his custody.

Soon after, my friendly neighbour, Michael, wandered over to the goldsmith because he had a business idea. He wanted to cut down trees and sell the logs to a carpenter in a neighbouring town. For this, he would have to buy an axe, a donkey and a cart, but he didn't have any money. The neighbour asked the goldsmith to lend him some money. He needed one hundred gold coins to buy the materials for his startup venture.

The goldsmith immediately realised the opportunity. He knew that he had one hundred of my gold coins in his safe. He knew that it was unlikely that I would ever come back to ask for all of the coins at once. He figured, at most, I might ask for ten gold coins. So he held back ten gold coins and told Michael, "Look, I can lend you ninety gold coins at twenty percent interest. After one year you will have to pay me back one hundred and eight coins. This includes the return of the capital (ninety coins) plus interest, at twenty percent, (90×0.20), which comes to eighteen coins."

Michael agreed and the transaction was concluded.

A year later, I had deposited another one hundred gold coins with the goldsmith. I never did come back to ask for the original ten gold coins that the goldsmith had kept aside. And my neighbour, true to his word, came back with one hundred and eight coins. The goldsmith had made eighteen gold coins profit from *my* money. My neighbour had created a good business carting logs all over the area. And I was none the wiser. Everybody was happy. It was not obvious that I had been told an untruth. However, the money that I considered to be mine, in fact now, belonged to the goldsmith, and all that I was left with was a claim for a similar amount.

In the meantime, the business of banking was born. From this story let's extract a few important banking terms.

Deposits: The initial one hundred gold coins, which I had saved up with the goldsmith, as well as the second lot of one hundred gold coins, which I later gave him for safekeeping (for ease of illustration this second lot of one hundred gold coins is ignored in the Balance Sheet example noted below).

Interest: The eighteen coins that the goldsmith charged my neighbour to let him use the ninety gold coins for one year.

Interest rate: Eighteen gold coins divided by the loan amount of ninety gold coins, that is, 20 percent.

Loan Amount: The ninety gold coins that my neighbour borrowed.

Reserve Ratio: This is the number of gold coins that the goldsmith decided to keep in his vault to meet any demand of gold coins I might make. In this case it was ten percent (the ten gold coins that he held back and did not lend to my neighbour). This system, whereby a bank holds only a fraction of its customers' deposits in cash, and lends out the rest, is called a *fractional reserve banking system*.

The above explains the basic framework of a bank. It takes in deposits from depositors like you and me, and it lends out the same monies to other customers, also like you and me. It holds back a reserve amount of cash for any daily demands from its depositors. In our example, the bank kept back ten percent and lent out 90 percent of all the deposits it received. If the goldsmith had put in five dollars of his own money to start the bank, this amount would be called the *capital* of the bank.

See below for what the balance sheet of the bank in the story above would look like.

Figure 10

Balance Sheet of Prehistoric Bank (Ltd)

Assets

Cash on hand:	$15
Loans receivable from customers:	$90
Total assets:	**$105**

Liabilities and Equity

Owed to depositors:	$100
Capital:	$5
Total liabilities and equity:	**$105**

It all looks fine up to this point. As long as the economic system is functioning properly, the bank can continue to operate. The bank can continue to take money from one person and lend it to a different person.

But there are huge problems lying in wait. A bank could never hand back all the deposits if they were demanded at one time, although it has promised to do just that.

Let me explain.

What if all the depositors showed up to withdraw their money at the same time? The depositors are owed $100 (see Figure 10) and want it immediately. But the bank does not have all that money available. It only has $15. What then? The bank goes bust; it closes its doors and all the people standing in line at the teller's window lose their money. (For the sake of simplicity, I have skipped some details. However, the foregoing explanation is sufficient to explain the problem with the current fractional reserve banking system where you are promised all of your money back. Although, the reality is that you can only get a fraction of your money back at any point in time).

Can this happen in real life? Of course! It happens all the time. There are far too many examples for me to mention. Recent incidents of banking crises include the UK's Northern Rock (September 2007) and the Cypriote banking crisis (March 2013). Each time the respective governments jumped in to bail out the banks. Conclusion: Banking is an inherently fraudulent activity made *legal* by the governments of the world.

Bankers will jump on me, clamouring: "No, no, you're wrong, banking is legal." However, that's only because the governments deem it so. In my view, it is questionable. Be very cautious about your dealings with this very dangerous institution.

Let me expand. When you deposit money into a bank, you have a claim on that money, but it has become the bank's property. It's not as safe as you think. If the bank goes under, you're out of luck. Basically, when you put money into a bank, you are taking on what the financial services industry calls *counterparty risk*. It's a big risk.

In addition, there's potential for enormous financial havoc. As an example, let's specifically cast our eye on the U.S. Federal Reserve, the central bank of the USA, which we shall call the "Fed" for short.

The Fed was formed in 1913. But strangely, it is neither a bank, nor does it have any reserves. It is simply a cartel[31] dominated by the larger banks[32] posing as the central banking authority.[33] Some of its activities are dark and dangerous. The problem is that these activities influence our lives in very real ways.

For example, the Fed can print money out of thin air.[34] I have provided a basic explanation of how and why this is done in Appendix VI.

What does this mean for you? The Fed's printing of money impacts you in two ways. The first is that the money that the Fed prints, which is known as *fiat money*, as opposed to *gold-backed money*, known also as *commodity money* ends up in your local bank (no matter whether you are in the US or abroad).[35] That bank then makes every effort to lend it out to the unsuspecting public. As the public takes on loans, its finances become stretched (that is, the public has taken on too much debt and at some point cannot afford to pay back the loans). At some point, the entire economic house of cards comes crashing down (including the banking sector).[36] As hordes of businesses go bust, millions of people lose their jobs and their homes. They get crushed financially. After a while, the Fed repeats the process, called reflation, which again ends with the same result.[37] The most recent reflation exercise began in 2008,[38] and we have yet to see how it will play out. The end result is likely to be very bad for the whole world.

Hence, you should be wary of trusting anybody who works for the Fed. I am talking about the higher-ups, those that are in the know of what's really going on. Those who are in the lower ranks are just carrying out orders. Of course, they should be aware of what's really going on because it affects them as much as it affects you and me, ordinary humans just trying to make a living, raise a family and retire securely.

Let me give you another example of the Fed's deceptive antics. Consider their use of the term *quantitative easing*. What is *quantitative easing*? It is the same thing as printing money. Because the Fed knows the negative connotations associated with the term *printing money*, it will not use it, replacing it instead with an obscure term such as *quantitative easing*, which only financial types will understand.

Somebody from the government sector might say: "But printing money is not the official terminology of quantitative easing; the official terminology for quantitative easing is *the expansion of the balance sheet of the Fed*." Yes, I know that. But 99 percent of the world's population would not understand the term but they would understand *printing money* much more easily. So why not use terminology that helps every day people to understand what's really going on?

Here is another example of a financial industry term designed to mislead you: *haircut*. The term *haircut*, which was most recently used in the instance of defaults on Greek debt during the Greek debt crisis in 2011, simply means *loss*. The financial media could just as well have said that bondholders of Greek debt would incur a loss; instead they said that the bondholders would incur a *haircut*. There is no need to hide the truth; it is simply because it's the way of the financial services industry.

Similarly, it is important for you to be wary of trusting any central bank. I'm going to show you how to deal with their potentially lethal antics.

Beware: Our success at becoming financially independent is hugely affected by what the Fed does, but only if you are in the *system*. That's the key. If you are a pawn in the system of the Fed, then you are in trouble. You need to work hard to get out of the system, and then you will be fine. Explaining how to do this is a major objective of this book. Understanding the Four Steps Millionaire Formula is how you avoid being hit by the Fed's shenanigans. Become financially independent as fast as possible, then you are out of the system. If you don't have bad debt, or depend on a job, or need to pay for your over-sized house, big car, or fabulous vacation, then you will be the last man standing, while others are dropping like ninepins all around you when the next financial storm hits.

The second way that the Fed's printing of money impacts you is via the spectre of inflation. Consider the following: There are two people in a room, you and me, and there is just one pencil. We both want to buy the pencil. If we both have exactly ten dollars each in our pockets, the most we could offer to the seller of that pencil would be ten dollars. However, if by some magic, the government was able to print another twenty dollars and put those newly printed twenty dollars into our pockets—ten dollars each, then we could bid twenty dollars each for the pencil. All of a sudden the price of the pencil went up from ten dollars to twenty dollars. That is inflation.

By printing money, the U.S. Fed has created a huge inflationary problem in the US and in the rest of the world. This impacts our lives horrendously. Poor people become poorer and the middle class gets hollowed out, while the rich get richer.

Let's look a bit deeper into inflation. Simply put, inflation means your paycheque is getting smaller.

The poor and the middle class have to work harder, run faster, and make more money. Families feel immense financial strain just to survive, spouses start fighting over money matters and then divorce. This printing of money is tearing up the very fabric of society all over the world.

Some economic commentators will point to the official rate of inflation in the U.S. and say, "Not so, inflation is well under control." Well, as Jill Keto explains in her book, *Don't get caught with your skirt down—a practical girl's recession guide*, official inflation numbers out of the U.S. are questionable.[39]

I suspect this goes on in many parts of the world. We feel the inflation. Prices keep going up, from utilities to food to everything else.

Therefore, we should be wary of believing government numbers. Almost nothing coming out of the government is believable, any government, anywhere in the world.

As I have previously stated, get out of the system. I don't know if the system has been intentionally set up to enslave you, or if it is just massive mismanagement on the part of the central banks. There are proponents for both sides of the argument. However, either way, it's a problem. The shenanigans of government are shoving people into modern serfdom all over the world.

Again, get out of their system. That's it. And the way out, again, is the Four Steps Millionaire Formula. That's why I've spent so much time discussing it. One of the major objectives of this book is to teach you how to escape from poverty.

However, it won't happen if you succumb to sneaky marketing and buy clothes that you can't afford. It won't happen if you succumb to the siren call of the banks for you to take out personal loans. It won't happen if you use your savings to buy retirement accounts such as 401(k)s in the US, RRSPs in Canada, RAs in South Africa or BRPs in Botswana. Retirement accounts may go under a different name in your country, but they are all WFD—Weapons of Financial Destruction. It won't happen if you don't invest the time to become financially literate.

But it will happen if you get financially educated. It will happen if you follow the Four Steps Millionaire Formula or Four Ways Business Formula. Neither Four Steps Millionaire Formula nor Four Ways Business Formula are pie in the sky get rich quick schemes. These are strategies that take time and effort to implement, but will place you on solid financial footing.

Then you will be out of the system. If you don't have a loan with a bank, it can't touch you. If your money is spread around in companies and trusts, the government will have a harder time lifting your money out of your bank at will. If you have cultivated the fortitude to say "No!" to sneaky marketing then you won't go broke.

In the introduction to this book I mentioned that it is important to know how to tackle inflation. The answer is not in some magical security like an *inflation-indexed bond*. Those are indexed to the government's figures of inflation. We don't necessarily believe these numbers. For real people down on the ground, trying to make a living and keeping our heads above water, the answer is that to beat inflation you need to implement ... the Four Steps Millionaire Formula. That's the only way out. As long as you have more passive cash coming in than you need to live on (i.e. PI>LE), you will be fine. If you are not in that position you are in trouble.

Question: How does President Nixon's 1971 act of cutting the tie between the U.S. dollar and gold affect us?

Answer: That action was the basis for the U.S. being able to print unlimited dollars.[40] Prior to 1971, all major currencies were tied to gold. The issuers of those currencies could not create money out of thin air. Simply put, now the monetary authorities have the license to wreak havoc on the public. The result has become boom and bust cycles around the world.[41] As I write this book, we are probably in another such cycle. The U.S. Fed has been printing money and creating debt like crazy since 2008, flooding the world with liquidity (cash). As a result we seem to be on an asset price increase frenzy. The stock markets are up; the prices of properties are up. But the debt has to be repaid. How this will end, nobody knows. So, as discussed earlier, prepare now to get out of the system. Even if the storm never hits, you are better off being on the solid footing that the Four Steps Millionaire Formula affords you.

Question: Going forward, could we get deflation instead of inflation?

Answer: Certainly. Deflation is when the overall prices go down rather than up. This is entirely possible. If the new credit bubble currently in progress implodes, people will again be without money and that could cause deflation followed by a depression. So the solution is: Don't be without money. How? Get financially independent as fast as possible. And for this important purpose, just follow the Four Steps Millionaire Formula. If you have money in your pocket in a deflation, you are a king. You can buy up assets at fire-sale prices. In any crisis—inflation or deflation—the people who have sorted out their financial matters will win big time. If no such crisis hits, as I just said a little earlier, you are still better off being on the solid footing that the Four Steps Millionaire Formula affords you.

Chapter 12: Trap #4: Your friends

I am referring here to peer pressure. It is one of my favourite topics, because it causes so much financial damage. What is peer pressure anyway? I define it as pleasing others, even when you don't want to.

I call it the Peer Pressure Trap (PPT).

Peer pressure gets in the way of financial security. You spend money that you shouldn't be spending. It's money that you should be saving and investing, as fast as you can, so that you can build your ark of financial independence, so that you can be free. Free from money stress, free to choose how you want to live, free to buy all the stuff you don't need. Spend as much as you want on frivolous things—the electronic gadgets, the vacations, the clothes as long as you are doing it *after* you are financially independent. Before that point, you are potentially creating a life threatening situation for yourself.

Why do people succumb to the Peer Pressure Trap?

To fit in. To impress others. To please others.

Like drinking beer. Lots of youngsters will drink beer to fit in because their friends are doing it. They get drunk and into trouble. I always warn my kids not to do things that can get them into big trouble. Small trouble is okay; it will be painful, but it won't be life threatening. Not doing house chores can be a problem. But big trouble will be a problem. What can get almost anybody into big trouble? Alcoholism, fornication and drugs. Consciously make a decision to stay away from these life-threatening activities.

For example, drunk driving. What if you killed someone? How will you ever shake the guilt from your mind? Or, a one-night stand that results in a pregnancy. If you are forced to marry that person, is that the person you would have chosen to marry in a sane moment? Or smoking?

Quitting smoking is a monumental task that I wouldn't wish on my worst enemy. The best thing, of course, is never to start in the first place.

Peer Pressure Trap is slavery. When you buy the bigger car or the bigger house to impress others, long before you can afford these luxuries, it enslaves you to the bank and to your rich friends.

Break free of peer pressure. Feel free to be yourself.

Have you thought about why we have become a society that runs faster and faster every day? We try to cope with numerous commitments just to please others. We fear rejection and criticism. Sometimes we end up burning ourselves out. All for what? To please others?

So kindly cease and desist. Stop pleasing others.

And that's your motto to fight off peer pressure: Stop pleasing others. When you do or say something that does not meet with the approval of other people, and your friends think it's not *cool*, just say, "I like it, I am happy."

That's it. You're done. Nobody can argue with your feelings. They're yours. If you're happy, so be it. End of story.

Think about it!

One more thing: Learn how to say "No." This is one of the most important words in the English language. Don't get dragged into other people's agendas. Work on your own. Don't do anything that moves you away from your goal. Just learn to say "No." Of course, figure out a polite way to say it, but don't be scared to say it. Here's how I say it, "Sorry, I'm just a bit busy."

Chapter 13: Trap #5: Big Business

The worst thing about big business is its sneaky marketing. This is one of the biggest obstacles to saving.

The art of marketing has come a long way. Marketers have figured out how to make us feel compelled to buy things. They do this by linking the purchase of goods and services to our emotions—love, prosperity, belonging, status.

For instance, I once asked a sales clerk who worked in a clothing store why the shape of jeans changes so often. She mentioned to me that the fashion gurus change the design and then start a new trend. And people want to look trendy, so they buy the new jeans.

The trendy button is all about emotion, the peer pressure emotion. We want to please others, so we buy what we think will impress them. And then what happens? We use our hard-earned money—or worse, we use our credit cards—to buy a pair of jeans we didn't really need in the first place.

If you can afford "trendy," it's no problem. Buy the latest fashions. But, because I know what's happening in the real world—99 percent versus one percent, I can tell you that most of my readers cannot afford to buy trendy clothes. You need to be saving your money so that you can get to the "I" step in the wealth building process (MSIP). Once you've built your wealth, then you can go back to building a lifestyle. And if you do that, what a lifestyle it'll be. No financial worries. You'll actually be able to enjoy all the toys and luxuries you buy, not spend the nights lying awake worrying about how you are going to make the monthly payments on your credit card.

And, in the overspending scenario above, if somewhere along the line you lose your job, you are truly in deep trouble.

Sneaky marketing is one of the greatest enemies of financial independence. You need to learn how to say "No!" to the barrage of bad advertising that tempts us daily to buy, buy, buy.

Once you can say "No!" that should give you the time to think through the marketing coming at you. Do you really need the stuff? Even if you think you do, put it off until the next day. Then see if it was just temptation, or do you really need the object that's being marketed to you?

In other words: think before you buy.

Part V: What stage of the life cycle are YOU in?

Chapter 14: Teenager

Mr. or Ms. Teenager, you are in the best position of all the age groups to achieve the success that you desire, whatever that may be. Academic success? You can do it. How to find a job? Sure. How to get rich? No problem. I'll discuss five things that are important to you; there may be more, but these are a good place to start learning about the real-life challenges that lie ahead.

1. Getting good grades in school

Concentrate on your studies and do as well as you can. Forget about everything else. At this stage of your life getting rich should not be your major goal. Why? If you have a formal education, then you can learn entrepreneurial skills by yourself anytime. Entrepreneurial skills are what you'll need to get rich, but these are within your grasp any time. A formal education is not. With respect to a formal education, it's now or never.

When I finished my B.Comm at the University of Toronto my immediate thought was to re-join my parents, who were living in Botswana at that time, and start a business. I had always wanted to be in business, ever since I was young. I have always been itching to be rich, and I figured that going into my own business would be the shortest route to get there.

Immediately, there were two things wrong with my line of thinking. First, I knew nothing about how to start and run a successful business. As a result, trying to start a business would almost certainly have ended in disaster and would have been a bad financial move. Second, my motive, at that time, for getting into business was *money*, money for me. Unfortunately, as I have learned the hard way over the years, the craving of money is not the ingredient that makes for a successful business. A business will be successful if its *first* motive is to serve other people, to solve other people's problems. This is an important concept that we have already discussed in Chapter 5 (*How to Make Money*).

As it turned out, I did not return to Botswana. My father, a medical doctor, working for the Government of Botswana, had other plans for me. He was intent on my pursuing a post-graduate qualification. He said, "Son, I don't want you to come back to Botswana just now. Business, you can get into anytime in your life. But you are still young. And you are single. This is a great time for you to continue your studies. You will not get this opportunity again in your life. Get a post-graduate qualification first and then we'll talk about a business for you."

That was one of the best pieces of advice I have ever received in my life. And I am repeating it for your benefit. Keep your studies going as long as possible; at a minimum, at least until you get an undergraduate degree. I know that many obstacles can come your way, but if you have a big enough *why*, you'll blast through any obstacle to get what you want.

Many of you are on the cusp of leaving high school and entering university. Here's a bit of advice for you: When you enter university plan on just one thing—getting your degree as fast as possible and getting out of there.

I went horribly wrong on this account. The point is best explained with a story: I started my university career at the Institute of Business Administration at the University of Karachi in Pakistan. After three years, I transferred to the University of Toronto. Imagine a 21-year-old Pakistani man, coming from a conservative (at that time) Pakistani society, who finds himself in Toronto, Canada, an open society. All of the benefits of an open society are available to him ... as well as the vices.

Well, with no parents around to monitor the young man's activities, it was easy for him to *get distracted*.

I spent more time partying than studying. Because of that I reduced my course load and my university career started to stretch out.

When I related this story to my teenage son as we were driving along one day, he did a double take. "What? You Dad? A party animal?" I understood his disbelief because today I am exactly the opposite. I have a great home life. I'd much rather sit at home and watch a movie with the family, or light a campfire in the backyard, or read a good book, than go out partying. I realise these activities might seem incomprehensibly boring to young people. I am just making a point—that partying can be bad for you.

Luckily for me, my partying spree did come to an end. God came to my aid. One day, upon awakening from sleep, out of the blue, I said to myself, "Stop this nonsense! Your Dad is using his hard earned money to send you to university in a foreign land. How can you waste it?" Well, with that bit of self-talk, I immediately cut myself off from the friends that I felt were taking me down the wrong path. I refused to see them or to return their calls. Immediately, I buckled down, focused on my studies and finished my university degree.

So, to my son, who, God willing, I suppose will shortly be going to university, I say, "Son, when you go to university, I will not be around to watch over you. Remember to be careful of three distractions—women (boys in the case of my daughters), drugs and alcohol. These three things will kill you. Remember you are going to university for one purpose and one purpose alone—and that is to get an education. You must focus on your studies and nothing else."

2. How to find a job?

This is a pretty big topic, and I've covered it in detail in Chapter 15 (*New Graduate*).

3. How to get rich?

In Chapter 4 (*The Four Steps Millionaire Formula*), I revealed the Four Steps Millionaire Formula, or MSIP for short. Understand the formula and follow it if you want to get rich. That's all you have to do. Of course, it's not as simple as all that; it's a process. It will take years to get rich, but if you follow the roadmap you increase your chances of getting there and reduce the time it will take. However, pay attention to your studies first. Learn about the Four Steps Millionaire Formula in you spare time. Go over the Four Steps Millionaire Formula once to understand the big picture. After that, focus on Chapter 6 (*How to Save Money*). Ignore everything else. Learn how to save and practice frugality. Learn to enjoy saving money. That's what rich people do. This habit will serve you well. Get through university and then work on the Four Steps Millionaire Formula topic in earnest.

In addition, do not multitask. That is, don't try to be good at your studies and simultaneously start a successful business. You will not be good at either. Focus on your studies, and in the summer months, if you are not studying you can try your hand at a part-time business. The best approach, however, is to focus full-time on your studies and related employment, such as an internship, get it done, and then you're free to start a business if that is what you choose to do.

Most importantly, prepare your mind for wealth, which means reading this book and any other personal finance book you can get your hands on. You are at an age where the quicker you cultivate the garden of your mind with good information the quicker you will achieve positive outcomes in life.

What irks me the most is that our educational system stresses the term *job*. It wants to train young people in math, science and computer skills to make them successful at finding a job. What it doesn't warn kids about is that jobs are fast disappearing. The future lies in understanding entrepreneurship and financial education. Who's teaching that to youngsters? No one; it is up to you. Learn those skills by yourself and get ahead earlier and faster than the rest.

4. How to get motivated

Lack of motivation is a problem that hits everybody, no matter the age. We all come to a point where we figure "Ah, forget it. Why do anything?"

I've been there, I know how it feels. But there is a solution.

You need to have a big enough "why." The only reason that I was able to get out of bed every morning when I was writing this book is that I had a big why. I, too, was hit with doubt and depression at times. I didn't even know if I could write a book. What if I couldn't finish it? What if nobody liked it? But I had a huge "why." I knew that there were people out there who needed my financial advice otherwise they may die. I also knew that there was bad financial advice permeating the world that I just had to break apart. Once I knew these things, getting out of bed was a cinch.

You have to figure this out for yourself. For instance, if you are questioning why you are trying to get good grades in school, ask yourself the question: "Why am I studying so hard?" And then think through the answers. Maybe you want to be a doctor and save lives. Maybe you want to be an astronaut and explore the heavens. Maybe you want to own a hi-tech company and rival Microsoft. What is your *why*? Figure it out and write it down somewhere. It will keep you going when the going gets tough.

We have already covered *long term view*. To be successful in life you have to be thinking many years out. If you give up your studies today, sure, it might feel a lot easier, but you will regret the decision in the future. Many more options are available to you if you complete school. But your dreams won't just fall into your lap. You have to *do* stuff to achieve your goals.

And here's another hugely important point. If you recall we have already discussed the three *Entrepreneur Traits*. Let's discuss the first and the third ones in light of where you are in your life. These traits apply to every *successful* person in his or her life.

A successful person has decided that he will rely on himself to achieve the progress he seeks (Entrepreneur Trait #1). He has made the decision to upgrade his skills and knowledge so that he can do that. Once he has made that decision he now has to live with the consequences of that decision, which includes not knowing the outcome of his efforts in advance (Entrepreneur Trait #3).

For example, when you sit for your exams, you have no clue about the outcome. All you know is that you've prepared for the exam. And now, what will happen, will happen.

This is the route that every successful person has taken—be it a successful entrepreneur, a doctor, or an academic. If you are driven to be successful then you don't have a choice. You have to live with this phenomenon. You have to go down a path where the outcome is unknown.

This doesn't mean that you take this step without adequate thought. No entrepreneur likes to take risk. In fact, entrepreneurs always try to reduce risk. And that's exactly what you are doing, reducing risk. How? By studying hard. You have no idea how you are going to perform on your exams, but if you study hard you know that you have reduced the risk of failure.

That's all you can do. It's enough and you are a *superhero* for having done that much to achieve the success that you desire.

"But what if I don't get all As? My teachers will be so disappointed."

"Oh no!" you think. Doubt, depression and tears.

This is where you have to learn how to conquer the Peer Pressure Trap. It is a skill that will hold you in good stead all your life. What's happening is that the fear that you are feeling of not living up to the expectations of others *is* hurting you. By wasting your time in doubt, depression and tears you are taking away valuable time that you could be spending studying (or even relaxing to refresh yourself). And if you walk into the exam room with that burden it could adversely affect your performance in the exam. So you need to be aware of it and deal with it.

Here's how:

Recognise that you can't control the minds of other people. If they have a certain expectation from you, so be it. Most likely they love you and they want you to do well. But you can't go to them and say "Hey, don't put me under this pressure." They won't stop. It won't help.

Hence, I am going to give you the most powerful words you will ever hear in your life. Only please yourself.

(This does not apply to God or your parents!)

If you think that you have studied hard enough, that's all that matters. If that level of work gets you As or it doesn't, then so be it. You are not an-swerable to anyone else, as long as you can honestly say to yourself: "I did my best."

These are powerful words of wisdom that I've shared with you. Let me recap:

1. To get motivated, find your "why."

2. Understand that as a future successful person you have taken the decision to depend on yourself. That automatically

means there are no guarantees for you in life. Control the
risk of failure as much as you can, but live with it.

3.   Stop pleasing others.

4.   You are a superhero.

Now go out and do your best!

5. Life's real struggles

I love it that I am catching you so young. Because there is an adage that
says: prevention is better than cure. I wish that I had received this advice
when I was just starting out. It would have saved me from so many mistakes. Mistakes are both good and bad. Good in that you learn a lot from
mistakes. Remember that there are no failures in life, only mistakes. And
one must learn from one's mistakes. But you can't avoid all mistakes. They
are part and parcel of living on earth. Don't fear mistakes.

But mistakes can also be bad. They can be expensive. Where possible, you
should try to avoid them. Why try to reinvent the wheel? Learn from those
that have gone before you, and you will save a lot of time, effort and
money. The more of your resources—time, money and effort—you save, the
more you can allocate them to creating a better life for yourself.

With that said, let's look at the three biggest challenges you are going to
face in your life: Wealth, Health and Relationships. Reading this book
enables you to conquer the Wealth matter. Now comes Health. Discussing
this topic in detail is beyond the scope of this book, but let me just briefly
say:

1.   Watch what you eat. Avoid foods with empty calories. For in-
     stance, when you eat an apple you are consuming calories,
     but you are also getting great nutrients like vitamins, miner-

als and fibre, which help your body in staying healthy, strong and productive. But if you eat pastry instead, you are eating empty calories—heaps of them, which have no beneficial nutrients. Your blood sugar spikes, you can't burn off all the calories and they become excess body fat.

2. Exercise as often as you can. Get away from TV and the Internet, go outside and get some exercise. Any movement: a walk, a jog, a game of some sort.

3. Take care of your body now and it will last you for a long time.

And then there's Relationships. This is a topic on which a detailed discussion is beyond the scope of this book, but I've touched on a few essentials in Chapter 16 (*Marriage Time*) and Chapter 29 (*Don't Trust Anyone*).

Chapter 15: New Graduate

As much as I am a protagonist of entrepreneurship, the job option is an appropriate route to follow early in your career. It will help you find your passion.

How do you find your passion? Well it won't just fall into your lap. You have to consciously think about it. You have work for a while to get a feel for what you think you are good at and what interests you. Then you have a better chance of deciding what it is that will hold your interest for a long time. As you go on this journey, be aware that entrepreneurship is the way of the future. Look for the careers that can take you down that path.

For instance, later on you could become a consultant in a particular area of expertise. You could provide consulting services to the company you initially worked for, or to other companies in your field. Lots of computer people will find consulting opportunities that could be lucrative.

Or you could become a supplier of products to the other companies in your field.

Let's return to the topic of how to get a job. I will give you my insights from having been both a job seeker and an employer. I graduated from University in 1989, and I subsequently set up my own shop in 1999. So I have ten years of experience as a job seeker and twelve as an employer. As an employer, at the peak of our business, we employed eight people. During the twelve-year course of our business we employed a total of fourteen people. So I can share with you a bit about how to get a job from the job seeker's perspective, as well as tell you a bit about what an employer is looking for when hiring a new employee. The first thing you need as a job seeker is a curriculum vitae (CV). A simple chronological CV will work best most of the time. It gives the employer, at a glance, all the information he needs to make an initial assessment of your *interview-worthiness*. Here's an example.

Figure 11

CURRICULUM VITAE

John Doe
P.O BOX 1X, Gaborone
CELL PHONE: 1234567
Email: johndoe@email.com

CAREER OBJECTIVE

Chartered Accountant seeking to help the organisation achieve its goals. I have over 4 years experience in accounting roles and over 3 years of experience in auditing.

EDUCATIONAL BACKGROUND

Chartered Accountant: Botswana Institute of Chartered Accountants, 2013

Bachelor of Arts: University of Botswana, 2009

IGCSE: Gaborone High School, 2005

PROFESSIONAL EXPERIENCE

XYZ CHARTERED ACCOUNTANTS: 2010 to present

STAFF ACCOUNTANT

JOB RESPONSIBILITIES:

- Provide accounting, tax and auditing services.

- Evaluate record keeping procedures.

- Improve procedural efficiencies.

EZ ELECTRICAL: 2009–2010

ACCOUNTS CLERK:

JOB RESPONSIBILITIES:

- Preparation of bank reconciliations.

- Preparation of trial balance.

- Preparation of Financial Statements—Balance Sheet, Income Statement, Cash Flow Statement and Notes.

COMPUTER PROFICIENCY

Proficient at Spread Sheet, Word Processing, Accounting and Tax Related Software, including:
EXCEL, WORD, INTERNET.

HOBBIES AND INTERESTS

- Best Photographer award for filming cricket event, 2010.

REFERENCES:

Available upon request.

CV preparation tips:

1) Do note that the above CV is not a model CV. It's just an example to illustrate the chronological format; writing a good CV will require that you refer to a CV writing service or read a book on how to write one. It will take a bit of time to get a CV done. Take your time because it is important that it communicates your qualifications and skills clearly.

2) Do ensure there are no spelling errors. A spelling error immediately creates a doubt in the mind of the employer with respect to your competence. You want as few strikes against you as possible when sending in your CV.

3) Also, ensure complete truthfulness of your resume. A worthy employer will check your history.

4) Your CV should be accompanied by a cover letter, which introduces you to the prospective employer. It is an opportunity for you to sell your skills and qualifications. Because a cover letter will vary depending on the reason for your submitting your CV, it's best you consult with a CV writing service, or read about how to do one.

Once you have prepared your CV, try to get it in front of a prospective employer. If the economy is in a recession, you will have a tough time landing an interview. Your best bet in a tough economy is word of mouth referrals. Call people that you know who are working in companies or industries that you would like to work in, and ask them to keep an eye open for you should a job opportunity come up. Twice in my job career, I've gotten a job through contacts rather than through sending my CV in response to an advertisement.

Once you manage to land an interview, here are the essential tips.

1) Dress smartly. Not over the top, but neatly and professionally.

2) Try to find out as much as you can about the company in advance. Prepare one or two questions that will demonstrate your interest in the company you wish to join.

3) In Appendix II, I have laid out some questions that an employer might ask when interviewing a job candidate. There are many different questions that an employer could conceivably ask, but these are my preferred ones. Prepare and practice your answers.

4) What personality traits is an employer trying to assess in an interview? There is a checklist of these items for you in Appendix III. Don't get too overwhelmed by this checklist, just be aware of it. Prepare for what you can prepare for, for example, your appearance. Don't be too worried about the other soft factors like "confidence." Just be yourself. Be polite, and above all, be present. Don't be thinking of anything else during the interview. Before you enter the interview room, take a deep breath, exhale and say to yourself: "Be present." Then resolve to listen carefully to the interviewer and to give your answers as honestly and as carefully as you can. By being present, you will be putting your best foot forward.

5) If you pass the first interview, it is likely you will be invited for a second interview, as well. If you get to the second interview it usually means that the company is interested in your candidacy. But don't let your guard down. Be just as careful to prepare for the second interview as you did for the first one. You are still in the process of trying to sell yourself to the company.

6) With the help of Appendix II and III you can have a good idea of what's going on in the mind of your prospective employer. It's job hunting gold. Once you know that, you know what he's looking for, which helps you prepare for your interview by including things he may want to hear.

For example, you know that your interviewer is interested in examples of your ability to do the job. Offer him examples of what you could do for him. Don't be shy about it. Don't wait for him to discover it. Tell him. Help him see who you are. Of course, wait for the appropriate moment to bring these attributes to the interviewer's attention. He may ask you a question that allows you to segue into the topic. If he doesn't, then find an excuse to mention what you think is going to be important for the interviewer to know.

With this type of preparation, your level of preparation has gone up a few notches. And that will show. Also remember not to be too desperate for the job. After going through the interview process *you* may be the one to reject the opportunity if it doesn't seem right. Use your sixth sense—your gut—if it warns you to beware.

How do you listen to your gut? By going silent, being still, closing your eyes and quieting the mind. Then take a deep breath, exhale and ask yourself the question that you are seeking an answer to. Then just listen. It takes some practice, but after a while, you will feel that you can hear your gut (your sixth sense) talking back to you. Try it and see if it works for you. If not, ignore it and use your judgment, which is the same thing.

How to make more money at your job

Assume you did well in the interview and now you have an offer from the employer. You agree on the salary and you accept the job. How do you succeed at the job and continue to grow within the organisation? As much as I am a fan of entrepreneurship, there is no reason that you can't become financially independent while working for someone else. It's likely going to take longer because you can't control your income growth, but here are a few tips that should assist you in making the most out of the opportunity.

1) Arrive to work on time. Arriving on time shows that you are a responsible person. This trait is very important to any employer.

2) Keep your word. If you promise something, keep your word. If it seems that you may not be able to keep your word then inform the other party immediately. You may be worried about the reaction, but it's always better to let the other party find out sooner rather than later.

3) Act like an owner. Align with the interests of the company. Think how you can a) increase the profits of the company or b) lower the costs of the company. Ask how you can contribute in these areas.

4) Speak up. Holding back your thoughts will help no one, especially yourself. But always do it politely.

5) Find ways to make yourself an indispensable employee. If cuts come, yours will be delayed as much as possible, and you may even survive until the next economic boom.

6) Work hard. When you are at work, work. Don't waste time chatting needlessly with your colleagues. And when it's time to go home, stay late an extra half hour.

As a new graduate you probably want to buy lots of toys. If it's not too expensive then do it. But remember, if your ultimate goal is to "become totally financially independent," as one new graduate told me, then you have no option but to follow the Four Steps Millionaire Formula. And therein, there is no room for spending on nonessential items. A little bit of pleasure spending is fine, but not a lot. The rest of your money should go into MSIP.

You may be a little sad that you couldn't buy yourself a new pair of jeans this month. The money had to be saved for the down payment on your investment property. But look at it this way. Big Business wants you to feel that way. They have conditioned your mind so that you feel *deprived* if you don't buy that dress. Well, it's time to fight back. As you refuse to buy the dress, think about the dollars piling up in your Financial Freedom account.

If you can say no, you will increase your chances of becoming totally financially independent. Otherwise, you may just not make it.

"Hey Faiz, you're taking away all the fun from life," you may complain.

OK, let's think through this.

As an example, think about how it may be twenty-five years into the future.

We have the person who spent all his income when he was a new graduate and is now living hand-to-mouth. He doesn't have enough money to pay off his credit card bills. He can't buy a new pair of jeans, nor can he afford to go on a vacation. Daily he fights with his wife over money matters. The parents divorce, the children are devastated. The money problems are still there.

On the other hand, there is the person who saved like mad when he was a new graduate. He lived on less. He didn't run his life according to the expectations of his friends. He didn't go to the movies. He brown-bagged it to work. He bought his first investment property and then another. He makes more money each month from his rental properties than from his paycheque. His children's education is taken care of and he spends time with his wife and family. They take vacations and live a modest but comfortable life.

So who's having more fun? You decide.

Keep in mind the discussion on *long term view*. That's what it's all about. Think twenty-five years out. If you are 25 years old today, the day will come when you are 50. What will your situation be then? What would you like it to be? Then work your way backwards. You will know what you have to do today, not ten years from now, when it's already too late.

I'm forty-eight as I write. I've never felt better in my life. God Bless. Touch wood. If you look after your health, you should have good quality of life long into the future. But you also must have the money to enjoy your health. If you are fifty and financially independent, that's much better than being fifty and broke. In addition, it seems that humans are living longer. That's great, but it could also be a problem. Where are you going to get the money to survive the longevity? You've got to think about it today. Right now. Or you're done for. Toast.

And if that happens, you'll ask: Whodunit? Answer: You*self*, of course.

We've talked a lot about why entrepreneurship is the superior career choice in the long run. But you may be concerned if you have never taken business courses in university. You might question whether or not you will be able to get into your own business. Of course, yes. As Brian Tracy reports, according to a Babson College study: *Most people who graduate from business school actually end up getting a job, not starting their own business.*

What a waste of all that entrepreneurship training. In the real world, a businessman is born the moment he embraces the Entrepreneur Traits. That's it. A businessman can learn everything else as he goes along.

How to invest

Make full use of your potential; maximise your moneymaking abilities. Do well in your job, or start a business. Then hold onto the money you make. Then buy real estate. It's just MSIP.

Really, it's that simple.

Chapter 16: Young Adult

Get out of debt

You're now in your thirties. Nobody told you about the dangers of credit card debt. You may be up to your neck in credit card debt as well as student loans, car loans and a home loan. All you do is dream about being debt-free. How do you do it?

There are two ways. One, you can declare bankruptcy. For those so deep in debt that this is the only solution, you need to seriously think about it. It's a drastic option. Your rights could be curtailed. I can't advise you further on this route, though; you'd need to see a lawyer to figure out the pros and cons of declaring bankruptcy.

For others, there is another way. Be aware of the problem and realise that it's a long way back. You must come to grips with the fact that you will have to pay off every penny of your debt. It's your past. You have to deal with your past before you can begin to design your future. There is no way around this other than declaring bankruptcy.

Hence, the first step is to know that "when you are in a hole, stop digging." Therefore, no more debt. Create a plan to pay back that debt. Depending on how deep the hole is, it could take a few months to many years. But you have to pay the price of your indiscretion. If you work hard at the repayment, there is a light at the end of the tunnel.

Don't despair. Many people have climbed out of debt, but have still gone on to live very successful lives. Donald Trump, the American billionaire, is a famous example. In the early 1990s he faced bankruptcy. He never declared bankruptcy,[42] but fought his way back. He's my hero when it comes to demonstrating to people that if you are in debt, a will of steel can get you out.

Yes, you have to be determined to do it. I'll help you with the plan, but only you can make it happen. Here's my three-step plan:

1. First, you need to master the psychology of saving. Realise that Big Business is out to empty your wallet by making you feel happy to spend. As I explained in Chapter 13 (*Trap#5: Big Business*) Big Business does that by attacking your emotions. Ultimately, though, if you are in debt, it's not the fault of Big Bad Business. You had a choice, whether to spend or not, and you made a decision to spend. So if you are in debt, it's entirely your fault.

The good news is that it's also entirely in your hands to stop spending indiscriminately.[43] You need to make that decision today. You need to become happier to save rather than to spend.[44] Say "No!" to the barrage of spending temptations, which are constantly being thrown at you, and imagine how good it would be to feel that your bank account is filling up with money.

2. Second, pay off your debts by allocating as much money as you can to the most expensive loan you hold. After you pay off that loan allocate money to the next most expensive one. What makes a loan more expensive than another loan? It's the interest rate being charged. Generally, credit card loans have higher interest rates than car loans or house loans.

That is so because the credit card loans are *unsecured*. This means that if you default (refuse to pay back the credit card debt), the credit card company can't just grab your car or house and sell it to recover the debt. It has to go through a long and expensive process of debt collection and may end up with nothing if it can't get anything from you that it can sell to recover the credit card debt.

> **Question:** Faiz, you say if we can't pay our credit card debts, the credit card company will come take our house, car, etc. What if all these things are under a trust? They can't touch them can they?
>
> **Answer:** No.

> **Question:** So what do I care if I can't pay them back? They can't take anything from me because it's protected by a trust?
>
> **Answer:** Technically, you're right. But you don't want to go down the route of bankruptcy* if you can avoid it.

Let's assume you have two loans—a credit card loan and a car loan. You need to pay off the credit card debt first.

In the meantime, you will have to live miserly. Make a plan to cut out all the luxuries from your life. Yes, it will be hard, but just imagine the freedom you will have when your loans are paid off. Just imagine the weight lifting from your shoulders. Just imagine the victory. And of course, you will have learned a big lesson that you will never repeat: no overspending.

Every time you feel depressed about not being able to spend your money on trinkets and frills, remind yourself of the great battle you are waging. It's an honourable crusade you are on. You are a superhero. Pick a superhero of your choice. Then proclaim, "I'm XYZ superhero, conqueror of debt!" Maybe you are the only one who knows about your struggle. So what? If you fail, no one is coming to help you anyway. So you might as well get the best possible results. In life, you are on your own. Say *no* to any kind of pressure from your friends to live beyond your means. Get rid of that debt. That's job number one.

3. Third, find some hidden cash lying around. You may have some trinkets that you acquired in the past that you do not use. Have a garage sale.[45] Then put any money you get from the proceeds towards your most expensive debt.

Only after your (bad) loans are taken care of will you be able to move on to designing the bright future you really want. You can beat your debt.

Marriage time:

This is also the time in your life when you may want to consider marriage. It's a good idea. There is nothing like a good marriage to enhance your financial future. All the time you will spend dating, wooing, breaking up and doing it all over again can be put to more productive, moneymaking uses. So get married, and get married soon. I recommend marriage. But there is a right way and a wrong way to go about marriage.

I am no marriage expert, but my wife and I have been married for nineteen years. We have raised three children, two of them teenagers and one pre-teen. We've learned quite a bit about having a successful marriage along the way, both from our own marriage as well as from studying and counseling other couples. My son once said to me, "I'm scared to get married." I said, "Why?" and he answered, "What if it doesn't work out? How will I know that it will work out?"

That was my cue for a speech on the Law of Cause and Effect. Success in marriage is not about happenstance or falling into a fairy tale story of everlasting love. You have a much better chance of having a successful marriage if you manufacture the success yourself. Just like getting rich can be manufactured. As I explained to you earlier that if you do (the cause) what the rich do (effect) then you stand an excellent chance of becoming rich yourself. However, if you don't know the *route to financial success*, you stand an excellent chance of getting lost and never becoming rich.

It is the same thing with marriage. Find a couple that is successful in their marriage, find out what they do, and then if you do the same thing, you, too, stand an excellent chance of having a happy marriage. Model successful people, then you, too, will be successful. It's really that simple. The Law of Cause and Effect.

That's exactly what I did when I was about to get married. I interviewed several couples, some of whom were having a good marriage and some that were not. I learned a lot from both groups. I distilled the lessons down to four rules of how to have a successful marriage. Those four rules have served my wife and me well over our nineteen years of marriage. We discussed and agreed to implement them the very night that we were married. Before I share them, I will caution you that these are probably very specific to a Pakistani culture and may not be relevant to other cultures. My wife and I are both originally from Pakistan and we had an arranged marriage. We met one week before we were married. So I suggest you talk to couples in your own culture to see what works and what doesn't. It worries me that young people get married without adequate training on how to have a successful marriage. No wonder the divorce rates are climbing. Marriage is not a joke. It is a wonderful experience if it is done right.

Before we move on to The Four Rules of a Successful Marriage, I'd like to mention an important point: My wife and I both feel that when it comes to finding a partner, one shouldn't focus on looks. Beauty is skin deep. Sometimes people date and then get married because of lust. But that is the wrong reason to get married. As one of my former bosses in Canada once said to me, "The love wears off in four months, and then the farting under the covers starts." Sorry. Very crude, but it's a proverb. It's exactly right. After four months, real life starts, and how you deal with the real life side of marriage will determine how successfully your marriage goes.

The Four Rules of a Successful Marriage:

1. Never leave home when having a fight.

Four months after we got married, we had our first big fight. It was a Sunday, my day off from work. I became quite angry and promptly left home. I came back after six hours with a lame excuse that I had to go visit my uncle in hospital. It was true and that's where I was, but there was no urgency for me to have done it on that particular day. My wife reminded me about our rule and said, "Look, the problem is still there. Nothing is solved. And you promised not to leave home if we had a fight." I broke the rule. We talked about the issue, and after a while we were fine. Thinking back on the events of the day, I realized I could have resolved the issue many hours earlier and spent the Sunday in a much better frame of mind. What a waste of valuable leisure time. Lesson learned: Leaving home in the middle of a fight does not solve the problem.

2. Have explicit trust in each other.

We decided right from the beginning that we would only trust each other. So even if someone showed me a photograph of my wife with someone else, or vice versa, I'd ask my wife about it and not the person revealing the information to me. Ditto for my wife. We were so adamant about not listening to any innuendo from anyone else, that soon people stopped trying to interfere in our lives.

3. Never go to bed angry.

We returned to Toronto about one week after we were married. It was January and I was immediately into tax season, meaning that it was the time of year when tax returns were due, and as an accountant I was working long hours. I'd leave home at seven in the morning, and return home at eleven at night. After about a week of this, one night I noticed that my wife was not talking much to me. She plunked down my food on the table and then sat there in a pout. My temper flared up, and I responded by keeping my mouth shut. Soon it was time to go to bed, which brought a challenge. But rules are rules and I said to her, "Look, we have agreed not to go to bed angry. I do have to sleep now, so tell me what it's all about." She blurted out that she never saw me anymore. "Is this how life is going to be?" I breathed a sigh of relief and laughed. "No," I explained, "this is just for three months, until I get through the tax season. After that it'll be nine to five." And that settled it. Problem solved.

Why is this rule great? Because it forces the couple to resolve the problem then and there rather than to let it percolate into the next day, and the next and even to the next week and so on at which point, unresolved, it could become a big problem. In fact, my wife and I quickly realised that once I got home there was no point in fighting. We would have to make up before we went to bed, so what was the point in fighting at all. If there was an issue brewing, deal with it, sort it out and let's enjoy the rest of the evening. As a result we rarely fought after that. It created a great sense of understanding between us, which has grown over the years. But we're not perfect—every now and then, Krakatoa, she doth burst.

4. Have respect for each other in public. Never fight with or make fun of your spouse in public.

In Toronto, we lived in a joint family setup. My mother and younger sister were also living with us. My wife and I decided that if we were going to have any disagreements, these would have to be dealt with in the privacy of our bedroom. If we had a fight anywhere else in the apartment, my mother and sister would witness it. And, because my mother and sister would naturally take my side, that would not be good for my wife. We stuck to that plan and it worked well for us. We were never seen fighting in public.

As for making fun of each other, let me tell you this is equally as bad as fighting in public. I did it once, and then my wife told me it was hurtful to her. How would I like to have the same treatment? I never did it again. I come across couples that make fun of each other in public. Not a good idea. Instead, praise your partner in public, and private for that matter. Give the other respect and the other will repay you with ten times the respect you give them.

Below you will find an acronym to help remember the points above. L E A P

Where:

L = Never **L**eave home when having a fight.

E = Have **E**xplicit trust in each other.

A = Never go to bed **A**ngry.

P = Have respect for each other in **P**ublic. Never fight with or make fun of your spouse in public.

Children:
Children are wonderful. In their younger years they are cute and cuddly and help to hold the family together. In later years, they become helpful to

their parents. Now that my children have grown up somewhat, they are extremely helpful around the house. If my training works out over time, then I suspect that as my wife and I become old and doddering they will be there for us.

However, the expense of raising children must not be ignored. If you can't afford children financially ... then do not have them. One of my clients, a very successful businessman, has one child. He categorically told me that if he had more than one child he would not have been able to survive the early years of establishing his business. He would've had to set aside his dream of owning a business. Instead, he would have had to find a job to support his family. With just one child in tow, he and his wife managed to scrape by until his business was on its feet. Today he is a grandparent and his whole family is financially secure. The family planning paid off.

Nigerians seem to have this concept down pat. I know of a middle-aged couple that has young children. I committed a faux pas by asking them how come their children were so young. Not skipping a heartbeat, the husband explained to me that in his culture the man must first establish himself financially before asking for the hand of a woman in marriage. Smart idea.

Another reason not to have any children is for environmental reasons. The world has too many people. All of these people desire a good life. All want cars, washing machines and refrigerators. After the "flattening" of the world since the Berlin Wall came down,[46] there are an estimated three billion new entrants into the capitalist based society. All of these new consumers want to have the same things that people living in the Western economies have already enjoyed for decades. Just imagine the havoc that mankind is about to wreak on the natural resources of the world.

Of course, it's not possible to reduce the numbers of people in the world. So the best solution is to control the growth of the population. It's the responsibility of the human race today to think about this problem seriously. There are millions of orphans around the world that need a good home. Why not adopt an orphan? That way you kill two birds with one stone: you have a child and you don't increase the world's population.

Or compromise: have one child of your own and adopt one.

How to retire young:
For many at this stage of their lives, retiring early is something they would like to achieve. Many young adults are ambitious people.

I was once spending a quiet Saturday afternoon at the Bokaa dam near Gaborone. It's an idyllic spot. Panoramic views. Big beautiful sky. Shimmering lake created by the dam. Typical short, tan-coloured African grass all around. Marabou stork, flamingo, ducks and Hammersmith Plovers landing sporadically near the water's edge. It is very relaxing to spend a lazy afternoon there. A few minutes after I arrived at the dam, a young man drove up in his bakkie (South African terminology for a pickup truck), pulled up near me, threw a large pipe into the lake and started to pump out water. I walked over to him and started chatting. He told me an interesting story. He lived on a nearby farm and was taking back water for his goats. As for drinking water for human use, he would take it from a tap in the nearby Bokaa village.

He said to me the farm life is good. No noise like in the village. "What about snakes?" I asked. "They are our friends," he said. "We don't chase them away. They come in the house. And then they go away." "What type of snakes?" I asked. "Cobras and Black Mambas. But sometimes they eat the chickens, the Cobras they swallow the eggs. That is a problem, so we use snake poison, which we buy from the vet and sprinkle around the chicken coop." He had completed his high school education having done his Cambridge 'O' Levels from another village near Gaborone called Mochudi. Now he was working on an electrician's license from The Public Procurement and Asset Disposal Board (PPADB) in Botswana.

After that he was hoping to win a government tender. "I want to be a big man," he said, spreading out his arms as the words came out of his mouth. I asked him "Why?" He said he wanted to make lots of money. I asked him why he needed the money? "To build a hospital for the elderly," he replied. "Because they are suffering. Their kids are not taking care of them ('don't know why,' he said)." Therefore, he decided that he wanted to take care of them, the Masadi Mokgolo (old women) and the Munna Mokgolo (old men). I told him that his is a big "why," and that he would be successful.

The main point of the story is that young adults are dreamers. They dream big, as they should. Of all the age groups they have the best chance at cracking the poverty problem. They want to secure their own families and take care of their parents as well.

But they must start now. The older one gets, the lesser are the chances of making big wealth. Your energy and determination start to drop. That's why I will re-direct you to Chapter 8, and the *How to Win Big*, idea. Do not waste your resources. Upgrade the use of your resources to the highest productive use.

How do you retire at a young age? The answer is in the Four Steps Millionaire Formula, or the MSIP. That's all there is to it. If you have the energy and guts to start a business, you could achieve the desired results a lot faster. If not, you can still do it while holding down a job. But follow the steps to a "T." Godspeed.

I recently met a young woman at a seminar who was a medical doctor. She asked me the question: "I want a career, children, family and to retire early with passive income. How is it possible?"

The answer:

The answer is you can't get everything all at once. If you put your hand into the cookie jar and try to take all the cookies out at once you will break the cookie jar. Without breaking the cookie jar, the only way to get the cookies out is one at a time. When you apply this example in real life, it's saying that you have to be patient.

Since you are young and can work hard at this age, you can start your career and your family together (with a one year hiatus to take care of the newborn). But don't focus only on your career. Perhaps work half a day. As you grow, your career will grow, your children will grow, and your experience will grow. The first five to ten years will be hard. But you won't mind it, because your target is passive income. The hard work you put in now will pay you back in the future.

By the time the children are older, career-wise you are in a better position than when you started. At that point, you will have more time to spend on your career because your children are going to school.

Hopefully, your spouse has also been working. If both of you have been adhering to the tenets of the Four Steps Millionaire Formula, then you have been saving money. You were not buying brand name clothes, handbags, shoes or designer makeup. Brand name anything costs double the money.

At this point in time you may think of going into a business with your spouse, or just continue in your individual careers. Either way, you would likely generate greater savings. These savings can be used to buy a small house for your family to live in, as well as to start investing in assets per the Four Steps Millionaire Formula.

By the time one reaches the mid-fifties, a hard working person who has saved well should have some savings, a passive income, a family and a career.

Thereafter, you can slowly acquire the luxury items you want. All this is the result of patience and having a game plan.

You may have the odd fight with your spouse now and again, but since you have money, generally speaking you will not be fighting with each other. Also, you and your spouse are both focused on acquiring passive income, so you know the lifestyle sacrifices that have to be made, and you will fight less over trivial things. In any event, this plan requires understanding between the spouses.

When you have your children when you are young, you have the energy to enjoy them. As you get older, your children reach adulthood. Had you concentrated only on your career in the beginning years, and decided to get married later on then it may have been too late to have children, or if you did have children in your later years, it may become more difficult for you to manage them. When you are young you can work hard. And it's just a matter of say five to ten years or so of struggle. In your fifties the hard work you put in early in your life in managing both career and family pays off.

You can retire young, possibly in your late-fifties.

Here's how you can help your kids do even better than you did: When one of your children gets married, don't have a lavish wedding. Don't succumb to peer pressure. In addition, think about renting before buying. For example, the wedding dress or the jewelry can be rented. Save the money that you would have spent on buying these things. Give it to your children instead, and have them put the money on a down payment for a house. Encourage the guests who attend the wedding to give cash gifts rather than boxed gifts. Pool the money with yours and put it towards the down payment for the house. No need for a lavish honeymoon either. Put that money towards the down payment, as well.

The newly married couple should then rent out the house that they just bought with all the money thus saved and live with the in-laws, instead. In no time, the house will be paid-off. As well, in-laws are a great blessing. They have wisdom for the newlywed couple on how to look after the grandchildren. Also, the in-laws can babysit the grandchildren, and therefore, allow the parents (the newlyweds) to progress so much faster down the road to financial independence.

Chapter 17: Pre-retirement

You are now in your fifties. Getting rich is not high on your priority list, but you want to be financially comfortable. Finding time to be with the family is high on your priority list. Time to relax and do the things you have wanted to do all your life is also high on your priority list.

The problem is you never allocated any money for higher education for your children. And that expense is looming large. The house mortgage also needs to be paid. You keep hearing about retirement planning, but you know you've not done enough to retire comfortably.

You want to be healthy. It is a big priority in your life. You don't know much about investing and need advice. You are frantically looking around for a financial advisor that you can trust.

If the above is your situation, you've got a whole host of problems. Let me put it to you straight. By fifty-five, if you are not already financially independent, or don't think you will be very soon, then you are in trouble. But at least you have plenty of company: 99 percent of the world's population is with you.

That said, let's see if there is a way to treat this predicament?

You will need to start all over again. Sounds awful, but that's the only way out. You can go into a depression, or you can start working to claw your way out of the hole you're in. I suggest the latter. Make a budget. Start saving and investing in cash flowing investments. It's the Four Steps Millionaire Formula route.

If your children's education isn't taken care of, you will be facing a tough decision. Do you offer your child what you can afford even though it may be inferior to what you would have liked to provide? Or do you allow your child to get into debt through student loans to fund higher education?

Very serious problem. It's best to avoid getting children into student loans. Perhaps you've heard about the huge student loan mess in the USA. Thousands of students who took out student loans are without jobs and can't pay off their loans. One has to be ultra careful. In my view, if your child wants to get a student loan to get a college degree, she must give careful consideration as to how she is going to pay off her debt. You will need to educate her and explain that the loan has to be paid off before she can start moving ahead with her life.

Every child must have a plan on how to pay off the student loan within the first five years after graduation. If your child is educated in this way about the seriousness of the student loan, then she may even try to earn some money during her university years to reduce the amount of the loan. Ultimately, it's a big risk. But armed with the knowledge that a student loan is very dangerous, hopefully your child can use her ingenuity to pay off that loan as fast as possible after university.

If you, unlike the person in this chapter, are well on your way to becoming financially independent, congratulations! Although you do have other financial issues to take care of, they are not as problematic as not having enough money. Here are your pre-retirement checklist items:

1) Do a will. Many people find it difficult to contemplate death. But death is inevitable and how your loved ones will survive

your loss will be affected in great part by whether or not you have a will. The will is a written document legally indicating how your estate is divided. When I was practicing as a financial advisor, the majority of people who walked through our doors did not have wills. I recommend you sort this one out immediately!

Your best option is to keep your first will simple. Once you have a simple first will, then you can always work on a more comprehensive one later on. In the meantime, at least you have something, so that if—God forbid—you do happen to die, you do not leave a huge problem for your family. To help you come up with a simple will, I have provided below a *Will Checklist*. Complete this document and take it to an attorney to have a will drawn up. It is not in your best interest to prepare the will yourself. There could be serious errors in it.

Will Checklist

Testator(s): _____

Executor: _____

Relationship: _____

Contingent Executor: _____

Relationship: _____

Beneficiaries:

Name	% Share

*Appointment of Guardian of Minor Children:*_____

Explanations:

Testator (s): This is you (or, in the case of a joint will, you and your spouse).

Executor: This is the person who will handle your estate's affairs after you pass away. My suggestion is that it should be your spouse if your spouse is financially literate. The master of the high court would insist upon the spouse being assisted by a professional (an attorney/banker/chartered accountant) in any event. Upon the passing away of the surviving spouse, it might be best to let a professional handle the estate to guard against delays caused by friction amongst the children, which might happen if one child is created executor and the others aren't.

Note: In your will it is not a good idea to dictate how to deal with your remains because the children or spouse may only find the will later, and if they have made arrangements contrary to the will, it will give rise to distress on their part.

Contingent Executor: In case your executor dies or is not able to handle the winding up of your estate, you could name another executor.

Beneficiaries: These are the people you want to benefit from your estate. Simply list their names and the percentage of your assets to be given to each.

Another important issue to consider when writing a will is to think about what will happen to the assets of each spouse, should either one die. We all have the tendency to think that the older spouse will die first. The reverse may happen. If the Will did not take this into account, then the remaining spouse could have a problem.

For instance, say the family home is in the name of the wife and she is the younger of the two spouses. Let's say that she wants the house to go to the children when she dies. However, if she predeceases the husband, then he might possibly be without a house to live in. The children probably would not evict him, but it degrades his financial condition. Therefore, you must think through what can happen if either spouse dies, regardless of their ages.

Appointment of Guardian of Minor Children: Whom should I appoint as the guardian of my children? Every will where the testator or testatrix has minor children must have a clause that has a guardian for those children. The importance of the point can not be overemphasized. If there is no guardian, family fights can ensue. Choose wisely and well. This is the person that must replace you in circumstances where your children have suffered a tremendous loss.

Ensure that the guardian has sufficient cash flow to look after your children. An insurance policy is a must, and the funds of that policy should be protected by a special trust within the will.

Make sure that you have spoken to your chosen executor, contingent executor and guardian and they have agreed to carry out the roles that have been assigned. Also, make sure that once the will has been completed they know exactly where it is. For example, my executor knows exactly where my will is located and so do my beneficiaries.

Along with a few standard paragraphs, the above information is sufficient to draw up a simple will. In Appendix V, I have provided an example of a simple will. Don't get too caught up in the legal jargon. That is your attorney's job. The will in the appendix is there to give you an idea of what a will looks like, and for you to get a sense of what is involved. It usually is a very simple procedure.

To work on a more comprehensive will you should ask yourself several additional questions. The following list is by no means complete, but it will get you thinking about what you want to accomplish, and what kind of legacy you want to leave behind.

- What assets will not be dealt with under the will (for example, trust assets or an insurance policy with a named beneficiary)?

- What happens if my spouse and I die at the same time, for instance, in a common accident?

- Do I need a buy-sell agreement for my privately held business? This is necessary to provide business partners with a process to buy out the shares of the deceased, while providing an easy way for heirs to access the value of the company.

- Do I want to establish a testamentary trust?

- Who should be my Trustee?

- Which asset should go to which of my beneficiaries?

- What personal items do I want to gift? To whom?

- What are my debts? Who do I owe money to?

- Who owes me money? Do I want the debt forgiven upon my death?

2) Have a *Centralised Assets and Liabilities Schedule*, and an *Estate Archive System*. One of the biggest problems that occurs when a person dies, even if the deceased had prepared a will, is his beneficiaries are not aware of what his assets are, or where to locate them. For example, the will may say that the deceased wants all of his assets to go to his spouse. But the spouse may not be aware of what comprises assets of the deceased.

To avoid being in such a situation, namely, where your beneficiaries may not easily locate your assets, you need to implement the following two-fold solution:

First you need a *Centralised Assets and Liabilities Schedule* (CALS). The CALS would list of all your assets and where they are held. For example, if it's a bank account then you would name the bank; if it's a property investment, then you would indicate who owns it, and so on.

Assets that are held in trust are also included in the CALS because it is important that the survivors are made aware of the existence of them, notwithstanding the fact that such assets are trust assets and cannot be dealt with under the will.

CALS would also list all of your liabilities, that is, monies you owe to anyone. For instance, all of your credit card companies should be listed. In that way, your executor can sort these liabilities out before distributing any assets. Please see Appendix IV for an example of CALS.

Second, you need an *Estate Archive System* (*EASy*–the "y" is there just to create an acronym that you can remember). You need a place to store your important personal documents, such as your will and your life insurance documents. I use a large, wallet-type folder with several compartments with an index in the flap. Then, in accordance with the index, in the first compartment, I've put my will, in the next, my life insurance documents, and so on. The folder is in a place that my executor and beneficiaries know of. This type of folder is called a *document wallet*.

See below for a sample picture.

So basically, I'm ready to die. (But, if God gives me life, I'll take it!)

3) Power of Attorney:

What if you are not dead, but say, God forbid, you had an accident and you are in a coma? And you needed money to pay the hospital bill? There is no way that you can access your funds. You may therefore die. However, if you had a Power of Attorney in which you had appointed a person to act on your behalf that person could go to the bank and authorise a payment from your account to the hospital. Depending on the jurisdiction, however, the Power of Attorney may be invalidated by the lack of contractual capacity of the person who issued it (for example, mental incapacity). And if that is the case then your lawyer must assist the person you appointed in the Power of Attorney to become a Curator of your estate.

You may not need a Power of Attorney if your money is sitting in a structure such as a trust. But it's best to check with a competent attorney about whether or not it will be necessary to have a Power of Attorney. If so, get it done. It's usually best to appoint the same person who is the executor of your will as your power of attorney.

There are several other matters to be thinking about like how to invest, what currencies to invest in and how to choose a financial advisor. These are discussed in the next chapter—Chapter 18 (*Retirement*).

Chapter 18: Retirement

You are seventy and your spouse is sixty-five. You dream of retiring and having financial security for the rest of your lives. Nice goal, but do you have enough money to retire? This is the most important question you need to answer. So let's figure it out.

However, before I get to that, I need to address another problem: Confusion. You may be so confused about how to figure out what lies ahead, that you just keep putting it off. However, the solution is not just going to fall into your lap. You have to attack the problem to get to the solution.

You are probably afraid to attack the issue of whether or not you have enough money to be financially secure for the rest of your life for two reasons, the first of which is because you don't know how to address the issue. However, I am about to tell you how. And second, it may be that you are too scared to find out the truth, which could be that you don't have enough to retire on. Then what? We'll get to that too.

One more piece of advice.

You need to know how to create time to work on your financial future. In the twenty-first century our lives have become very busy. And in this chaos, you need to figure out your financial future, and you need to set aside the time to do this. It is not possible to say you'll spend an hour every day for the next two weeks working on your retirement plan. Earlier I mentioned that I was a financial advisor, and practically nobody who walked through our doors had a will because nobody had the time to do one.

So how do you find the time? Utilise a concept that we talked about earlier, namely, that of *block time*. Find a chunk of time, two to three days, in which you will do nothing else.

Once you have decided to block off the time, do not schedule anything else during that time. If there are too many distractions in your home then try to leave for two to three days. Go to a resort. Take your essential paperwork with you, and get to the rest when you get back. That way, if you've got the bulk of the work done, then you can polish it up at home later on.

Will your money last?
How can you figure out if you have enough money to retire on?

Step 1: Create a budget. See Chapter 6 (*How to Save Money*) for assistance. This is imperative, even if you only do a rough budget. Come up with a rough estimate of how much it's going to cost you to live.

Then add 20 percent to the figure that you came up with. As mentioned earlier, it's just a fact of life that people underestimate their living expenses. I discovered this when I used to do financial plans for clients. They would be amazed at their cost of living as revealed by our budget. It would be much higher than what they thought they spent every year. After the 20 percent has been added, you will have a real figure to work with.

Let's say the figure you arrived at for your total annual expenses, after adding the 20 percent suggested above, is $100,000 per annum.

Step 2: Next you need to figure out your sources of retirement income. Let's say it comprises of the following:

1. Property Income from your Revenue Producing Property: $20,000 pa

2. Pension income. This, however, is a tricky one. Pension plans are in trouble around the world, and you may find that your pension plan runs into trouble and cannot pay out the promised pension income. To allow for this we will attach a 50 percent risk factor to such income; that is, discount it by half. If it's expected to pay out $30,000 pa, we'll use only $30,000 × 0.5 = $15,000 per annum.

If those are the only two sources of retirement income, then you have a total of ($20,000 + 15,000) $35,000 coming in. That is your passive income.

Step 3: Figure out the shortfall in required income—that is, how much do you need to fund from other sources. In our example, the amount of shortfall in required income is (expenses of $100,000 pa less passive income of $35,000 pa) $65,000 pa. Let's say that in addition to the revenue producing property and pension plan mentioned earlier, you also have some savings in the form of cash (money in a bank account), as well as some savings in the form of a portfolio (money in an investment account).

Hence, the only way the shortfall of $65,000 can be funded is from the two sources above.

Please note that if you have an investment account, consider converting eighty percent of it to cash, or to Money Market mutual funds. One hundred percent conversion would be better. This would make it more realistic when calculating funds. If much of your investment account is in volatile mutual funds such as bonds or equities, it is useless for retirement purposes, as that money can vaporise rather quickly through a combination of withdrawals and bad markets.

The example above now shows that you require an additional $65,000 pa in retirement expenses.

Step 4: How big should your savings pot be to fund this amount? Multiply $65,000 by 100 minus the age of the younger spouse. Accordingly, if the younger spouse is 65 years old, the calculation is:

$$\$65,000 \times (100 - 65 \text{ years}) \ 35 = \$2,275,000.$$

This is roughly the figure that you ought to have in your possession as cash, or in a conservatively allocated investment account, or both taken together. This will enable you to survive your retirement years. This calculation totally ignores the effect of investment earnings or inflation. I suggest not including these in the calculation. It only makes the calculation more complex and it won't make much of a difference. Just keep a margin of safety. You will be surprised how much you spend in retirement. It's more than you think.

So here's what's happening:

Let's say you are seventy years old. Your spouse is sixty-five. Your life expectancies can be approximated by studying a mortality table. But given that medical science is enabling us to live longer and longer, even that is just an estimate. So let's just say a reasonable assumption of life expectancy today is living to be one hundred. This means your wife is expected to outlive you, and she still has thirty-five years left to go. As this is longer than your expected remaining life of (100–70) thirty years, we should use her age—sixty-five years—to calculate the retirement funds needed.

Let's look at it:

Your Expenses are:		$100,000 pa.
Your Retirement Income is:		
Property Income:	$20,000	
Pension Income:	$15,000	
Total:		$35,000
Shortfall:		$65,000

Hence, if you supplement your retirement income by taking a withdrawal from your savings pot each year of $65,000, you'll be fine: <u>$65,000</u>

Shortfall: <u>$nil</u>

We will assume for a moment that you have sufficient money in your savings pot to fund the shortfall of $65,000. Hence you have (35 years × $65,000) $2,275,000 in your savings pot. And the $65,000 pa shortfall comes from this pot. So when your spouse turns 100 years, the retirement pot will have been drawn down to nil. To get a visual demonstration of this, see Graph A in Figure 7 of Chapter 7 (*How to Invest Money*). If she dies before then, she'll be fine money-wise. Of course, we are assuming that she outlives you and you have already passed away at age 100, or prior.

The big problem you may face is that you do not have $2,275,000 in your retirement savings pot today. That's where your budget will come in handy. Scrutinise it carefully. Where can you save money? What expenses can you reduce? Let's say that you feel you can eliminate $15,000 in expenses. You now need less in your retirement savings pot. You need:

Step 1: Living expenses budget: $85,000.

Step 2: Passive income: $35,000.

Step 3: Additional funding needed: $85,000 − $35,000 = $50,000.

Step 4: Retirement savings pot value required: $50,000 × (100 − 65) = $1,750,000.

If that is what you have (or more) then you can retire. If you have less, then you have three choices:

1. Simply continue on working and saving until such age as the above calculation works out.

2. Consider Four Steps Millionaire Formula step 3—Invest in Cash Flowing Investments. Do you have the skills to buy and handle property investments? If so, you could pull yourself out of the hole much faster. But if it seems too big a task for you, consider sticking with option #1 above (continue working).

3. Seek advice on whether an annuity (I will come back to this product a little later) will sufficiently cover the income gap of $50,000.

If you are a teenager or a new graduate, note the great opportunity you have. You will not be stuck in this predicament when you are seventy years old if you save properly. Don't squander your opportunity. At age seventy if you don't have enough money, you may have to keep on working. Prevent this. Implement the Four Steps Millionaire Formula in your life as early as you can.

Choosing a financial advisor:
Be very careful when working with financial advisors. The problem is that one of the main products they sell—mutual funds—is simply snake oil. Revisit Chapter 7 (*How to Invest Money*).

In defense of financial advisors:
The one valuable product that a financial advisor sells is a protection

policy (insurance policy). However, few financial advisors sell protection policies because it is usually the purview of insurance salespeople.

Let's be forthright: you need insurance. As a minimum, you need life insurance, disability insurance, and the other usual types such as car insurance, home insurance and medical insurance. These are the only financial products you should own other than a bank account, good debt and a credit card—the credit card is for convenience purposes only. We will delve a bit more into the type of insurance products that you should own in Chapter 32 (*Buy Insurance—Before You Need It*).

How to invest

Aside from mutual funds, which are not a good investment, where else can you invest? Your main investment options are a business, real estate and cash. As I mentioned earlier, you could also consider an *annuity*. I will come back to this product a little later.

We have covered investing in a business earlier in this book. I will have more to say on this topic, as it relates to retirees, a little later on.

As for real estate, if you have reached the stage in your life where real estate sounds like a hassle, I don't blame you. It *is* a hassle. That leaves just one other "asset class" to put your money into: cash in the bank. Now there is a little more to this idea.

As I explained earlier, the banking industry is not the warm welcoming and friendly institution of the TV advertisements. Your bank can also go bankrupt. During the course of writing this book, Cypriote banks had to be bailed out by their government. If you live in the USA or the UK, should your bank go under, you could get some assistance through government deposit guarantees. But, if you live in Botswana, for instance, where there are no government deposit guarantee schemes, you stand to lose it all. Therefore, for those of you who live in countries that do not offer government deposit guarantees, you have to be smart about this.

If you have a substantial sum of money, you must not keep all of it in one bank. You must spread it out across two banks. That is enough. Using more than two banks will just increase the complexity of your life and not really add any more safety. After all, you have to leave some things to God. Let Him do His job also.

Alternatively, you can have some of your money in one bank and put some of it into a *Money Market* fund. Money Market is a term I've already used, and frequently, but let me explain it briefly.

Money Market Fund: A Money Market Fund is a term given to a mutual fund that holds only cash. It takes investors' money and distributes it into several bank accounts (i.e. cash). The money market fund is not allowed to hold stocks or bonds. Hence, it's not a highly volatile fund because the market value of the fund does not depend on stock markets. A money market fund is not flawless, but it reduces the risk of holding cash within a problematic banking system by automatically spreading your risk among several banks. That's more than enough diversification for your cash holdings.

Let's say, in our particular example, the money market fund distributes the fund's cash holdings throughout eight banks. Hence, the risk of holding all of your money in one bank is reduced. Subsequently, if one of the eight banks that the money market fund holds its money with goes bust, one-eighth of your money is lost. For example, if the value of your money market fund before the bust was $100,000, then after the bust, it's value would be one-eighth less, or $87,500. A lot better than if you had all your money sitting in that ill-fated bank that went bust and when you wake up one morning, it's all gone.

That is the purpose of a money market fund—to provide diversification in the holdings of your cash balance. You reduce the risk of losing all of your cash if your bank goes under.

The portfolio manager carries out the process of diversifying the holdings of the fund; you do not do it. You have given the money to the money market fund, and it will do the work for you. The portfolio manager is going to save you the bother of setting up eight bank accounts. He will do the administration work and get the desired result, the diversification of your cash holdings. The portfolio manager benefits, as well, because he charges the fund a portfolio management fee.

> **Question:** Am I allowed to withdraw as much money from the money market fund as I want to? Or is there a limit?

> **Answer:** Usually, one can draw much money as is desired. In rare circumstances, the money market fund may get suspended, in which case there may be limits.

At this stage of your life, preservation of your capital is of paramount importance. To know how much money you need to have saved up to retire, please see the earlier part of this chapter.

Annuities: I said I'd come back to this product. It's is an excellent product for some of your money. If you want to be sure you'll still have money coming in for life then you may want to consider putting a portion of your nest egg into an annuity. Also, if you are married, then consider a joint-life annuity, which will pay until the second death occurs.

What's an annuity?
This is a way to get income for life. Let's say that you had one hundred dollars and you didn't know how to invest it, so you handed it over to me. I promised to give you five dollars every year for the rest of your life. In

actual fact, you wouldn't hand the money to me; you would give it to an insurance company. Insurance companies offer annuities.

Note that the insurance company is betting that you will die before it has to pay the full one hundred dollars back to you. If that happens, it gets to keep the difference. But if you live longer than they expect you to, then you will beat them at their own game and you will collect five dollars each year for as long as you live.

Is this a good investment? Sure, it is. If you had the hundred dollars in your hands, you might spend it or lose it in one year. By handing it over to an insurance company, you are guaranteed to get five dollars every year. You just have to learn how to live on that five dollars.

In addition, an annuity can provide you with a higher income than the equivalent sum in a bank account.[47] The reason for this is rather obscure; it has to do with the fact that the product is issued by an insurance company. Consequently, if you die earlier than the insurance company had expected, your remaining money is used to fund the incomes of other annuitants. Therefore, they could collect more money than what they might have received from putting their money into a cash deposit. Of course, if you are the one living longer, and other annuitants die before their time, then the benefit of their monies comes to you.[48] In summary, an annuity can be a useful product to produce retirement income. A financial advisor (or insurance salesman) will help you with the details.

Do note that an annuity is a cash flowing investment rather than a capital gains type of investment. As well, there are many options you could choose from depending on what you need, for example, the annuity could be for a set period rather than for life, and it could also come with inflation protection.

Also, keep in mind that the "guarantee" part of the "guaranteed income" that the product provides is only as good as the strength of the life insurance company behind the product. Accordingly, as per the earlier warnings about banks, the same applies here. You cannot be sure if the life insurance company will be around for your entire life. Don't put *all* of your money into such a product.

Other financial pitfalls to avoid:
If you are retired, people may think that you have some money stashed away and will approach you with investment proposals. Not all of these have your best interests at heart.

My advice is that you deal in bank products (cash), annuities and property investments, which you own and control and nothing more.

If you plan to invest, be aware of fraudulent schemes. One scheme that you must never think about investing in is a *Property Syndicate*. These are not good for anybody, no matter what the age. A property syndicate is similar to a mutual fund in that a group of people pool their funds to buy property. Usually a property syndicate can be formed without having to go through any kind of regulatory oversight, unlike a mutual fund, which usually requires a license from a regulator. Not that the license makes the mutual fund any safer; in fact, the *regulatory approval* can hide the risk of the mutual fund to the investors' detriment.

A property syndicate is a dangerous investment vehicle, and so are any number of other exotic investment vehicles, for example, limited partnerships. Basically, you should not invest your money into any property investment that is not solely and fully controlled by you. Why? Because once you put your money into a Property Syndicate, you won't easily be able to get it out. You are not in control of the investment, and you have no clue how it's going to be run, or who's going to run it. Even if the administrative and investment matters are nicely explained in magnificent looking brochures, which make great promises, when your money disappears so will all of the charming people who sold you the investment.

The only time that you might consider getting involved in a property syndicate is if the members of the syndicate were close family or close friends. Even then, to avoid bad blood, all the details need to be spelled out in writing, especially how the members will receive income, the downside risks and the exit policies.

Starting a business when you're elderly

What if you have the notion of starting a business at this age? It's tricky. Because your health is a resource that may not be in as good a condition as you would like it to be.

I met a couple in their sixties who wanted to start a second business. They owned some vacant land and felt that putting up a business on the land would be its best use. However, that may have been a great idea some twenty years ago, but now it was a risk because the couple had health problems. They would not be able to put in productive twelve-hour days, as would be required by the new business.

People in their sixties have to be very cautious about starting a business. They should follow the procedures given in chapter 5 (*How to Make Money*) to assess their business idea.

The couple mentioned above did have other options. They owned other parcels of land, so another option they were considering was to build houses and rent them out. This could be a better option. The level of active effort required, eventually, after the construction of the houses was complete, would be less than trying to run the new business they had been contemplating.

In the meantime, they had no idea how to get a loan from the bank. They had been avid savers all their lives and had accumulated assets without incurring loans, buying assets with cash as and when the cash became available. Pretty good strategy if you ask me. "How did you manage to accumulate these assets without going into loans?" I asked them. "We have always had a culture of savings," the lady replied. "I don't spend a lot of money and neither does my partner." A great lesson for young people. A *culture of savings* strategy had helped the couple accumulate some valuable land assets, become debt-free, and boast a decent amount of cash in the bank. So, although they were not out of the woods as far as their retirement planning was concerned, they were not in big trouble either. They had options.

When it comes to getting a loan, instead of trying to find a consultant to prepare the paperwork for you, the best way is to approach the bank directly and ask them what they need. In the case of a construction loan, the bank will usually require approved plans and a *valuation* of the project from a recognised valuer. The valuer will provide an estimate of the total cost of the project. The bank will also want to know how much you will be contributing from your own pocket, and how the loan will be serviced (paid down) during the construction phase and thereafter. Usually, banks will not require servicing of the loan (repayments) to start until the construction is complete as they realise that the loan will be paid for by the rental income.

For this couple, building houses on their vacant parcels of land was the fastest way for them to create sufficient passive income to retire. They would still need to go through the step I outlined earlier in this chapter to assess what their income requirement would be during retirement. Following that, they would need to figure out how best to create the passive income as soon as possible.

If you are hesitant about getting into a property project so late in your life, let me tell you that several of my former clients have done exactly that. Some had started projects in their late sixties. It's not so hard after you've done one. And it's the best way to ramp up your passive income. You may also want to consider involving your children. Maybe they can help you with the property management.

If this still sounds like too much work, after you have done the retirement calculations, and you have ascertained the capital you will need to have in cash to retire, keep on working until you have accumulated that amount of cash. Do not try to short-circuit the advice by trying to invest in mutual funds or property syndications or any other scheme that a financial advisor or other such consultant wants to sell you.

This is not the time in your life to be ignorant. So don't be.

Stick with cash, and if you wish, annuities and/or property investments. That's it.

If you have mutual funds outside of a retirement account convert them to cash (money market) mutual funds.

If you have mutual funds in retirement accounts, convert at least 80 percent of your portfolio to money market funds (100 percent would be better). That would lower the risk to an acceptable level. Then start your withdrawals as per what is allowed under your tax scheme and as per what you need to withdraw to live on. Your withdrawals from the retirement account will be in addition to the income from other sources.

For example, let's say your retirement account is $200,000 and you are required legally to withdraw a minimum of five percent (or $10,000) each year, then, incorporating this information into the example we saw at the beginning of this chapter, the following scenario would unfold:

Your Expenses are:		$100,000 pa.
Your Retirement Income is:		
Property Income:	$20,000	
Pension Income:	$15,000	
Withdrawals from Retirement Account:	$10,000	
Total:	$45,000	
Shortfall:		$55,000

If you supplement your retirement income by taking
a withdrawal from your savings account each year of
$55,000, you'll be fine: $55,000

Shortfall: <u>$nil</u>

Currency Diversification

This issue affects developing nations more than it does developed nations. In Botswana, for instance, a constant worry for people is whether they should keep their savings in BWP (Botswana Pula), ZAR (South African Rands), USD (US Dollars), GBP (Great Britain Pounds) or E (Euros).

In developed nations such as the USA or Great Britain, because of the stability of their currencies in relation to the currencies of other nations, the issue is less problematic.

But if you live in a developing nation, there may be a problem. Let's take the example of Botswana. The reason that the currency diversification issue is a major issue in Botswana is that the currency of Botswana has depreciated significantly against the major currencies over time. Let's consider the devaluation of BWP vs. USD over the last ten years. At the time of the writing of this book, the BWP had depreciated by 75 percent over the last ten years. Let me explain:

The BWP:USD ratio in July 2003 was 4.83, meaning that it would have cost BWP 4.83 to buy one USD.

The BWP:USD ratio in July 2013 was 8.46, meaning that it would have cost BWP 8.46 to buy one USD.

Therefore, total depreciation of BWP vs. USD over those ten years is:

4.83–8.46 = −3.63

−3.63/4.83 = −0.75,

or 75 percent.

Hence, if I lived in Botswana and I had my savings placed in BWP cash for the last ten years, it would be worth 75 percent less than the same savings placed in USD cash. So having my savings in the right currency has a huge impact on my financial well being, and that's why it's such a hot topic in Botswana.

The way to control this situation depends on where one intends to spend his retirement years. It also depends on whether that country is a developed country or a developing one. Let's say he intends to retire in country A, which is a developed country, for instance USA or Great Britain.

Traditional currency allocation techniques say that the retiree should allocate some percentage of his money in the currency of country A, and some percent internationally. When I was a practicing financial advisor in Canada in the 1990s, the foreign currency allocation allowed in an RRSP (Registered Retirement Savings Plan) was twenty percent. That is a reasonable guideline to use. The reason to have twenty percent outside of the home currency is to achieve a hedge against the local currency losing ground against the foreign currency. If the local currency depreciates, imports would become more expensive and the retiree's cost of living would increase. If you are living in a developed nation, place 20 percent of your savings in a foreign currency.

What would be the best course of action if the retiree were to retire in a developing nation such as Botswana? For guidance on this issue I'll draw on the Government of Botswana's recommended currency allocation with respect to local pension funds. Local pension funds are allowed to invest 70 percent overseas and 30 percent must remain in Botswana. As per my discussion with a local Asset Manager, the reason for this is that Botswana has a small economy and the investment opportunities are limited, so the government has permitted the local pension funds to invest the bulk of their money overseas.

The answer for a developing country is almost the exact reverse of that for a developed country: keep 30 percent of your savings in local currency and 70 percent in major currencies such as USD, GBP and Euro. As for the foreign currency allocation, meaning how much to split between USD, GBP and Euro, I'd suggest a simple one-third, one-third, one-third split.

So if I had BWP 100,000 (approximately USD 12,000) in savings I would just leave it in BWP. The amount is not worth diversifying. I'd focus my time on plans for making more money to increase my savings. If I had BWP one million or more, I'd allocate it as follows:

30 percent—BWP 300,000 in BWP

70% percent—

BWP 234,000 in USD

BWP 233,000 in GBP

BWP 233,000 in Euros.

We have already discussed placing your cash funds. You would either use two banks or one bank and a money market fund. Since we are talking about being in a developing country, let's say the cash funds are in your local currency. In the above case, the figure is BWP 300,000 and that's how you would place the BWP 300,000. You would either split the money into two banks or one bank and a money market fund.

How about the foreign currency funds? In this case the GBP, USD and Euros that were mentioned above. How should you store these? The first question is whether you keep the funds inside your country of residence or outside your country of residence.

The answer depends, first, on whether the local tax authorities can confiscate your money. If they can, then keep your money outside your country of residence. Second, it's just common sense to keep some of your foreign currency outside your country of residence. Even the USA, the bastion of freedom and the bastion of rule of law, usurped its citizens gold in 1933.[49] If the confiscation of people's wealth by the government can happen in the USA, it can happen anywhere.

The safest place to have your money these days is the UK, or any of its off-shore centres such as Guernsey, Jersey or Isle of Man. This is not to say there is an iron-clad guarantee that these locations are the safest in the world, but it's one of the best places to have your money. Plus you have the advantage of government deposit guarantees offered by the UK government, or the Crown dependencies, in the case of Guernsey, Jersey or Isle of Man, as they are called.

Accordingly, once you have opened your account in one of these places, you can then have the money that is in excess of the limit for deposit guarantees placed in a money market fund. For instance, if the deposit guarantee figure per deposit holder is GBP 50,000 and you have a joint account with your spouse, then, should the bank fail, you are covered for GBP 100,000 by the UK government (or Crown dependency government such as Guernsey, Jersey or Isle of Man). If you have monies over that fig-ure, have it placed in a money market fund offered by the same bank. That will reduce the risk on the funds over and above the deposit guaran-tee figure of GBP 100,000.

Should there be instances of bank failure, and you have money in the bank's money market funds then the same scenario applies as discussed earlier, namely that you may lose a portion of your money market fund, but it is unlikely that all of it would go up in flames.

By keeping an amount in cash that is somewhat equivalent to the govern-ment deposit guarantee scheme and any excess in money market funds offered by the bank, you have greatly reduced your risk of losing money. Now relax; leave the rest to God.

Another important point about *offshoring* is that you should not put your money into the *investment policies* of offshore mutual fund companies, or the *investment policies* of offshore life insurance companies. These "investments" are really just a form of "gambling." If you come across a financial advisor who is offering you "offshore financial products," and it turns out that these are investment products, my advice to you would be just say "No!"

If the financial advisor offers you a "protection" product such as life insurance, it's a slightly different matter and we will discuss this in the chapter on life insurance Chapter 32 (*Buy Insurance—Before You Need It*).

Now, do be aware that even the bank where you have your money is not to be totally trusted. A bank is not a charitable organisation and doesn't have your best interests at heart. It wants you to move some of your cash savings into its investment products. That's how it makes money from your money—by finding ways to charge you commissions and fees. Its representatives will hound you for this. But, do not go there. Politely refuse. And beware: the bank's representatives are persistent. You need to be equally strong in saying "No!" "But the investments are bank guaranteed," they'll plead. "No!" you'll firmly reply. You just need the bank's cash products, for instance, a chequing, savings or a fixed deposit account.*

As a final note on currency diversification, do realise that the aforementioned allocations are not carved in stone. You can vary them according to what you are comfortable with, but it is advisable to incorporate some element of currency diversification into your asset mix.

I don't know enough about financial issues

Not only do I hear this refrain from people who are about to retire, but also from people throughout the age spectrum, from teenagers to eighty-plus. It is a very valid worry. I hope that after reading this book, though, you will have resolved your biggest financial issues. That is my purpose. This book is meant to provide information regarding all essential financial matters. It is not meant to overwhelm you into *analysis paralysis*. The advice is kept simple so that the information is actionable.

Health Issues

As you grow older, your health becomes a priority. I am no health expert, but here are some financial matters related to health issues to keep in mind:

If you live in a country where you have to pay for your own medical insurance, do not let it lapse. This is the time in your life that medical expenses, specially unexpected ones, can become more prevalent. You do not want to be caught off-guard and have to dip into your retirement fund to pay for medical expenses.

If you travel to another country, ensure that your medical insurance will cover you. If not, then arrange for *travel* medical insurance *before* you buy your ticket. If you do not buy it before you buy your ticket, you may encounter a problem. Being without health insurance is too risky.

I know of a person who went on a trip from Botswana to another country, but did not buy travel medical insurance. His trip was scheduled to last one month. When he got to that country he fell ill with a serious disease. It was several months before the traveler was cured, including many a visit to intensive care. Total cost, well over $100,000. Such a huge financial hit could potentially wipe out many a person.

Therefore, never leave home without your travel medical insurance. Arrange for it in advance of purchasing your ticket. That way when you get the ticket in your hands, your travel agent will already have purchased the necessary travel insurance and will deliver both items to you simultaneously. On your trip, make sure that the travel medical insurance policy is readily accessible.

What do I want from life?

Many couples face this dilemma in their retirement years. Until that point, it was about making enough money to live, to feed the family, send the children to school and so forth. For those retirees who have their children living close to them, they are very lucky. Others will have to plan for a retirement of self-dependency.

As a couple goes through a financial analysis, both parties might disagree on the appropriate course of action. For instance, in the example of the couple earlier in this chapter—the one about the couple who owned a few parcels of land—one of the partners was insistent on starting a second business, while the other was insistent on building property investments. They realised that they couldn't do both because they didn't have the time to run both operations. They couldn't agree on what would be the best course of action, and as a result the matter was continually postponed.

This can happen. The solution to this is to come to a conclusion that you can both live with, and then implement it. Both parties need to be flexible. Stubbornness will not help. Realise that nobody really knows how a decision will work out. A friend once told me: "*Kal kisne dekha hey?*" This is a Hindi proverb meaning, "Who has seen tomorrow?" But if you've put serious thought into the decision, then you've increased the chances of your success. Thereafter, let the chips fall where they may. Don't rebuke each other, don't taunt each other and later on don't say: "I told you so."

You are physical adults; now become economic adults as well, where you both take joint responsibility for whatever decision you decided to implement.

Whom to ask for advice

You may need to involve trusted advisors and see what they have to say. Trusted advisors could include children, or friends, or an accountant. Do not consult with a financial advisor or a consultant that sells financial products. You know what his advice will be—give me the money and I'll invest it for you. That may not be what you want.

However, if you want to buy an annuity, you will need to consult with a financial advisor or an insurance salesperson. However, *you* decide how much money to put into this product. Do NOT disclose all your assets to the financial advisor. Under the guise of doing a *financial plan* for you, he will find out how much money you have in your name and he will probably try to get you to invest that money with him.

I am going a little over the top here because, in fact, the financial advisor does need the details of all your assets and liabilities to give you holistic financial advice. And certainly, there are instances where people have greatly benefitted from the advice of financial advisors within the financial services industry. However, in order to maintain financial safety, do not be convinced that it is necessary to have a financial advisor do a financial plan for you. It's simply a tool for drumming up business.

So *you* decide how much of your money you would like to put into an annuity.

How do you do that? Well, first, let me repeat that you wouldn't put all of your money into one—only a portion of your retirement income should be coming from an annuity. Hopefully, the rest of your income is coming from other sources such as cash or property income. Accordingly, let's say you have decided that you'd be happy with $30,000 pa coming from an annuity. Ask a financial advisor to provide you with a quote for what such an annuity will cost. Then tell the financial advisor to get you the best annuity for that much money.

The other way to do it is to decide how much cash you would like to allocate to an annuity. Tell the financial advisor to get you the best annuity for that much money. Of course, your financial advisor should explain the product to you in detail. Do not disclose to the financial advisor how many other monies you have.

Chapter 19: Eighty years young

Congratulations if you've made it this far in life. It's an accomplishment. I hope that your finances are also able to cope with your longevity. Longevity is great, but it's also becoming more and more of a problem if you do not have the financial means to support yourself. At this stage of your life, if you lack financial means, you may be dependent on others to support you, perhaps the government or family members. However, often-times, governments have a tough time supporting the elderly of their society. As for your children, if you are not financially stable, do you think that you were able to give them the financial education necessary for them to become financially stable and able to take care of you? It is highly unlikely.

This is a sad state of affairs, but it's the reality for many of today's elderly people, as well as their children. I once met a Caucasian woman on a flight from New York to Johannesburg. She was in her eighties. We were sitting next to each other. She seemed to be a wonderful person, bright as a button. She had many fantastic stories to tell me of her life and the wisdom of her years poured out of her. She was returning to South Africa after visiting one of her children who lived in the USA. I asked her if she had family in South Africa and she said "no."

"Then why are you living in South Africa?" I asked "Why not join one of your children and live with him or her?"

She explained to me that some of her children were going through divorces and were having a hard time supporting even themselves. Her child who lived in the USA had a reasonable life, a spouse and young children. But the child could not afford the medical insurance for the mother, so the mother was not able to stay in the USA. "They cried when I left," she said, "my child and my grandchildren. But there's nothing that any of us can do. That's life."

I was sad. She deserved to be with her loved ones, not cooped up in an apartment all day without the comforting sounds of her family around her. But … "that's life," as she said … unfortunately, for many elderly people.

If you are financially secure, count yourself lucky. Talk to your children about your remaining life. You need to be able to trust someone, and probably your best bet is your children. Families should be able to talk to each other about money.

Your children likely have your best interests at heart. Take them into your confidence. Don't be shy about it. You are going to need their help as you get older. Your mental capabilities as well as your physical capabilities are going to deteriorate. No avoiding that. When you start to forget important things, you need someone else to pick up on those issues for you. Be open. Let them know which of the children is going to get what asset. Where your will is located. Do you have a trust? Let them know everything. Ask for their advice and follow it.

Part V: Financial Advice for Certain Groups of People

Chapter 20: Celebrities and Sports Athletes

I love celebrities and sports athletes. They make our lives so rich. They give us joy, passion, heartbreak and excitement. They are awesome.

So when I see a celebrity in financial trouble, I just hate it. I once saw a famous Pakistani film comedian of yesteryear on television. He was an old man and he was destitute. He was sick and had no money for medical treatment. He was dependent on gifts and donations from others.

I was shocked. I would have imagined that this man would have surely been a multi-millionaire. With his fame and humungous fan base, he should have been.

I was sad.

What went wrong? I don't know the specifics about his case, but I imagine for many others it's the same story, over and over again. People do not know enough about financial management. A celebrity has the potential to earn a lot of money during his career. If he does, but does not hold onto his wealth and invest it wisely, then he will not become financially independent.

A celebrity's career is particularly difficult to predict. It could be long or it could be short. It depends on the fan base. How long will they love him? A celebrity should look at his career as a lottery winning. In essence, the lives of celebrities and lottery winners are similar. A celebrity or sport athlete has no clue as to how long he or she will be popular, so they have no way of knowing when the paycheques will end. If you are a celebrity or sports athlete please save your money. Accumulate your capital, and don't spend it. Look at your capital as the golden goose that will lay the golden eggs. You are only allowed to spend the golden eggs (the passive income gener-ated from your capital) not kill the golden goose (your capital). This is the key to financial security for you.

Along with professional career advice, the financial education of celebri-ties and sports athletes is of the utmost importance for their overall suc-cess. And the financial education that a celebrity needs is exactly what has been laid out in this book—the Four Steps Millionaire Formula.

That's all there is to it. If you are a celebrity or sports athlete, build your financial ark as fast as you can. Once you are there, then spend the excess passive income. But not until you are in a position to know that you are generating passive income in excess of your living expenses. Of course, if you are too busy with your career to figure out how and what to invest, just accumulate cash. Buy a personal house as a minimum, though. After you are past the most hectic part of your career, you'll have ample time to invest cash to earn passive income. Investment opportunities will always exist. Focus on your career and save as much cash as you can. Religiously follow the "Save" step of MSIP.

However, if you fall into the Peer Pressure Trap you're doomed.

Capish?

How to stop match fixing

Like millions of ardent sports fans around the world I condemn match fixing. It mars the pleasure that fans derive from the sport. But I'd like to take this discussion one step further. I am privileged to have learned a lot about personal finance in my life and I'd like to draw upon that knowledge to suggest how to combat this evil.

Let's get to the root of the problem. It's all about the Law of Cause and Effect. What is the root cause of this crime? Is it greed? Is it avarice? Is it a criminal mentality? I don't think so. I feel that it is simply a lack of financial education. That is the cause, and the effect is poverty-consciousness. My guess is that many top players in any sport come from humble financial beginnings. And, as kids, they probably neglected their studies and spent most of their time playing sports. Not a good idea in my book. However, they somehow managed to climb to the top of their chosen sporting activity. That is no mean feat. In fact, full credit to them for somehow recognising their genius at an early age and sticking with it.

At the same time, I am not suggesting to other students that they neglect their studies and follow their sporting passion. The chances of success in such an endeavour is so infinitesimally small that it's best left alone. Only the lucky few make it to the top levels where there is good money to be made.

Athletes that are competing on the world stage in any sport are unique individuals. They are so unique that they have an incredible opportunity to make big money. They should not even be thinking about match fixing. So where does this disease come from?

As I said earlier, it is probably a matter of poverty-consciousness. Like the celebrity who squanders his money and ends his life destitute, or the lottery winner who lost it all in a few short years, the problem is that these people do not know how money works. It comes to them and it goes from them. It flows like water through their hands.

Whereas, if you compare sports athletes to self-made millionaires, you'll find that the self-made millionaire is very careful with his money. Why? Because he has learned about how to hang onto his money. Or, if was he very lucky, he grew up in a rich family and learned the lessons of money the best way possible—over many years, by observing how his parents managed their money.

Where is the information gap for sports athletes that can keep them out of the clutches of match fixers? Simply, it's financial ignorance.

And not only are sports athletes ignorant about how to get financially independent, they are also not aware of how easy it is for them to accomplish such a goal given the potentially high incomes that they can earn in their careers. As I've said earlier, your income plays the biggest role in your financial success. If they learn and apply the Four Steps Millionaire Formula, they can achieve a passive income in excess of their living expenses, and probably fairly quickly at that. Then they can be financially free. All they have to do is save the money they earn, avoid the Peer Pressure Trap, invest it properly in cash flowing investments, and in virtually no time they will be out of poverty. Freedom beckons!

The Peer Pressure Trap is particularly insidious for sports athletes. A sports athlete may see his fellow sports stars, whether in his own country or in a foreign land, "appear" to be making the big bucks. And, accordingly, possessing all the material accoutrements of the big lifestyle—big house, big cars, lots of gold jewelry hanging around their necks, which is totally fine. If people have put in the hard yards, they have every right to spend their money any way they like. The problem comes when the sports athlete who doesn't yet have all these goodies, starts to wonder how he can get his hands on them, *quickly*.

The sports athlete could then fall into the trap of trying to make a quick buck via match fixing. What he has done, instead, is literally lit a match to the huge amount of money he could have earned in his lifetime, both through his sporting career and later through his growing passive income. All with his own hands.

If you know a sports athlete, please pass this book along to him. Save his or her life today.

Now, if this book "hath" come into the hands of a sports athlete a bit too late, meaning he has already committed the sin of match fixing, don't despair. Get out, fast. Confess to the crime, take the punishment, and move on because there is a huge opportunity waiting on the other side. It's a prize that could be even bigger than the prize you could have earned in your sporting career.

How, you may ask? Here is the answer: You have an opportunity to both make a difference in the world and possibly earn a living, even a fortune, doing it. Talk openly about what happened to you. The world wants to hear it. Young people want to hear it: FROM YOU. Imagine the impact you could have, the millions of young lives that you could save by telling your story of how you were done in by the match-fixing slime-bugs.

How could you make money at this venture? You should write a book (a slim volume would be fine). Then go on the road and teach students and other sports athletes how they can avoid falling prey to this evil. If you do this sincerely and consistently, you will make money both from the sales of your book and from your keynote speeches. Who knows? Your book may become a best seller and you may become rich after all.

"But I don't know how to write a book!" you exclaim. No worries, neither did I. Just know that when the student is ready the teacher will appear. If you seek guidance it will come to you. Start searching for this knowledge today.

I've just given you a million-dollar idea. It's up to you to implement it.

Chapter 21: Widows and Widowers

When one spouse passes away, if he or she had taken out life coverage during his or her lifetime, than the surviving spouse will likely receive an insurance payout. It is crucial that the surviving spouse handle this money very carefully.

The surviving spouse should put it to its maximum use by first saving it. Do not spend it. Then understand the Four Steps Millionaire Formula. Figure out if you are capable of investing the money into a Revenue Producing Property. If not, just preserve the funds in cash form. Then check out Chapter 18 (*Retirement*) and do the calculations. If you are able to retire on the insurance money plus your other savings, you are safe. If not, then be ultra careful with this payout and keep working until you can retire.

The other things you need to do in a hurry are a will and a Centralised Assets and Liabilities Schedule (CALS). If the money is big, it's also advisable to consider setting up a trust. We have spoken about trusts earlier in the book.

Chapter 22: Doctors

Doctors are close to my heart. I served many a doctor client in my practice in Canada and Botswana. My father, too, is a doctor (retired now). Hence, I grew up close to that profession. What I saw in my financial planning career, though, is that very few doctors actually make it to financial independence. That was a great mystery to me. With their income producing power, doctors should easily achieve financial independence and very early in their lives. Instead, I observed that many doctors just kept on working all their lives; some could not ever afford to retire.

Why was this? One reason, I discovered, is that doctors spend a lot of money on trinkets. They make a lot of money, but they also spend a lot. What's worse, they take on bad debt. They want to own every goody on the planet on a "buy now pay later" basis. Of course, this is a common malady amongst the entire world's population. And exactly what I am trying to combat in this book. Recall the commandment of "saving" in the Four Steps Millionaire Formula, or the commandment of saying "No!" to marketing. Those are the steps doctors miss big time.

So again, it comes down to the Four Steps Millionaire Formula. Doctors have little or no knowledge of this process. The little financial education that they do get is about how to buy mutual funds, which we know by now is not a sound financial strategy.

In what follows, I am going to discuss the Four Steps Millionaire Formula in relation to how, in my financial advisory career, I saw some doctors implement it successfully. And then I'm going to spend some time on the Four Ways Business Formula Strategy and see how that can be applied to a doctor's practice.

The story is of Doctor John Doe. It's a true story even though the name is fictional. Dr. Doe's big advantage is that he grew up in a business family. He had already learned about money matters from his parents as he was growing up. As a young man, he was told that as soon as he qualified as a doctor and opened his own practice, the first thing he had to do was to own his own office building. So that's what he did. While I was busy buying new (almost new anyway) Land Cruisers, the good doctor, also an off-road enthusiast, was driving a beat-up old 4x4. It did the job. It took him into the bush and back. Not in the same style as my much newer Land Cruiser, but he knew he was winning on the financial front. I, on the other hand, was totally oblivious to the race that I was losing—the financial race.

He was saving furiously, and his savings were going into buying cash flowing assets, like his office building, whereas mine were going into buying liabilities like my beautiful Land Cruiser. Four years after he bought his office building he had paid it off. The way he accomplished that was by renting out part of the building to other tenants while he used the remaining part of the building for his own medical practice. But he knew there was more to do on the financial front. He soon bought other properties. Ten years hence, he was done. He had more income coming in from his property investments than from his medical practice. He was in his forties.

How about that? Forty-something and financially independent. Isn't that an awesome result? Isn't that something not only doctors but the rest of us should also aspire to?

That's one way for doctors to achieve financial independence. Follow the Four Steps Millionaire Formula system. The above is not an isolated event. I know several doctors who achieved that exact same result. Some did it in their forties; some took longer, achieving financial freedom in their sixties. The doctors who accomplished it in their sixties took longer to figure out the plan. No matter. At least they got there.

This is an excellent way for doctors to achieve financial independence. Create passive income through ownership of real estate. And make sure you keep doing it until your PI>120% of LE.

Now, how about the Four Ways Business Formula? Can that apply to a doctor's practice?

Four Ways Business Formula, step 3 is about how to move the owner from operations into administration. With respect to a doctor's practice, the idea is to hire another doctor to bring in the income, while the original doctor can spend less and less time in the practice and engage in other activities instead.

Whether this is possible all depends on the laws of the country. If the medical authorities allow doctors to set up a practice easily, meaning that practice licenses are easily obtainable, then there is little incentive for one doctor to work for another (however, even in that case, it may still interest him to work as a locum for another doctor, as I'll explain shortly). He might as well set up his own practice.

If there are restrictions on obtaining licenses, then the licensed doctor has an opportunity to hire another doctor and have him work for the hiring doctor. Let's call the hiring doctor Dr. John Doe, and the hired doctor, Dr. Mark Locum.

In this case, Dr. Doe can remunerate Dr. Locum by salary or a percentage of the gross revenue. The percentage of revenue is the better idea. It will motivate Dr. Locum to generate more revenue, both for himself and for

Dr. Doe. Since the practice is paying for all the medicines and overhead such as staff, electricity and premises, Dr. Doe must take these into account when deciding what amount to split with Dr. Locum. Likely, 45 percent of the daily revenue generated by Dr. Locum should go to Dr. Locum and 55 percent to Dr. Doe. After paying off the bills, Dr. Doe may remain with 15 percent for himself. This is just enough to compensate Dr. John Doe for the risk he is taking and the effort he is expending in running the practice. And Dr. Locum should be happy with the 45 percent, as he does not have to handle the administrative matters of the practice.

Even though a doctor could set up his own practice, it may still interest him to work as a locum for another doctor for three reasons: First, the locum doctor would have no worries about the administrative matters of the practice; he can avoid those hassles almost entirely. Second, he can take stress-free vacations knowing that since the owner-doctor is taking care of his patients they will still be there when he returns. And third, while he is away or unavailable, his patients will be taken care off and not "die of pain."

The locum doctor would have to be compensated using a commission structure to give him sufficient motivation to work as a locum rather than to set up his own practice. And it's imperative the locum doctor not be cheated (for example, being told that his fees for seeing a particular patient are not applicable because the patient came back with the same ailment and the owner-doctor had to handle it) or receive delayed pay. Keep the locum happy and the owner will make money off him.

Here then is a way for a doctor to create passivity in his practice: Bring in locums to work for him.

> **Question:** How can you protect your practice from losing patients to the locum? That is, if the locum decides to open a practice down the street?

Answer: You could have a *non-compete agreement* with the locum doctor. For example, you could make an agreement that if he leaves you, for the next five years, he cannot open up a practice within a 10 km radius of your practice.

Can such a practice be sold? Again it depends on the laws of the country. If such a transaction is allowed, then there's no problem, and the sale of the practice is an option that is open to the doctor. If the medical authorities do not allow it, they need to re-think their laws because they are closing down an excellent option for the doctor to fund his retirement. An option that he should rightfully have full access to. The doctor has spent a long time building up his clientele and, therefore, has built up significant goodwill therein. The only way for him to cash in on that hard work and the goodwill therein is to sell the practice.

Let's say that in a particular country selling a practice is allowed. If Dr. Doe decides to sell the practice, he will first need to get it valued. Dr. Doe will then have to work out a payment plan, as it is unlikely the purchasing doctor will be able to pay the whole purchase sum in one go.

As for the purchasing doctor, it is imperative that he include a *non-compete* clause in the purchase contract so that Dr. Doe (the selling doctor) does not decide to immediately turn around and open up a new practice down the street. That would not be fair to the purchasing doctor. This does happen. Not just with doctors, but with many other business ventures. Be aware and bring it to the attention of your attorney when drafting the Deed of Sale for the practice.

Question: Do you have a formula for calculating the sale price of a medical practice?

Answer: I'll give you my suggestions, but it's best to see an accountant to sort this out. It's possible to value the practice based on gross income, say, on three months of gross income. The monthly income used for this calculation would be the total annual income in the past year divided by 12. For example, if the annual income for the past year was $240,000, then the monthly income to be used is ($240,000/12) $20,000. So the value of the practice is ($20,000 × 3) $60,000.

Other factors that could affect this value include:

1. Number of patients the practice caters to.

2. Number of years that the practice has existed.

3. The location of the practice.

4. The fee scale of the practice (general practitioner versus specialist practice).

These factors could add further value to the $60,000 calculated above and increase the sale price.

Question: Now from the perspective of the locum doctor, should he be satisfied with the monetary reward of being a locum, or should he try to set up his own practice?

Answer: Running a practice is not easy. If the locum doctor can get a good income without the hassles of running a practice, this is a good thing. In addition, there are other benefits of being a locum. But here's the KEY: It's not the ownership of the practice that will make you rich; it's the knowledge of how to spend, save and invest your income. That aspect has been covered in detail in this book under Four Steps Millionaire Formula. My advice to the locum doctor: If you are getting a healthy income as a locum, then just keep working as a locum, but make sure you apply the Four Steps Millionaire Formula to grow your wealth.

Is everyone happy now (that is, both the owner and the locum doctor)?

Chapter 23: Expats

Expatriates are a very big group of peripatetic people. These people will have left their home to work temporarily in a foreign land. Some end up enjoying the foreign land so much that they don't go back. But for the purposes of this discussion let's focus our attention on the expatriates that do intend to return to their home countries eventually.

If you fall into this group, your financial strategy is rather restricted. If you are intending to remain in a particular foreign country for ten years or longer, it is conceivable that you could follow the Four Steps Millionaire Formula. In that case, you would follow the "I" step—invest in the cash flowing investments step of the Four Steps Millionaire Formula system and buy property in the foreign country. When you leave you'd sell it and repatriate the cash proceeds to your home country. But there are pitfalls to be wary of. If you are not sure how long you will stay in the foreign country, or if it's difficult for you to predict tenure of at least ten years, then you may wish to stay away from buying property.

The reason for this is that to benefit from a property investment you need to be able to commit to a long-term horizon, say, at least ten years. With a ten-year horizon you will likely be able to pay off the property, and if the markets gyrate because of economic conditions in your country, you would have a good chance to ride out the gyrations so that you are not forced to sell at an inopportune time. Remember, you are not buying the property for the capital gains aspect. You can never predict what's going to happen to the price of the property with certainty. You are buying it for the cash flow and that someone else (the tenant) will help you to pay off the loan.

However, it's worth mentioning that if you did hold property for ten years, it is likely that the price of the property would have increased. The reason for this is that rental income should have increased over that time because of rental increases from inflationary adjustments (for example, if inflation is five percent, you can increase the rents by five percent each year). Hence, the price of the property should also increase accordingly, but don't count on it. If the economy is not in good shape, the value of the property can decline.

Hence, don't look for capital gains as the primary way to make money from a property investment. A property investment is really meant to be held forever, and for you to make cash flow returns forever. These cash flow returns should be increasing at the rate of inflation and will likely be higher than the rate of interest on a bank deposit. Once the property is paid off you use the rental cash flow to acquire another property asset. That's the whole idea behind property investments.

Some of the richest people I know in Botswana would be loathe to selling their property investments to you. In fact, you'd best be advised not to even bring up the idea of buying a property from them. They know that the rental income from their property investments is their life-long financial security, and they would not trade it in for a cash lump sum.

Therefore, if buying property in the foreign country appears like it's going to be risky for you, what should your financial strategy be? You have two options:

1. First, you could buy a property in your home country. This is a good idea, but there is one major pitfall. When it comes to

owning property, long distance management is difficult. For example, in the early 2000s Dubai had become the destination of choice for people wanting to own property outside of their own country. The companies that were promoting the property developments offered to manage the properties, as well.

For a while the plan worked. People invested in Dubai and then enjoyed a decent six percent return after all management costs. No problem there. Additionally, most of these people were buying properties as a permanent investment, so the huge decline in Dubai property values that occurred at the time of the Great Financial Crisis around 2007-2008 did not affect them. They were not looking for capital gains or to make money from just flipping property. Flippers got massacred; some went bankrupt.

However, according to my recent discussions with people who have property investments in Dubai, some of the original promoters and property management companies have exited the business, leaving the property management burden to the property owners. This creates a big problem because the owners are far away from the cash flowing investments. The investors have no way of collecting their money or looking after their property.

So now you have the difficult decision to decide whether you shutter the property and let it sit empty, sell it, or make expensive trips there to do the work of managing the property yourself. If the property is valuable to you in that you think you'll live in it at some point in the future, then shut it down and let it sit empty. Otherwise sell it. The management hassles and expenses are just not worth it.

So for the expat who wants to invest in his home country, unless you have family that can look after the property for you, it's best to just buy the property and leave it empty.

I know of a gentleman from India, who has accumulated a port-folio of well-situated properties in that country. These properties have increased in value. However, he does not rent them out be-cause, apparently, the laws of India are not conducive to that business. He could incur tenant hassles if he is not there to manage the business himself. However, when he returns to India, he knows he has a ready-made passive income. He just has to sell properties, as needed, and live off the proceeds. In this way he will have enough money to live on for the rest of his life.

2. Second, you could place your savings in cash. Do not invest in offshore investment policies. The problems are the same as in-vesting in mutual funds.

Also, as previously discussed, if your savings are sitting in a bank account for a number of years, you could expect a loss of pur-chasing power (that is, inflation eating into your money), say five percent per year. That is a far more acceptable risk than losing 50 percent of your money to the stock market or 100 percent to a fraudulent investment scheme offered to you by some clever salesman.

Note that if you are regularly saving money, then you are in-creasing your savings balance anyway. That is better than invest-ing your hard-earned capital in an offshore investment policy. But you could use an offshore bank. Please refer to the discus-sion under Currency Diversification in Chapter 18 (*Retirement*).

If you are a one-percenter and are able to own property in sev-eral jurisdictions, then please note that because the property owner may be a different tax entity in each jurisdiction, owning property in several jurisdictions may be a very good strategy from a tax point of view. Of course, this will depend on the double tax agreements in place between the various jurisdictions. If each parcel of rental income is taxed in its own jurisdiction, the tax results could be very pleasing.

For example, if you owned property in Gaborone, Johannesburg, Windhoek and Harare, you pay tax in each respective country at the disaggregated lower rate. Hence, you can split income with yourself. Any time you split income you save tax. It's the only true way of saving tax.

Chapter 24: Lottery Winners

What follows is advice is for lottery winners. People do play lotteries and occasionally they do win. However, my advice is don't waste a lot of your money on lotteries. Your chances of winning are infinitesimally low. You are better off spending your time learning the wealth building ideas in this book and then working them. That will give you a much better chance of achieving the wealth you seek.

For lottery winners, here are my twelve tips for you:

1. Don't touch the capital (that is, the winnings). Think of the capital as the golden goose. You will live off the money that the golden goose produces. Do not kill the golden goose (that is, spend the capital). Otherwise you will not have the golden eggs.

2. Simply put the capital into either A) a Money Market fund, or B) buy a house to rent out.

3. Live off the interest on the money market fund or the rent from the house.

4. Do not touch the capital—remember it's the golden goose ... it will continue to give you golden eggs for as long as you live.

5.	If you've won a lot of money, then you can give some away. But not a lot.

6.	You may give away money from the interest earned or the rent earned. If you are a student, the interest or rent could constitute a lot of money. You can spend some, say a third; save a third; and give away a third to family, friends or charity.

7.	If you are earning any interest or rent, don't forget there will be some tax to pay to the government. Pay this amount first, every month and get it out of the way. Otherwise you may have spent the tax money on goodies and when tax time arrives, you will not have the money to pay the taxman. Do not pay taxes from your capital. You don't want to touch the capital.

8.	Most importantly: Do not "invest" the money into shares, mutual funds (other than a money market fund) or offshore investments. You could LOSE your money, despite what the charming financial advisor will say to you to convince you otherwise. There are other, less risky ways to grow your money. Read and understand the Four Steps Millionaire Formula. That's your best course of action. As you get more comfortable with your money, and you become savvy about the traps that could make you lose it, then, if you wish, you can look at stock market investments like shares and mutual funds. Don't be in a hurry. You don't need such investments instantly.

9.	Go to a lawyer and draw up a will immediately. In due course, ask him about corporate structures such as companies and trusts. Depending on how much money you have, and what types of future businesses or activities you get involved in, you may need to spread out your money into these types of structures to secure yourself from potential lawsuits. These are called *asset protection strategies*.

10. Once you have increased your financial literacy, you may want to figure out how to use your financial bonanza as a launch pad to multiply your money. Your roadmap to multiply your money is the Four Steps Millionaire Formula, and its extension, Four Ways Business Formula.

11. By that time, you should be less likely to lose your money to swindlers who prey on people with the twin weaknesses of newfound money and little money sense.

12. You have a golden opportunity to become and remain financially independent for the rest of your life. Don't mess it up.

Chapter 25: One-percenters

One-percenters need to be reminded of the fundamentals of wealth preservation. Otherwise they could lose their wealth.

First, let's just understand who is a one-percenter? It's a rich person, as defined in Chapter 7 (*How to Invest Money*).

Now, as a reminder, financial independence can be achieved in two ways. One way is that you have investments in place that will throw off an income that will cover your expenses for life. This is represented by Graph B of Chapter 7 (*How to Invest Money*). Technically speaking, do note that your expenses will increase over time because of inflation, so you would need to bring inflation into the picture. To counter inflation you would simply need to have a margin of safety, for example, ensure that your passive income is greater than your living expenses by a margin (to be safe, of at least 120 percent).

The other way to achieve financial independence is to have sufficient cash savings such that if you take monthly withdrawals then the capital would deplete over time, but the capital would last longer than you live. This is represented by Graph A of chapter 7 (*How to Invest Money*). Again, to counter inflation you would increase your withdrawals each year. You should work with a margin of safety when calculating how long your money will last. Ensure that you have enough cash to last longer than your life expectancy.

Most one-percenters would like to be in the situation depicted by Graph B. However, there is nothing wrong with being in the situation depicted by Graph A either. Sure, you will "eat into your capital," but there's nothing wrong with that. I bring this to your attention because one-percenters sometimes think that their money must be "invested" in order for them to be able to have enough money to live on without working. Such thinking can force you to invest your money into hare-brained schemes sold by a smooth operator who is willing to promise you the world. Beware. You must guard your wealth zealously, or else you could lose it. Pay attention to the old saying: 'A fool and his money are soon parted.'

With respect to how to invest your money, one investment solution is to invest your money into property, which you alone own and control. Alternatively, if you don't want to get into property investments, cash in the bank is fine. Remember to spread the cash into two bank accounts or one bank account and a money market fund. Also consider annuities; you can allocate some money there, as well.

You also need to make sure that all your estate paper work is sorted out, for example, a will and/or a trust.

Don't forget to review the Four Ways Business Formula system in Chapter 5 (*How to make money*) and investment advice for one-percenters in Chapter 7 (_How to Invest Money_). These could be relevant to you.

What follows is strictly for the über-wealthy. So for the rest of you, please, it's censored information. Do not read further and skip to the next chapter.

OK, I'm just kidding. Read on if you wish.

Family Office

If your wealth has grown past $50 million, then you need to consider if a family office setup can benefit you.

> **Question:** What is a family office?

> **Answer:** A family office is the term used to describe a service dedicated to helping very wealthy people look after their wealth, for the benefit of themselves and their families.

You can either join an existing family office or institute one under your own auspices. The former is called a "multi-family office." Here a third party provider, such as a bank, offers family office services not just to you but to many other customers, as well. The latter is referred to as a "single family office" where you build it yourself from scratch.

The purpose of a family office is to help you to streamline and manage your personal and business affairs. If your wealth is over $50 million but less than $150 million you would likely not be able to afford a single family office, and would opt instead for a multi-family office. A multi-family office usually takes care of the following matters:

1. It offers complete management of the financial aspects of your wealth, meaning the gathering and reporting of financial data.[50]

2. It provides inheritance and succession planning services, for example, advice on how to pass the family wealth down from one generation to the next.[51]

3. It provides investment management services.

Once your wealth zooms past $150 million, consider the single family office concept because it could provide additional services such as:

1. Educational programs for the family members in areas such as financial education, business, leadership abilities and life and wellness skills.

2. Implementation of charitable giving.

3. Concierge services such as finding properties or schools, making travel arrangements and buying tickets to sporting events.

4. One advantage is that the advice you receive from a single family office would be independent, with no conflict of interest issues. For example, a multi-family office run by a bank may be intent on pushing the bank's products to its customers. However, one disadvantage of a single family office is that it is only dealing with issues specific to one family, and therefore, it may not be exposed to industry best practices. Hence, with respect to family office issues, it may not be on the innovative edge.[52]

5. Any other tailor-made solution to your problems, such as handling drug-afflicted children if the parents are deceased.

One difficulty with family office setups is that they are sometimes located in offshore centres. The main reason for this is that offshore centres usually offer a low or zero tax regime.[53] This is a huge advantage, but one problem you need to be aware of is whether or not you will be able to easily access the offshore location in physical terms. Here are a few more things you need to think about when selecting a location for your family office:

1. Local talent: Is there enough competent local staff for you to fill positions in your family office?

2. Quality of professional services: Is there sufficient third party expertise in professional services such as accounting and legal services available?

3. Quality of banking services.

4. Political climate: Is the government prone to extremism or is it democratic?

5. Ease of obtaining work permits for skills you cannot fill from the local staff pool.

6. Quality of life—safety, climate, education, entertainment, housing and hospitals.

Examples of offshore centres would include Bahamas (often used by wealth creators based in the US time zones), Isle of Man (often used by wealth creators based in the European time zones) or Mauritius (often used by wealth creators based in the African time zones). It's also a good idea to have a family member down on the ground in the offshore centre to look after your single family office.

How not to lose your wealth
You've worked hard to accumulate your wealth. The last thing you want to do is lose it. So how could you lose it? The answer is that a deficiency occurs. It could arise in any one or more of the following areas:

1) Overspending. Ensure that your expenses are in control and well within your budget. If you haven't done a budget see Chapter 6 (How to Save Money).

2) Bad investment decisions. Stick with cash, property investments that are wholly owned by you, and annuities. If you are really big, then you may consider investing some of your

wealth into mutual funds, public company stocks and private company stocks. Keep in mind that capital preservation should be your main goal. With the assets that you have in place, reaching for returns is not necessary. It's not about getting richer, but preserving what you got.

3) Claims against you, for example from liability risk such as harm caused to others. When it comes to protecting your assets from such claims, you could buy insurance to cover the problem, for example, auto insurance. You should be prudent about taking on such risks in the first place, for example, don't drink and drive.

4) Taxation. Specialist HNW (High Net Worth) solutions could help to reduce the loss of wealth owing to the effects of income tax, capital gains tax and/or inheritance tax.

5) Claims and legal fees from conflicts. For example, divorce or law suits by disinherited heirs. If you do not own the assets yourself, but have put them in the proper asset protection structures—for example, limited liability companies and trusts—this problem can be mitigated.

6) Property loss. We will look at this in Chapter 32 (Buy Insurance—Before You Need It).

To find out more about a family office setup that can work for you, it's best to get a referral from a friend who has already gone down that route. Otherwise, sources of information on family offices would either be from a global accounting or a global law practice.

Part VI: More Tips for Financial Success

Chapter 26: Money and Marriage

Money is an integral part of a successful marriage. It is often said that money problems can lead to divorce. With that in mind, let's look at two financial pitfalls to avoid in marriage.

No money

One of the problems is a lack of money. The reason? Simply not knowing enough about financial management. No surprise here. It seems to be the general malaise of the whole world's population. The pattern starts with overspending. As the couple overspends, their debt load grows. Soon they are having difficulty making repayments. Add school fees to the mix and the tension and stress of not having enough money starts to have a deleterious effect on the marriage. The love starts to dissipate, and the couple starts to move apart. Soon, problems are no longer about money—they are about the marriage itself!

Lack of communication

The other problem is a lack of communication with respect to money matters. Couples need to talk about money matters openly as much as about anything else that pertains to their marriage. If they are not sharing their thoughts on this matter then one partner could be pulling in one direction and the other partner in the other direction; and the good ship "Wealth Builder" will go nowhere.

Here are a few suggestions on how to avoid these difficulties:

Educate yourself on the Four Steps Millionaire Formula

Both spouses should become familiar with the Four Steps Millionaire Formula. If they are both speaking the same "money-language," then it becomes so much easier for them to cooperate on money matters. Ultimately, the couple's goal should be more money in the bank. More money in the bank means less stress and more love.

Plan as a Team

I know of couples that worked together as a team during their married life. They worked at their businesses together and at their family finances together. Eventually, they became financially successful. Without both partners committing to the same cause, I doubt if they would have made it out of poverty.

Communicate:

Husband and wife need to talk about their finances openly and freely. If financial mistakes have been made in the past, they need to be cleaned up. Then the couple can move on.

The reason that wives sometimes feel insecure is that they don't know what's going on financially. The husband needs to educate his wife about basic financial planning. If he does that she'll be secure and not give her husband any stress.

Let me give you an example with respect to my situation. If I died tomorrow, my wife is aware of the whole financial picture. She knows exactly what she has to do to survive. She knows that she will already have a certain amount of passive income coming in. With my life insurance payout (we will talk about life insurance shortly) she will buy additional cash flowing assets to increase her passive income. Then she'll be fine for money. Not that she will be living in the lap of luxury—I didn't want to buy so much life insurance that she'd be happy if I die (!)—but she'll survive. Every night I sleep peacefully, knowing that if I didn't wake up the next the morning ("hey now, honey, don't get any ideas") she would be able to take care of herself and the children, at least until they finish university. After that, the children can contribute towards the family income if required.

This is what I've shared with her. And she's happy. She's not stressed out because she knows that if I'm not around, she'll survive.

The basic financial planning issues that a wife must know are:

1. What is the yearly family income and expenses?

2. Whom to contact for financial matters if the husband dies. Let her consult with your accountant.

3. How much is the savings?

4. Where the Will, Centralised Assets and Liabilities Schedule (CALS) and Estate Archive System (EASy) are located.

Harmony around money matters will lead to a happier married life. Take the time now to forge a healthy relationship between money and your loved ones. It can be one of the most rewarding things you do in life and a source of continued strength in your marriage.[54] And that is one of the best investments you can make!

Chapter 27: Take care of your Parents

For the people who are the sandwich generation, meaning they have to take care of their children as well as their parents at the same time, here are a few words of advice:

As your parents get old, they will get senile. This is a fact of life. But be aware that this not the time in their lives that they need you to be disrespectful to them. In fact, it's quite the opposite. You need to show respect and caring. It's not an easy task to keep your cool when their mental and physical faculties start failing. Also, you need to realise that your parents have been independent souls all their lives. They feel nervous about becoming dependent on their children. One of the delicate subjects is money, especially inheritances. But I believe that once parents are in their late seventies (or even earlier), these subjects—money, wills, and inheritance—are subjects that need to be talked about. You may want to refer your parents to the section in this book where I urge older people to trust their children and enlist their children's help to chart out the remaining years of their lives: see Chapter 19 (*Eighty Years Young*). I hope it will help to open up the doors to having a candid discussion about wealth, health and relationship issues. It is better to discuss all of these openly rather than obliquely. Once these issues are out in the open, the problems, if any, can be resolved. Without clarity on the problems, how can good solutions be crafted?

Chapter 28: The Taxman Cometh

My admonition to you is to make sure you pay your taxes. The hands of the tax authorities are long and they will find you and nail you, so don't mess with your taxes.

By all means you should take every opportunity to legally reduce your taxes. That's called tax avoidance. It's totally legal. Knowing you owe taxes and not paying up is illegal. That's tax evasion.

If the taxman audits you, just play ball. The taxman will tell you that he is very lenient with matters where the taxpayer volunteers information rather than where the information is discovered by the taxman. So hide nothing.

How do you know if you are paying the right amount of taxes? This is a tricky question. You need to find yourself a good accountant or tax consultant. Unfortunately, not all accountants or tax consultants are created equal. It is a process of trial and error. You need to be vigilant about your financial statements and your taxes. You need to keep on top of your accountant or tax consultant to ensure that he is doing things right. However, there is no way to be completely sure. Be aware that there could be mistakes brewing; be prepared for such an eventuality.

One way to be on top of your tax situation is to make sure that you file each and every one of your source documents (the documents generated in the course of your business activities): contracts, invoices, fee notes, receipts, quotations, statements and delivery notes, as well as all correspondence from the taxman. File everything and keep it all in date order. These will come in handy for accounting and/or tax audit purposes.

Chapter 29: Don't trust anyone

This is a tough topic, but it may save your life. There are people that you should not trust, at least not fully. The problem here is that we are conditioned to trust these people. And when they betray that trust, it creates a problem for us, sometimes emotionally, and sometimes financially. The emotional problem you'll overcome in time. The financial one is more troublesome because it could damage you permanently. Be cautious from the beginning and you may prevent a problem before it happens. Prevention is always better than cure. So in that spirit, it's better to be cautious about trusting people, until you have reason to trust them.

This applies to everybody you meet. The world can be a dark place, and you will learn that. However, learning the hard way can leave indelible marks on your mind and/or wallet.

First, be careful about trusting the professionals you work with, for example your accountant or attorney, until you've been working with them for a while. It is most important to figure out as quickly as you can what their professional limitations are. For instance, you may find that an attorney is great at real estate matters, but may not know enough about tax law. Always try to judge whether or not the professional you are working with has the expertise to handle your affairs.

It is a good idea to politely probe the professional to determine if he can handle your problem. For example, you can ask: "Mr. Professional, is this within your area of expertise?" and *wait* for the answer. Asking good questions, and *waiting* for the answer will save you from a lot of unnecessary problems. Don't second-guess the answer. Don't put words in the mouth of the person you asked the question. Always ask the question, and then wait. Even if the subsequent silence is deafening, refrain from being the first to speak. That way you will get high quality information, which you can use as the basis for good decisions.

Second, be careful of trusting your friends. Everything is fine until money is involved. Then be careful. If you go into business with a friend make sure that all matters are documented, including exit procedures, in case the business relationship doesn't work out.

Don't lend money to your friends. You will lose the money and the friendship.

Also, if you want to be financially successful, limit your friends to just a few. For all practical purposes, we can develop close relationships with only a few people.[55] Make your spouse the number one priority with whom you are going to do this. Spending time with your spouse is invaluable, and the emotional and financial returns will be most rewarding. As for the rest of your acquaintances, limit how much time you allocate to them. Too much time spent with your friends could hurt you.

Third, do not trust co-shareholders and/or business partners. You must always have shareholders' agreements and/or partners' agreements (and think about what could go wrong). Have the agreements reviewed regularly by a legal professional.

Try to ensure that you can buy out your co-shareholders or partners at any time.

Fourth, be cautious about trusting anyone who wants to sell you an investment product. Do your homework thoroughly. If it doesn't seem appropriate for you, just stay away. Politely refuse to buy the investment product. Don't sign anything before you read a document *in full*. Even that little slip that comes out of the electronic machine at the cashier's till. Read it in full. It could spell trouble. I never expected any mistakes from that little slip, so I used to sign such slips without checking them. Then once I was charged with an incorrect amount. Avoid such errors.

Always read the small print before signing legal documents. Whoever it was who said something like "the small print from hell" knew what they were talking about. Don't fall prey to the small print. Read it.

Be cautious. Be skeptical. Don't trust anyone unless you have to. This strategy may save your life.

Question: How do you trust a trust?

Answer: Again, as I said above: "Don't trust anyone unless you have to." Don't put all of your assets into one trust. If you are rich enough, use two trusts, obtained from two different trust companies. Also, keep some assets in your own name and that of your wife and children. Diversify the holdings of your assets rather than concentrate them in one place. That should be good enough.

Question: Can a trust be attacked?

Answer: When trusts have been attacked, they are mostly not attacked because of their wording. Each and every trust is basically similar to all the others. Trusts can be attacked if they are not administered properly. This means the trustees do not meet on a regular basis and possibly one or more beneficiaries runs the show, which might result in the trust being declared as the alter ego of the main trustee or founder.

For a trust to work properly, all the trustees have to apply their minds to trust issues. Where the trustees blindly follow the directions of the main trustee or founder, they act as agents for the founder. This results in the trust becoming something akin to a partnership and not a true trust.

Chapter 30: In defense of the Gruesome Trifecta

Just as much as we have to attack the causes of obesity because obesity can cause diabetes, similarly we have to attack the Gruesome Trifecta—government, big business and the financial industry because they can cause financial disease.

As I mentioned in Chapter 1 (*The New World*), the Gruesome Trifecta has certain downsides; let me touch on the downside of these institutions. You need to be aware of the downside of these institutions so that you can protect yourself from their deleterious effects.

Government: They seem to allow problematic institutions like banks and mutual fund companies to come into existence. They manipulate statistics and the money supply. Governments are basically a front for Big Business. Through lobbying,[56] Big Business can get Government to do its bidding. How do you protect yourself from Government? Be very wary of trusting them.

Big Business: They bombard us with bad advertising tempting us to buy junk that is of no use to us. How do you protect yourself from Big Business? Have the gumption to say "No!" to all the bad advertising being thrown at you.

Financial Industry: They promote Weapons of Financial Destruction (WFD)—mutual funds, credit cards and loans. How do you protect yourself from the Financial Industry? Don't get involved with mutual funds and bad debt, and learn never to abuse your credit card.

To be fair, we do need to have ... some ... element of the Gruesome Trifecta around.

Take government, for instance. Any country would be in chaos without government. People need to have an environment in which they know certain systems are stable and will work on a daily basis without them having to think about it. There are many examples: traffic signals, the courts and police among others. We need government, but the call should be for an honest government, one that fights corruption, doesn't waste taxpayer's money or destroys freedom.

This is no easy task. But let's start to instill such ideals in our children today. If these children grow up to be government officials, maybe the governments of the future will be better. We should start right away on the long journey of creating honest government officials. We should inculcate in our children the idea that they can bring about change, even single handedly.

Sure, massive change can be brought about by just one person. Imagine if Martin Luther King decided that one man was not enough to bring about the ideal of equality for blacks, or Gandhi thought that the massive subjugation of sub-continent Indians by the British could not be ended by one man, where would we be today? These men changed history. Single handedly.

Let's train our children to believe in themselves and in making a difference.

As for Big Business, why do we need them? We need big business to pull off large capital-intensive accomplishments like drilling for oil and building planes. But when big businesses move too far afield from providing a valuable service or product to mankind, we as individuals need to rein them in. Don't forget the power of your wallet and how we, as individuals, can use that to inflict lethal damage on Big Business institutions that we feel are harming the financial well being of humans or the environment. All we need to do is to simply stop buying their products. "Wallet Power" is a powerful weapon, which we must be aware of.

That leaves financial services. We need banks. As I've mentioned earlier, they provide services that we need such as bank accounts and good debt. We also need other financial services companies such as Life Insurance companies.

As I mentioned in Chapter 1 (*The New World*), you also need to know how you can profit from the Gruesome Trifecta's system. Play their—the house's—game and you will win.

For example:

Government: If you become an entrepreneur, you can save on taxes. Sit with your accountant and figure out what your tax breaks are (tax breaks are expenses that you can claim). You will find that entrepreneurs get more tax breaks than employees. For instance, if you are an entrepreneur and if this book helps you to increase your income, you could write-off the cost of this book. In general, a self-employed person can write off far more expenses than a salaried person can. Going into debt to avoid tax is not very clever. The only true way to save tax is to split income. So give a thought to splitting the income amongst family members and possibly across jurisdictions.

The reason that entrepreneurs get tax breaks is that government wants to promote entrepreneurship. More entrepreneurs means more jobs, and hence, more taxes for government. Another instance—property investments. Property investors, too, get tax breaks. Again, the reason is that government needs property development to occur and instead of doing it by themselves, they want to encourage entrepreneurs to partner with government to put up more property.

Big Business: As a small entrepreneur you can compete with Big Business. The Internet has leveled the playing field. Learn Internet marketing and you can be off selling products, which previously only big businesses could sell. With a good website, you can reach customers on a worldwide level. You could jump from being a local entrepreneur to being a global one, previously the domain of large companies with multi-country presence. Now armed with just a laptop you could have the same reach.

Financial Services: Don't buy mutual funds or get involved with bad debt. Stick to cash deposits and good debt and you'll be playing the banking system to your advantage.

This was one of the main missions of this book, to teach you how to protect yourself from the Gruesome Trifecta, and at the same time to think about how to profit from their system.

Chapter 31: Financial Planning for Muslims

A word on financial planning for Muslims. Let me say right in the beginning that I am no expert in Islamic Finance, but this is how I read the situation. Muslims have specialised needs with respect to financial matters. For example, the need to avoid dealing with "interest." I would like to offer a bit of guidance in this book, lest I leave my Muslim brethren without an opportunity to avail the financial techniques explained in this book.

Islam forbids both the receiving and paying of interest.[57] So how do the things I've talked about in this book apply to Muslims? Just one change. Muslims need to substitute any "interest-earning" or "interest-paying" financial instrument for an Islamic alternative that is a "non-interest-earning" or "non-interest-paying" one. Or, speaking in broader terms, substitute any non-Islamic financial instrument with an Islamic one (for instance, a conventional insurance product with an Islamic insurance product). The rest of the strategies I recommend stay the same.

For example, one of my recommended strategies is the Four Steps Millionaire Formula. If you are a Muslim, the only thing that would change here is that if you are seeking a loan from a bank, you may wish to seek out an Islamic Bank, or a conventional bank with an "Islamic Window" that offers an Islamic "loan." I am using the term "loan" for the sake of convenience, but in actual fact the Islamic "loan" is not a "loan." An Islamic loan will not entail interest,[58] but will allow you to implement the same strategies as a conventional bank loan would. Without getting into too much detail, suffice it to say that although the details of the Islamic loan differ from those issued by a conventional bank, for all intents and purposes they are one and the same thing.

For example, if you were going to use the loan to buy a house, you would be able to buy a house and pay off the loan over time with both your tenant's money as well as your own. But your intention for taking out the loan must be the same as I've explained in the Four Steps Millionaire Formula; meaning, for good debt. A loan, taken out for the purposes of buying a trinket for personal consumption is bad, even if the loan is Islamic.

Similarly, my suggestion is you are not to buy Islamic mutual funds for exactly the same reasons as you wouldn't buy conventional mutual funds. They are all WFD (Weapons of Financial Destruction).

The wealth-building concepts taught in this book are universal, across the globe; no matter the country, culture or religion. Wealth can only be gotten in one of two ways: Four Steps Millionaire Formula or its extension, Four Ways Business Formula. Some of the financial tools may need to be modified according to your specific circumstances, but the concept is the same, no matter where you live in the world, your culture, or your religion.

Chapter 32: Buy insurance— before you need it

You need to protect yourself from the untimely loss of life, income or other assets. So, buy insurance—before you need it.

Let me explain. Let's start with life insurance. Assume that you are married and have two young children. To understand why you need life insurance, let's look at the following diagram (see Figure 12):

Figure 12: Why You Need Life Insurance

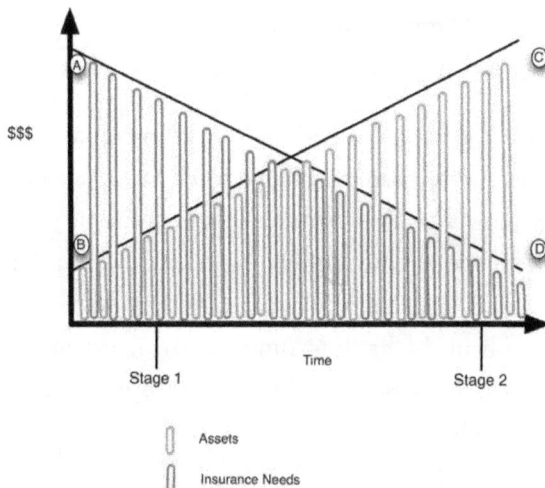

The diagram shows that early on in life your assets are probably low, as depicted by point B on the Assets Growth scenario B-C. Hence, your life insurance needs are high, as depicted by point A on the Insurance Needs scenario A-D. If you were to die at Stage 1, with hardly any assets to your name, you would create much hardship for your spouse and your young kids. To overcome this problem, you need to buy life insurance. If you are young, you would pay a small monthly payment, called a monthly premium, and you could get a decent amount of life cover. *Life Cover* refers to the payout your spouse would receive should you die. It's a way of creating an instant estate for your young family. ("Instant estate" meaning "instant wealth").

For example, if you had purchased $100,000 of life cover, and you died even one day after you bought it, the life insurance company would give your spouse a cheque for $100,000. It may not be enough for your spouse to live on comfortably for the rest of her life, but it would give her some breathing room to sort out her financial affairs.

If you had purchased one million dollars of life cover, and you died, she'd have a much bigger sum in her bank account. It would be much better than the $100,000. But you would have had to pay a much larger monthly premium to buy one million dollars worth of life cover; and maybe you could not afford it. There is a limit to how much life cover you can buy. It's based on how much premium you can afford to pay.

As life carries on, it is hoped that you are building up assets. The B-C scenario depicts this. As your assets grow, your life insurance needs drop. The A-D scenario depicts this. So what this means is that if you had one million USD in the bank, why would you need one million dollars worth of life cover? If you died and had no life cover, your spouse could use the one million dollars cash in the bank to fund her living expenses. Hence, later in life as your assets increase, your life insurance needs drop. Stage 2 depicts this on the graph.

That's the basic premise behind life insurance: should you die without many assets, life cover provides an "instant estate" for your family.

That is why you need to buy life insurance. I have seen people's lives saved because of it. That is, the lives of the survivors (wife and children).

This immediately leads to another question: what kind of life cover should you buy?

There are two types of life cover that you could buy: one is called Term Insurance, and the other is Whole of Life Insurance. Let's discuss each briefly.

Term Insurance:
In the case of term insurance, as the name implies, the life cover is for a specific term, that is, for a specific number of years. If you die after the term expires, your family gets nothing.[59] This is depicted in the diagram below (see Figure 13).

Figure 13. Term Insurance

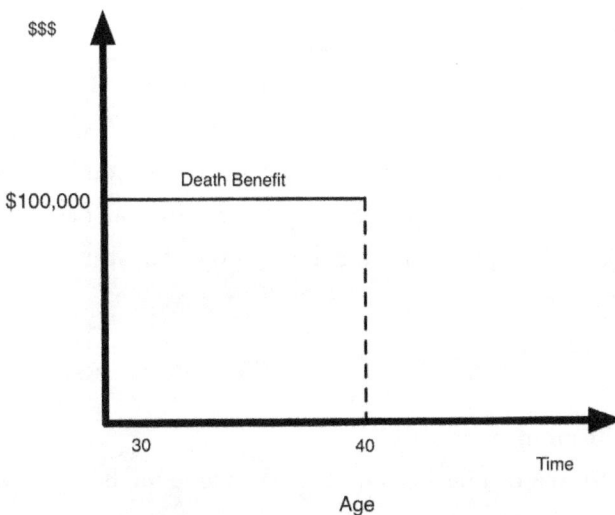

In this particular case, say you were thirty when you bought the term cover and the term you bought it for was ten years. If you died at the age of thirty-nine, your spouse would get paid out the sum of $100,000. But if you died at the age of 40 years and one day, then your spouse would get nothing. If so, would this policy have been a waste of your money? Absolutely not. It protected your family for the period of cover that you purchased it for; in this case, ten years. If you had purchased it for a period of twenty years of cover, it would have protected your family for twenty years. If you die at any point within the set period of cover, your family gets paid out. Hence, another name for an insurance policy is *protection policy*.

> **Question:** In term insurance, what happens to the $100,000 if I don't die within the set period? Do I lose it?
>
> **Answer:** Let's first understand something about the the $100,000 you are referring to. It is the amount of *cover* you bought. You didn't actually give $100,000 to the insurance company. You paid a yearly *premium*. A premium is the yearly fees for the life cover. Maybe it was $150 pa. If so, after ten years you paid ($150 × 10) $1,500 to the life insurance company. If you had died within the set period, the life insurance company would have kept the premiums of $1,500 and paid out $100,000 to your spouse in return. But if you didn't die within the set period, the life insurance company gets to keep the $1,500 in premiums, which you had paid over the ten years. And you lose the $1,500. However, as I explained above, actually you have not "lost." You bought protection for the period of ten years. It was a *cost*, not a *loss*.

Whole of Life Insurance

In the case of Whole of Life Insurance, as the name implies, the cover is for your entire life, regardless of when you die.[60] This is depicted in the diagram below (see Figure 14).

Figure 14. Whole of Life Insurance

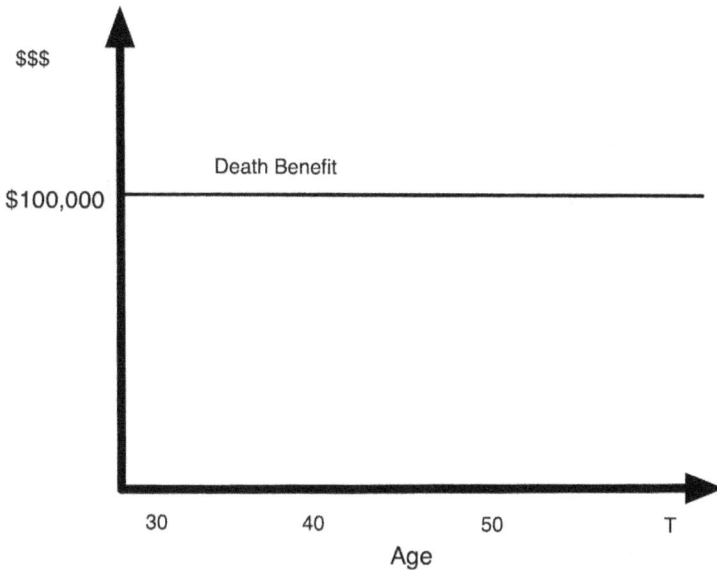

Because you are protected for life, this type of policy is more expensive than Term Insurance. This is because, no matter what, with Whole of Life, the insurance company has to pay out someday. They need to make enough money from you to do that.

To illustrate the difference in costs, let's say a Term Insurance policy providing life cover of $600,000 for a term of twenty years may cost you: $200 per month, but a Whole of Life policy providing life cover of $600,000 may cost you $500 per month. These numbers are examples, as they ignore age as well as health condition.

Because of the substantial difference in cost, a big decision to make when buying life insurance is which type of policy to buy—Term or Whole of Life? Before figuring that out, it is important to figure out how much life insurance you should purchase. A simple rule of thumb is that you should buy ten times your current annual income. So if your salary is $60,000 pa, then you need to purchase $600,000 of life insurance.

As per the preceding example, if you can afford $500 per month, you should buy the Whole of Life policy. If you cannot afford the $500 per month, then I still recommend that you buy a Whole of Life policy, but the amount of cover you would buy would be less. Perhaps you could afford only $200 per month, and that amount could only buy $150,000 of Whole Life cover, then that's what you should buy. You should avoid Term Insurance, because after the term expires you will not have any cover. The problem with Term Insurance is that when the policy term expires, if your health has deteriorated, you may not be able to buy life cover again. As a result, your family would be left without any life cover.

This may not be a problem if you have managed to build up sufficient assets. However, if you are still struggling financially, you may need a loan for a new venture and the bank may require that you provide a life cover policy to qualify for the loan. If your health condition is problematic, you wouldn't be able to get the loan because you wouldn't qualify for a life cover policy. Therefore, be on the safe side, and buy as much Whole of Life cover as you can afford.

Another important consideration is that both spouses must have life cover. Above we have discussed the situation for the case where the husband dies. What if the wife dies? If the husband was the primary breadwinner in the family, he still has to continue to be the breadwinner. But if he has young children, he will need to hire a nanny. If there were a life cover payout for the wife's death, such cover could take care of the housekeeping expenses that will arise, leaving the husband mentally and physically free to continue to earn a living.

Accordingly, both spouses need to buy life insurance. A smaller amount of cover could be purchased for the spouse that is not the primary bread-winner. For example, you may buy $150,000 of Whole Life Insurance for the husband and $100,000 of Whole Life Insurance for the wife, or, if the wife is the main breadwinner in the family, vice versa.

Another point is that your life insurance salesman will often try to sell you a new policy. He will make up some excuse or the other why you need an-other life policy. "Oh, the first one was to cover your family. But now you need one for key man insurance to cover your business." He may be right. Your life cover needs can change over the course of your lifetime.

However, beware of buying too many policies. You may not need them. The reason that the insurance salesman tries to sell you a new policy is that, when it comes to life insurance policies as opposed to investment policies, he is usually paid a one-time commission. With respect to in-vestment policies, the financial advisor could be getting an on-going fee. Consequently, for the insurance salesman to repeatedly make money from you, he has to sell you a new policy.

Also, know that insurance policies are not just "buy-and-forget" financial products. There is servicing that the insurance salesperson may need to do on an ongoing basis. For instance, what if you miss a premium, or the premium changes, or, God forbid, the life insurance company goes bust? The life insurance salesman needs to provide you with all necessary services.

The problem arises because he was only paid *once* for selling you the life cover policy. He doesn't get paid for providing on-going services. It is im-portant to discuss this aspect with your life insurance salesperson; ask him how he will service your policies without getting further payments from the insurance company. He may get a minute on-going stipend from the life insurance company, but it's hardly enough to pay for his efforts in servicing your policy. It would be appropriate for the life insurance company to provide salesmen with on-going fees. It would be excellent motivation to continue to service your policy. You may need to negotiate a fee, which you would pay directly to the insurance salesperson. Maybe that will keep him happy. But beware of being sold too many new policies, which you may not need.

There are many other types of insurance cover that you may need. I'll list a few below:

Critical Illness Cover: This is usually sold as a package combined with life cover. It is important to buy critical illness cover because you may be diagnosed with a serious illness. In such an instance, if you had bought critical illness cover then the payout from the insurance company could help you to get the treatment you need. Do note: If you avail yourself of the critical illness cover, the life cover will likely fall away. Therefore, you need to consider whether or not you have other financial means to pay for treatment. If you do, then do not take the critical illness payout; instead, continue to keep the life policy because you may not qualify to buy life cover again. But if you don't have other financial means to pay for the treatment, you'll be happy you had bought the critical insurance cover.

Disability Insurance Cover: According to the insurance industry you are much more likely to have a disability before the age of sixty-five than you are to die.[61] If you are disabled for a prolonged period, you could find it difficult to survive. Basically, what's happening is that you are not dead, but where will you find the money to eat if you can't go out and work? For example, if you are a surgeon or a dentist, and if your hands are not functional because of a major injury, how will you earn a living? Consider purchasing as much disability cover as you can afford. It is something every breadwinner should have.

Auto Insurance: This is mandatory in most countries around the world. As a minimum you need to purchase "third party" insurance, meaning that if you have an accident, only the other party's vehicle would be covered, not your own. In such an instance, you would have to pay for the repairs to your own vehicle. If you are rich, then this may be acceptable. But I recommend that everyone, including the rich, purchase *all perils* auto insurance. In addition to the third party's damages, all perils auto insurance will take care of your damages. It can save you money and provide you with peace of mind.

Medical Insurance: With the cost of medical procedures rising all the time, it's wise to have this type of insurance. It is especially important if you are caught in an unexpected accident or major illness, where the medical bills could be beyond the reach of the average person.

House (and Property) Insurance: Your house or investment property is a major asset. Should you experience a major hazard such as a fire it could destroy your most valuable asset. You want to be adequately insured against such a risk.

Depending on which country you live in, or the type of business you're in, there may be other insurance products you need. For example, in the USA, in addition to the above, it's advisable to purchase Long Term Care Insurance. In addition, if you are a very wealthy person, you may want to buy insurance to cover liability risks, such as guests injuring themselves while riding your horses.[62]

For a complete list of what types of insurance covers you need, it is advisable to consult with a competent insurance salesperson in your country. To find a competent insurance salesperson, ask for a referral from someone you know. Just like accountants and attorneys, not all insurance salespeople are alike. Some know more than others, and some provide better follow-up service than others. You need to find the best possible insurance salesperson to work with.

Also keep in mind that when buying insurance of any kind don't just compare the price of the insurance cover from one insurance company to the price of the insurance cover from another; also look at the strength of the insurer. As I mentioned when discussing annuities, the insurance cover is only as good as the strength of the life insurance company behind it. Try to get a feel for the strength of the insurer. Usually the bigger the better, but ask your insurance salesman, "How do I know if this insurance company will be around if my family or I need to collect on the insurance cover?" His assessment will be fine, go with it.

If you're wondering whether insurance is just another questionable activity like the banking industry or the financial services industry, the answer is "probably, yes" because they are all connected. But I think that the insurance industry is probably the best of a bad lot. Ultimately, there is no way to "guarantee" that your insurance company will be around if and when you or your family need to collect on the cover, but having insurance is better than not having it. There are many instances that I know of where the life insurance policy of the family proved to be of inestimable value at the death of the breadwinner. Life insurance is a must, but be careful and do not take the company or the intermediary at face value.

Offshore Life Insurance Companies

For those of you living as expats in the expat world, you too, need life cover. You could buy this from the country in which you are temporarily resident, or you could consider offshore life providers. Consider buying life insurance from offshore life companies. Buying life cover is not buying investments. Do not buy investments from offshore life companies. Regarding life cover, it is to your advantage to buy from an offshore life insurance company because you can then buy in international currencies such as GBP, USD and Euro. You will not be restricted to buying life cover in the currency of the country where you are temporarily resident.

Take Botswana for example. I had written earlier how Botswana's currency had lost 75 percent against the U.S. dollar over the last ten years. Therefore, if my life insurance cover were in Botswana Pula, and I died, my wife would get 75 percent less than what I had intended for her at the start. Consequently, if you are an expat, opt for buying life insurance cover from an offshore life insurance provider.

However, in doing so, you have to be very careful about which offshore life insurance company to use. You have to be particularly concerned with where the life insurance company is domiciled, that is, where its head office is located. If it is domiciled in a country with a robust regulatory environment, you are better off. Accordingly, if you are an expat, I would recommend that you take out life cover with a life insurance company domiciled in the UK or its offshore centres such as Guernsey, Jersey or Isle of Man. Also, the bigger the name the better, for example: Friends Provident International, Royal London or Zurich Life. At the time of writing this book in 2013, I'd be happy with any of these.

> **Question:** Only one-percenters can afford to buy all these insurance products you mention. I am a young person (or a 'not so rich' person). How can I afford all these insurance products *and* simultaneously create passive income streams?

> **Answer:** It's not going to be easy, but here's a plan. Your financial priorities are as follows:
>
> 1. First off, create enough income to live—that is, to eat, and pay for rent and transportation.
>
> 2. Then create enough income to buy health insurance, disability insurance and life insurance, in that order.
>
> 3. Then create enough income to start your passive income streams.

The point is to create enough income, and then to know how to spend it. If you follow the plan laid out for you in this book (as diligently as you can—you are a human and you will stray off course from time to time, but as long as you correct course occasionally you will be fine) then you will achieve the ultimate goal: Passive Income > 120 percent of your Living Expenses. It will not be easy and it will take time—maybe fifteen to twenty years. But if you stick with it, then in all likelihood you will get there.

Chapter 33: Multiple Sources of Income

If you've managed to implement the Four Steps Millionaire Formula, then you've already created two sources of income: first, from your job or business, and second, from your property assets. Wow! How does that feel? If you are laid off, or you fall sick, you still have money coming in from your property assets. You eat. You live. Fantastic.

You can expand on the "Multiple Sources of Income" theme to create more sources of income. One approach would be to increase the number of property assets you own. Each property asset then becomes an additional source of income. So if Property Number 1 is not generating any income, perhaps because it is temporarily without a tenant, no problem, Property Number 2 will generate money for you. And so on.

How about a second job?

No. This is not what we are talking about. We want you to create multiple sources of *passive income*—money that you don't have to actively work for, at least not a great deal. Remember after reading this book the thought of exchanging your time for dollars should be anathema to you. You must constantly be looking for opportunities where you can create passive income. Even if that means an initial period of struggle and an investment of time and money to get you into a position where, once the project is up and running, thereafter, the income generation from your project is substantially passive.

Here are a few more sources of income that you could setup:

1. Bank interest: If you have a big enough bank balance, you could live off the interest. But if you don't have a big enough bank balance to live off the interest, you could also tap into the capital. There is nothing wrong with that as long as you have done the calculations regarding retirement. Always consider how much cash you can pull out without running out of money before you die. Because interest is highly passive, this is probably the best source of income. You don't have to work for it at all, other than doing paperwork.

2. "Four Ways Business Formula," step 3. We have covered this one in detail earlier in the book. Consider how to turn your current business into a passive income stream.

3. Dividend paying stocks. Only buy individual stocks; do not put your money into a mutual fund, which specialises in investing in dividend paying stocks.

4. Do not put your money into other people's private businesses or into property syndicates. You will not get your money back. No matter how attractive the returns appear to be, do not invest in this way.

Part VII: Conclusion

Chapter 34: The Big Picture

We are almost at the end of our journey together. What was my goal for you in this book? To provide a highly actionable list of things that will make you financially independent faster. Let me recap, in big picture terms, the lessons to take away.

Build Wealth

First, it is about how to build wealth. This is the first thing that I wrote about. If you are early in your life, you stand a great chance of accomplishing this. If you are later in your years, don't get discouraged. I know of people who started in their sixties and still accomplished their wealth goals by their seventies. Thereafter, their retirement years were very pleasurable. The knowledge you need in order to build wealth is encapsulated in the following two tenets:

1. The Four Steps Millionaire Formula or MSIP.

2. And it's extension, Four Ways Business Formula, or MSIPPS.

Keep it

Second, I wrote about how to keep your wealth. Making money is one thing, but keeping it is a different thing altogether. For this you need to:

1. Understand the "S" step in MSIP. If you can't save your money, it won't matter how much money you make. You'll always be poor.

2. Understand how to protect your assets by placing them in asset protection structures such as companies and trusts.

3. Ensure that you do not trust anyone any more than you have to, and not until they've given you sufficient reason to trust them.

Live a life free of money worries

Finally, of what use is having money if you are going to fret over it? To allay your stress over having too much money, you need to know how to live a life free of money worries. This entails:

1. Having a will and/or a trust.

2. Having a CALS and an EASy, and making sure that you've shared the location of these with your executor and beneficiaries.

3. Having acquired sufficient insurance (life, disability, medical, etc.).

Chapter 35: Next Steps

Here is what you need to do in the next 30, 90 and 180 days:

Next 30 days:

1. Reread *Route to Financial Success.*

2. Do a budget.

3. Get healthier: Start a diet, exercise more and sleep eight to nine hours daily. This will give you the energy to start thinking like a winner.

Next 90 days:

1. Figure out how you're going to make more money. If more money is not your main target (maybe you are already a one-percenter), figure out how you are going to improve your life. What needs improving? Your health? Your relationships? Do you need more leisure time? Figure it out, write it down and make a goal to improve those areas of your life that need improvement.

2. If you are going to start a business, do a business plan. If you are already in business, update your business plan.

3. If you need certain skills to improve your income-producing
    ability then figure out how you're going to acquire those
    skills. For instance, take a course, read a book or get advice
    from a successful mentor.

Next 180 days:

1. Every day journal about a new business you can start. Walk
    around with a journal. Whenever a new idea hits you, write
    it down. If you don't write it down, you will lose it.

2. Start a business. Even if it's going to be a part-time business
    in the beginning. Or, if you are already in business, start fig-
    uring out how to buy revenue producing property. Maybe
    you can buy the building where you are currently renting
    space.

3. Memorise a personal finance topic from this book or else-
    where and teach it to your spouse, child or a friend. Do this
    as often as you wish. Try, perhaps, to do it at least once every
    month. That way, over the next two years or so, you will mas-
    ter a number of personal finance topics. Thereafter, the fi-
    nancial results you seek will come into your life so much
    easier.

Chapter 36: Last but not least

When you reach the end of your life, will you feel like you had made it financially? Or will you feel like you had messed it up? If you are like 99 percent of the world's population, it is highly likely that you will be saying to yourself: "If only I could do it all over again, how I would get it right!" "Get it right" meaning that you would either have had a lot of money at the end of your life, or at least, that you would have had "enough," enough to accomplish those things that meant a lot to you, such as enjoying a comfortable life and taking care of your loved ones.

None of us is going to get a second chance at life. Whatever we're going to accomplish, it's going to have to be done in this lifetime. Wouldn't it be better if you had the roadmap, instead of trying to figure it out on your own? Well, you have it now. That was the purpose of this book, to help you shorten your learning curve with respect to building wealth, keeping it and living a life free of money worries.

Now that you have the roadmap, don't waste another moment of your precious life. Go out and do it. Achieve the financial independence that you desire. And once you have it, teach others how to do it. Help ease their journey with what you've learned. If you've read all the way to this page, then you are one of the few people in the world who is dedicated to creating a better financial outcome for yourself. I honour you for that and wish you all the best.

Appendix I: Sample Lease

AGREEMENT OF LEASE

1. PARTIES

The parties to this lease are

1.1 Sample (Pty) Ltd, represented by Mr. Landlord Sample ("the Lessor").

And

1.2 John Tenant ("the Lessee").

2. INTERPRETATION

In this lease, except in a context indicating that some other meaning is intended,

2.1.1 "the Property" means The First Floor of (physical address).

2.1.2 "the Lease Period" means the period for which this lease subsists, including any period for which it is renewed;

2.1.3 "month" means a calendar month, and more specifically:

2.1.3.1 in reference to a number of months from a specific date, a calendar month commencing on that date or the same date of any subsequent month; and

2.1.3.2 in any other context, a month of the calendar, that is, one of the 12 months of the calendar, and "monthly" has the corresponding meaning;

2.1.4 "the parties" means the parties to this lease, and "party" means one of them;

2.1.5 "the Rates" means the assessment rates payable on the Property and includes any other charges payable by the Lessor to the local authority (such as, but not limited to, refuse removal charges or sanitary fees), but not charges for water, electricity or gas;

2.1.6 "year" means a period of 12 consecutive months, and "yearly" refers to a year commencing on the date on which the lease comes into operation or any anniversary of that date;

2.2 references to notices, statements and other communications by or from the Lessor include notices by or from the Lessor's agent;

2.3 expressions in the singular also denote the plural, and vice versa;

2.4 pronouns of any gender include the corresponding pronouns of the other genders.

2.5 Any provisions of this lease imposing a restraint, prohibition or restriction on the Lessee shall be so construed that the Lessee is not only bound to comply therewith but is also obliged to procure that the same restraint, prohibition or restriction is observed by everybody occupying or entering the Property or any other part of the Property or the Building through, under, by arrangement with, or at the invitation of, the Lessee, including (without limiting the generality of this provision) its Associates and the directors, members, officers, employees, agents, customers and invitees of the lessee or its Associates.

2.6 Clause headings appear in this lease for purposes of reference only and shall not influence the proper interpretation of the subject matter.

2.7 This lease shall be interpreted and applied in accordance with the law of the Republic of Botswana.

3. LETTING AND HIRING

The Lessor lets and the Lessee hires the Property on the terms of this lease.

4. DURATION

4.1 This contract commences on the 1st of May 2014 and will continue for a period of twelve (12) months.

4.2 After the period of twelve (12) months the contract will be renewable at the option of the parties hereto. Notice regarding renewal or termination of the agreement must be done three months before the end of the lease period.

4.3 The contract can be terminated by three months written notice from the one party to the other.

5. RENT

5.1 The rent shall be P 5 000(Five Thousand Pula) for each month of the_ first year of the Lease Period; and

5.2 the rental will escalate annually by 10% at the anniversary of the initial lease period.

5.3 The Lessee shall pay the rent monthly in advance on or before the 7th day of every month.

5.4 The Lessee will, within immediately after signature hereof, pay a deposit to the Lessor of P 5000 (Five Thousand Pula).

5.5 The deposit will be repaid to the lessee without interest.

6. PAYMENTS

6.1 All payments due by the Lessee to the Lessor under this lease shall be made to the Lessor at the Property or to such other person, if any, at such other place, if any, as the Lessor has designated for the time being by written notice to the Lessee.

6.2 The Lessee shall not withhold, defer, or make any deduction from any payment due to the Lessor, whether or not the Lessor is indebted to the Lessee or in breach of any obligation to the Lessee.

6.3 The rent and all other amounts payable by the Lessee under this lease shall be inclusive of value-added tax in so far as it is applicable.

6.4 The Lessee shall be liable for interest on all overdue amounts payable under this lease at a rate per annum 3% (THREE PERCENT) above the official prime rate per annum of the Bank of Botswana from time to time, reckoned from the due dates of such amounts until they are respectively paid.

7. ADDITIONAL CHARGES

7.1 In addition to paying the rent and other amounts, the Lessee shall reimburse the Lessor, monthly in arrear, within 7 (seven) days after receiving an account from the Lessor reflecting the amount(s) so payable, with the cost of electricity, water and gas consumed on the Property, determined at prevailing municipal rates in accordance with readings of separate sub meters.

7.2 All costs for the drawing of this contract together with all Stamp Duties payable in terms hereof will be for the account of the Lessee.

8. CESSION AND SUBLETTING

8.1 The Lessee shall not be entitled, except with the prior written consent of the Lessor to cede all or any of the rights of the Lessee under this lease or to sublet or give up possession of the Property, in whole or part, to any third party.

8.2 The Lessor shall not, however, unreasonably withhold its consent to a subletting of the whole or part of the Property to any third party.

9. SUNDRY OBLIGATIONS OF THE LESSEE

The Lessee shall

9.1 keep the Property clean and tidy;

9.2 not use the Property or allow them to be used, in whole or part, for any purpose other than commercial office space;

9.3 not bring onto the Property any article which, by reason of its weight or other characteristics, is liable to cause damage to the Property;

9.4 not contravene any of the conditions of title of the Property or any of the laws, rules or regulations affecting owners, tenants or occupiers of the Property;

9.5 not cause or commit any nuisance on the Property or cause any annoyance or discomfort to other tenants or occupiers of the Property;

9.6 not leave refuse or allow it to accumulate in or about the Property except in the refuse bins provided;

9.7 refrain from interfering with the electrical, plumbing or gas installations or systems serving the Property, except as may be necessary to enable the Lessee to carry out its obligations of maintenance and repair in terms of this lease.

9.8 take all reasonable measures to prevent blockages and obstructions from occurring in the drains, sewerage pipes and water pipes serving the Property;

9.9 provide at the Lessee's own expense all electric, fluorescent and incandescent light bulbs required in the Property;

9.10 not erect any radio or television aerial on the roof or exterior walls of the Property without the Lessor's prior written consent, which shall not be unreasonably withheld; and

10. <u>MAINTENANCE AND REPAIRS</u>

10.1 The Lessee shall at its own expense and without recourse to the Lessor throughout the Lease Period:

> 10.1.1 maintain in good order and condition the interior of the Property and all parts thereof, including (without limitation of the generality of this obligation) all windows, doors, fixtures and fittings contained in the Property;

10.1.2 promptly repair or make good all damage occurring in the Property from time to time during the Lease Period, whatever the cause of such damage, and including damage to any part of the interior of the Property or to any window, door, fixture or fitting, and replace all such items (as well as any keys) which have been broken, lost or destroyed (again regardless of cause); and

10.1.3 on the termination of this lease, howsoever and whenever it terminates, return the Property and all such parts thereof (including all keys) to the Lessor in good order, condition and repair, fair wear and tear excepted.

10.2 If the Lessee notifies the Lessor in writing within 7 (seven) days after having taken possession of the Property of the need for any repairs to or in the Property or of the fact that any part of the Property, including any lock, key, door, window, fixture or fitting, is damaged, missing or out of order, the Lessor shall promptly cause the necessary repair or replacement to be effected at the Lessor's own expense. If or in so far as the Lessee does not give such notice, the Lessee shall be deemed to have acknowledged that the Property and all parts thereof were intact, in place, and in good order, condition and repair when the Lessee took possession of the Property under this lease.

10.3 The Lessor shall be responsible for the maintenance of, and for all repairs and replacements becoming necessary from time to time in or to, the Building and all parts thereof other than those which are the responsibility for the time being of tenants or of the local authority, and the Lessor's obligations in this respect shall include the maintenance and repair of the structure of the Building, all systems, works and installations contained therein, the roofs, the exterior walls, the lifts, the grounds and gardens.

10.4 The Lessor shall not, however, be in breach of clause 11.3 in so far as any of its obligations there under are not or cannot be fulfilled by reason of any vis major or the acts or omissions of others over whom the Lessor has no direct authority or control, and where the Lessor is indeed in breach of clause 11.3, the Lessee's only remedy against the Lessor shall be a right of action for specific performance.

10.5 Should the Lessee fail to carry out any of its obligations under this lease with regard to any maintenance, repair or replacement, the Lessor shall be entitled without prejudice to any of its other rights or remedies, to affect the required item of maintenance, repair or replacement and to recover the cost thereof from the lessee on demand.

11. ALTERATIONS, ADDITIONS AND IMPROVEMENTS

11.1 The Lessee shall not make any alterations or additions to the Property without the Lessor's prior written consent, but the Lessor shall not withhold its consent unreasonably to an alteration or addition which is not structural.

11.2 If the Lessee does alter, add to, or improve the Property in any way, whether in breach of clause 11.1 or not, the Lessee shall, if so required in writing by the Lessor, restore the Property on the termination of this lease to their condition as it was prior to such alteration, addition or improvement having been made. The Lessor's requirement in this regard may be communicated to the Lessee at any time, but not later than the 7 (seven) day after the Lessee has delivered up the Property pursuant to the termination of this lease; and this clause shall not be construed as excluding any other or further remedy which the Lessor may have in consequence of a breach by the Lessee of clause 11.1.

11.3 Save for any improvement which is removed from the Property as required by the Lessor in terms of clause 11.2, all improvements made to the Property shall belong to the Lessor and may not be removed from the Property at any time. The Lessee shall not, whatever the circumstances, have any claim against the Lessor for compensation for any improvement to the Property, unless such improvements were made with the Lessor's prior written consent which compensation shall be limited to the costs of the improvement, or as otherwise agreed to in writing by the Lessor, nor shall the Lessee have a right of retention in respect of any improvements.

12. EXCLUSION OF LESSOR'S LIABILITY

Acts of God, or violent actions caused by agents not under the control of the lessor shall not give rise to any liability for loss to the lessee or any person connected to the lessee or the property of any such person held on the premises. Neither shall the lessor be liable for any other damages or losses caused to the above persons which loss may result from the occupation of the leased premises regardless of the cause.

13. LESSOR'S RIGHTS OF ENTRY AND CARRYING OUT OF WORKS

13.1 The Lessor's representatives, agents, servants and contractors may at all reasonable times, without thereby giving rise to any claim or right of action on the part of the Lessee or any other occupier of the Property:

13.1.1 enter the leased Property in order to inspect them, to carry out any necessary repairs, replacements, or other works, or to perform any other lawful function in the bona fide interests of the Lessor or any of the occupiers of the Property; or

13.1.2 carry out elsewhere in the Building or on the Property any necessary repairs, replacements, or other works, but the Lessor shall ensure that this right is exercised with due regard for, and a minimum of interference with, the beneficial enjoyment of the Property by those in occupation thereof.

14. SPECIAL REMEDY FOR BREACH

14.1 Should the Lessee default in any payment due under this lease or be in breach of its terms in any other way, and fail to remedy such default or breach within 14 (fourteen) days after receiving a written demand that it be remedied, the Lessor shall be entitled, without prejudice to any alternative or additional right of action or remedy available to the Lessor under the circumstances, to cancel this lease with immediate effect, be repossessed of the Property, and recover from the Lessee damages for the default or breach and the cancellation of this lease.

14.2 Clause 14.1 shall not be construed as excluding the ordinary lawful consequences of a breach of this lease by either party (save any such consequences as are expressly excluded by any of the other provisions of this lease) and in particular any right of cancellation of this lease on the ground of a material breach going to the root of this lease.

14.3 In the event of the Lessor having cancelled this lease justifiably but the Lessee remaining in occupation of the Property, with or without disputing the cancellation, and continuing to tender payments of rent and any other amounts which would have been payable to the Lessor but for the cancellation, the Lessor may accept such payments without prejudice to and without affecting the cancellation, in all respects as if they had been payments on account of the damages suffered by the Lessor by reason of the unlawful holding over on the part of the Lessee.

15. NEW TENANTS AND PURCHASERS

The Lessee shall at all reasonable times

15.1 during the Lease Period, allow prospective purchasers of the Property; and

15.2 during the last 3 months of the Lease Period, allow prospective tenants or purchasers of the Property, to enter and view the interior of the Property.

16. DOMICILIA AND NOTICES

16.1 The parties choose as their domicilia citandi et executandi the addresses mentioned in clause 16.2, provided that such domicilium of either party may be changed by written notice from such party to the other party with effect from the date of receipt or deemed receipt by the latter of such notice.

16.2.1 The Lessor: (postal and physical address)

16.2.2 The Lessee: (postal and physical address)

16.3 Any notice, acceptance, demand or other communication properly addressed by either party to the other party at the latter's domicilium in terms hereof for the time being and sent by prepaid registered post shall be deemed to be received by the latter on the 5 business day following the date of posting thereof. This provision shall not be construed as precluding the utilisation of other means and methods (including telefacsimile) for the transmission or delivery of notices, acceptances, demands and other communications, but no presumption of delivery shall arise if any such other means or method is used.

17. WHOLE AGREEMENT

17.1 This is the entire agreement between the parties.

17.2 Neither party relies in entering into this agreement on any warranties, representations, disclosures or expressions of opinion which have not been incorporated into this agreement as warranties or undertakings.

17.3 No variation or consensual cancellation of this agreement shall be of any force or effect unless reduced to writing and signed by both parties.

18. NON-WAIVER

18.1 Neither party shall be regarded as having waived, or be precluded in any way from exercising, any right under or arising from this lease by reason of such party having at any time granted any extension of time for, or having shown any indulgence to, the other party with reference to any payment or performance hereunder, or having failed to enforce, or delayed in the enforcement of, any right of action against the other party.

18.2 The failure of either party to comply with any non-material provision of this lease shall not excuse the other party from performing the latter's obligations hereunder fully and timeously.

SIGNED at Gaborone on this ....in the presence of
the undersigned witnesses.

1. _____

2. _____

_____
                                                        LESSEE

SIGNED at Gaborone on this .... in the presence of
the undersigned witnesses.

1. _____

2. _____

_____
                                                        LESSOR

Appendix II:

JOB INTERVIEW QUESTIONS AN EMPLOYER WOULD USUALLY ASK:

An employer is mainly trying to assess three things:

1. Are you intelligent?

2. Can you do the job?

3. Are you a nice person?

When it comes to the intelligence issue, as an employer, I would ask for all educational transcripts. This would tell me a lot about the IQ level of the candidate. I would then listen carefully to the questions the candidate asked in the interview. The more curious a candidate is, the more intelligent he probably is. The problem for an employer is that a dull candidate will not be able to do the job unless it's a purely menial job. Hence, an employer is always looking for signs of superior intelligence.

The next most important issue that an employer needs to assess is whether or not the candidate can do the job. As part of his assessment, he is likely to ask the following questions:

1. What were your responsibilities at your previous job?

2. Why did you take that job and did it meet your expectations?

3. Why did you leave that job?

4. How do you feel about working overtime if a project needs to get done?

5. Where do you see yourself in your career three to five years out?

6. What are your salary expectations? How did you come up with that figure?

7. What are your biggest accomplishments at your previous job and what did you learn from them?

8. What are your biggest failures at your previous job and what did you learn from them?

9. How can you guarantee that you can keep company information confidential? (This is a difficult question. But most candidates I asked this question to did really well with it. The response I often got was: "I can't guarantee it, but I know it's unethical to disclose company information outside the company. So I won't do it." Job done. It shows the candidate is honest.)

10. How are you going to manage studies and your job (if applicable)?

11. Why are you qualified to work here?

12. What is your greatest strength?

13. What is your greatest weakness?

14. Why do you want to work here?

15. Do you have any questions?

When it comes to assessing whether a person is nice, I would simply observe their attitude during the interview. If they seemed positive that was good enough.

Appendix III: Interview Assessment

These are some of the common assessment factors an interviewer will look for in a job candidate. After the interview is completed the interviewer will place a tick mark in the box he feels most closely aligns with the attributes of the candidate that he is assessing.

Assessment Factors	Poor	Average	Excellent
First impression			
Confidence			
Curiosity			
Personal appearance			
Skills match			
Communication skills			
Attitude			
Overall Assessment			

Appendix IV: Centralised Assets and Liabilities Schedule (CALS)

		27-Feb-13
	Date of Birth	Age
Mr. John Doe	7-Oct-51	58
Mrs. Jenny Doe	25-Sep-57	52
Jill Doe	22-Aug-81	27
William Doe	8-Feb-83	26
Business Assets		
Sample Couriers Ltd		
Share holdings:	John Doe	50%
Share holdings:	Jenny Doe	50%
Property Assets		
Residence		
Plot# XYZ, (in the town of)		
Share holding:	Doe Family Trust	100%
Revenue Producing Property 1 Ltd		
Share holding:	Doe Family Trust	100%
Property (e.g. Warehouse)		
Revenue Producing Property 2 Ltd		
Share holding:	Doe Family Trust	100%
Property (e.g. Flats)		
Cash/Investment		
Bank Accounts		
John Doe		XYZ Bank
Jenny Doe		ABC Bank
Retirement Accounts		
John Doe		XYZ Bank
Jenny Doe		ABC Bank
Liabilities		
Credit card—John Doe		XYZ Bank
Credit card—Jenny Doe		ABC Bank
Other Debts		
Car Loan		XYZ Bank

Appendix V: Sample Will

LAST WILL & TESTAMENT

We, the undersigned,

JOSEPH BLOGGS
And
JANE BLOGGS

Spouses married to each other out of community of property, and residing at Gaborone, Botswana, declare this to be our Last Will relating to all our assets whether in Botswana or any other country.

1 REVOCATION OF FORMER WILLS

We hereby revoke all former Wills, hereto made by ourselves either jointly or individually.

2. APPOINTMENT OF EXECUTOR AND ADMINISTRATOR

2.1 We nominate and appoint as Executor and Administrator of our Estate, the survivor of us. In the event of our simultaneous deaths or should we die within 30 days of each other, we wish to appoint Harvey Spectator, a duly admitted Attorney, of Pearston Hardwoman Attorneys, or failing him, the Senior Partner of Pearston Hardwoman Attorneys, at the time being or their Successor-in-Title, as Executor and Administrator.

2.2 We hereby give and grant to our said Executor and Administrator all such powers and authority as is required or allowed by law and especially that of assumption.

2.3 We direct that it will not be necessary for our Executor or Administrator to provide security to the Master of the High Court or other competent authority for the due and proper fulfillment of his/her duties in either capacity.

AS WITNESSES:

1) _____   _____

                                    JOSEPH BLOGGS

2) _____   _____

                                    JANE BLOGGS

3. **APPOINTMENT OF HEIRS**

We hereby direct that in the event of one of us dying, the surviving spouse will inherit our entire Estate.

3.1 We further direct that in the event of both of us dying simultaneously, or within 30 days of each other, we bequeath our entire Estate to our children, Popeye Bloggs, born on the 14th of February 1985, and Olive Bloggs born on the 12th of May 1987, in equal shares and per stirpes.

3.2 We further direct that in the event of both of us and our two children Popeye Bloggs and Olive Bloggs dying simultaneously without issue or within thirty (30) days of each other, then our Estate should be dealt with as follows:

> 3.2.1 Half of the Estate to the brother of the Testator, Sundance Bloggs.

> 3.2.2 The Residue of the Estate we bequeath to the brother of the Testatrix, Kasey Jones.

4. **CREATION OF TRUST AND APPOINTMENT OF TRUSTEES**

In the event of us dying before our children have reached the age of Twenty-One (21) years, such heirs' share of our Estate shall not vest in him/her, but shall be paid over to our nominated Trustee, until such time as our children have reached the age of Twenty-One (21) years respectively.

We then hereby confirm and appoint as Trustee of the Trust:

4.1 The person nominated as administrator in clause 2 of this our Last Will and Testament.

AS WITNESSES:

1) _____   _____

                                       JOSEPH BLOGGS

2) _____   _____

                                       JANE BLOGGS

4.2 **INVESTMENT OF TRUST FUNDS**

Our Trustee shall be entitled to retain the assets in the same form as they are handed to him/her or in his/her sole discretion may convert same into cash at such time and in such manner as he/she may deem fit, and invest or reinvest the proceeds thereof in such securities including equities of any nature, as he/she may from time to time in his absolute discretion decide with the specific power to acquire immovable property, mortgage same or grant mortgage bonds, it being our intention that our Trustee shall be un-fettered in his/her choice of investments, and that he/she will have the power to vary such investments as he/she shall think fit.

4.3 **USE OF CAPITAL AND INCOME DURING OPERATION OF THE TRUST**

Our Trustee shall utilise so much of the income accruing to the Trust Estate (after deduction of all fees, disbursements and, if any, taxes) as he/she in his/her sole discretion many deem necessary for the maintenance, education advancement in life, wellbeing and travel of our children.

We further give to our Trustee the power to make advances to an heir out of Trust Capital for such purposes as he/she may deem reasonable or desirable giving him/her full discretion as to what advances he/she makes from time to time, and such heirs' Estate shall not be obliged to refund any such advances should the heir die before attaining the age of Twenty-One (21).

AS WITNESSES:

1) _____   _____
                                    JOSEPH BLOGGS

2) _____   _____
                                    JANE BLOGGS

4.4 **PAYMENT TO HEIRS**

As soon as our children respectively attain the age of Twenty One (21) years their share of the Trust shall then be capitalised and the capital, together with the accumulated income, less advances made on their behalf in terms of Clause 4.3 above, shall devolve upon them entirely to deal with as they deem fit.
We give to our Trustee the power to defer the payment of any bequest or inheritance for a period not exceeding twelve (12) months from the date such bequest and/or inheritance is due in order to avoid liquidating our or the Trust's business interest or other assets or investments at the time when he/she, in his/her discretion, consider it inadvisable to do so.

4.5 **LIMITATION OF TRUSTEE'S LIABILITY**

Our Trustee shall not be liable to make good to any heir of our Estate any loss occasioned or sustained from any cause howsoever arising except such loss as may arise from or be occasioned by his/her own personal dis-honesty or other willful misconduct.

4.6 **PAYMENT IN CASH OR KIND**

Our Executor and Trustee shall be entitled to pay or make over any amount due to a beneficiary in cash or in kind and whether for the purpose of allocating assets or for the purpose of payment to a beneficiary, to distribute the assets of our Estate in such manner as he/she considers fit in accordance with the valuations made or obtained by him in his/her discretion, which valuation shall be final and binding upon all persons affected thereby.

AS WITNESSES:

1) _____

                                _____

                                JOSEPH BLOGGS

2) _____

                                  _____

                                JANE BLOGGS

5 **APPOINTMENT OF GUARDIAN**

In event of our deaths before our children have reached the age of Twenty-One (21) years, we request that the Testator's Brother, Mr. Kalahari Jack, care for our children as their guardian.

6 **LEGATEES AND HEIRS TO INHERIT FREE OF COMMUNITY**

Should any person who will benefit under this our Will be married, or get married, in Community of Property or subject to any law of Accrual, then, notwithstanding such Community of Property or Accrual, the benefits payable under this Will shall devolve upon and belong to them personally and shall not form part of any such Community of Property or Accrual.

SIGNED BY US AT GABORONE ON THIS THE 8th DAY OF MAY 2014 IN THE PRESENCE OF THE SUBSCRIBING WITNESSES ALL BEING PRESENT AND SIGNING AT THE SAME TIME AND IN THE PRESENCE OF ONE ANOTHER

AS WITNESSES:

1) _____   _____
                                JOSEPH BLOGGS

2) _____   _____
                                JANE BLOGGS

Appendix VI: How the Fed prints money

This is how it works (see Figure 15):

1. Consider that the U.S. Treasury needs money, for example to pay government bills such as staff salaries, or to newspapers for advertising.

2. So that it doesn't raise taxes, the U.S. Treasury could issue a bond. The bond is called a "Treasury."

3. The government then sells the Treasury bond to a commercial bank. The commercial bank gives the U.S. Treasury the money and keeps the bond.

4. The Fed then buys the bond back from the commercial bank. And gives it (the commercial bank) money created from nothing. Basically the Fed increases the reserves of the commercial bank at the Fed. The commercial bank can draw this money out anytime.

5. So this may increase the money supply. Note: The commercial bank has to be able to give the money out as loans. If nobody wants the loans then there is no increase in the money supply.

6. However, the commercial bank often aggressively markets the loans. Hence, this process is not guaranteed to increase the money supply, but it will likely do just that.

7. That's how the Fed prints money and creates more of it in the real economy. All without even the cost of ink and paper!

Figure 15: How the Fed Prints Money

Steps 2 + 3

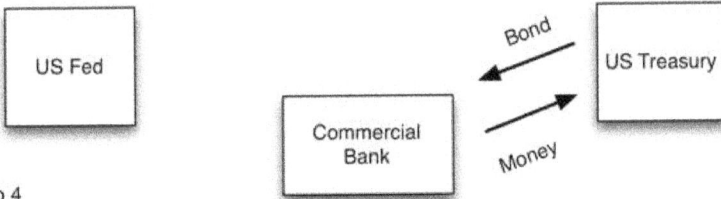

Step 4

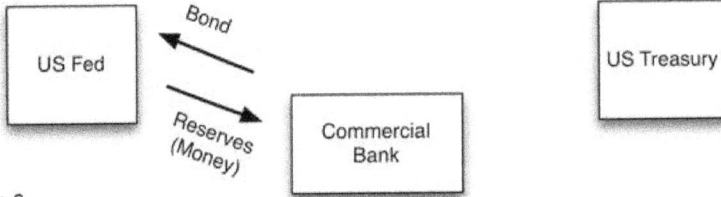

Step 6

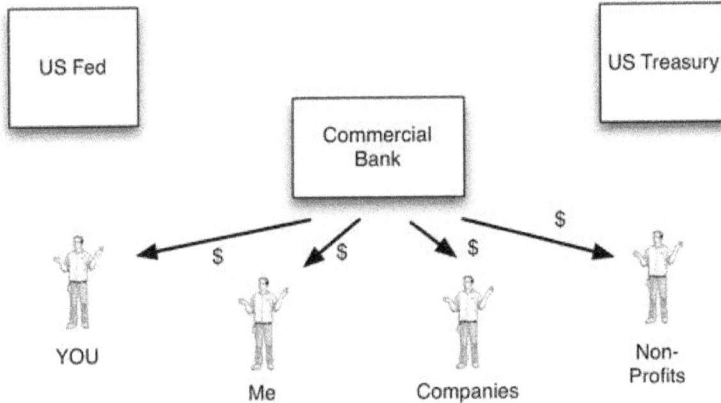

Appendix VII: Frequently Asked Questions

Please note that the following FAQs are in no particular order. Scan through them until you find what you are looking for.

What is downsizing?

This is when a company reduces its staff.

What is investing?

Investing is putting your money into something from which you hope to make a profit.

What is a recession?

That is when the economy goes bad. Then, for example, businesses often shut down. As a result there are fewer jobs and many people who were previously employed become unemployed. As a result there is starvation. The deeper version of a recession is a depression.

What is a credit bubble?

That is when too many people have taken out too many loans, and the whole country becomes over-indebted. At some point the people are unable to pay back their loans. They are then said to have "defaulted on their loan." The people who took out the loans go bankrupt, and the banks that loaned them the money also incur losses (some may go bankrupt). The credit bubble is then said to have burst. A credit bubble can lead to a recession.

What is Cash?

In simple terms, this refers to money in the bank. If you have a bank account and it has $100 in it, you have $100 of cash. If you don't take any money out, and if we ignore any interest earnings (interest rates are close to zero at the time of writing this book in 2013) for the following year, this balance of cash will be exactly the same. It does not fluctuate, unlike a stock or a bond. If the money is invested in a stock or a bond, the amount of money you have next year could be higher or lower, meaning it can fluctuate. You could make a profit or a loss.

What is a Bond?

This is money owed to someone. If you own the bond, it is money owed to you. If you issued the bond, it is money you owe to someone else.

For example, if I needed $100, I might ask you to lend me $100. In return for the loan, I could say to you that I'll pay you five percent interest every year for the use of your money, and at the end of the tenth year I would pay you back the $100. Therefore, over ten years you would earn five dollars interest every year for a total of ($5 × 10 years) $50. At the end of the tenth year you would get your $100 back.

You would give me the $100, and I would give you a receipt that says: "Faiz owes the bearer of this chit $100. Each year he will pay the bearer of this chit five dollars. At the end of the tenth year, Faiz will return the $100 to the bearer of this chit." That piece of paper is called a "bond."

In this example, you own the bond, so I owe money to you. On the flip side, I issued the bond, so I owe money to you.

Much can go wrong with this bond between signing time and ten years hence. There could be many a slip twixt the cup and the lip. For example if interest rates rise, and you had to sell the bond because you needed your $100 immediately, you would get less than $100 back. You might get only $90. That's a $10 LOSS! The value of a bond can go up and down. In other words, the value can fluctuate, just like a stock.

Accordingly, if you have a mutual fund that invests in a portfolio of cash, bonds and stocks, the point is that it will fluctuate. And the mutual fund may incur a loss when you withdraw your money. You have no control over the amount of money that can be lost.

What is a mortgage?

Basically, a loan to buy a house is called a mortgage.

What is a subprime mortgage (and what was the great financial crisis of 2007–2008)?

When I went to a bank to get a loan to purchase my home, the bank checked my financial situation to see if I could pay it back. Only once they were satisfied that I could afford to pay back the loan back did they give me the loan. However, during the early 2000s banks in the USA started to issue NINJA loans—meaning "No Income, No Job, or Assets." In other words, they were issuing loans to people in poor financial condition. This is a subprime mortgage, a mortgage granted to people in poor financial condition.

When all this started, the banks didn't care much. They were earning interest on the loans. And the bankers were getting paid huge bonuses depending on the interest income they could generate on paper (the more loans that were issued, the higher the interest income). Such is the greed of bankers.

In the beginning all went well. The property market started to boom. Because the banks were willing to lend out any amount of money, house prices started to rise. So the house that was initially worth $200, sold six months later for $250, then for $300, and so on, until soon it was selling for $500. Then the last person who bought that house lost his job, and could not pay his house loan. No problem. The bank repossessed the house and sold it off for $500. They got their money back. But soon, more and more houses started to come on to the market, and consequently the $500 house could not sell for $500. It sold for $400.

This was a problem, because the bank lost $100 on the loan. So let's see what's happening:

Let's say that the bank is allowed to lend out ten times its capital. This is called a 10 percent capital adequacy ratio. Therefore, if the bank had $100 in capital, it could lend out $1,000. See figure 16 below.

Figure 16: Bank Capital

	Capital		Can Lend Out
	$100	X 10	$1,000
Loss	$100		
	0	X 10	0

As you can see, when everything was okay, the bank was able to lend out $1,000. But now that it's lost $100, it's not allowed to lend out anything. So, it has to close its doors. Between 2008 and 2010, 187 banks failed in the U.S. because of the subprime mortgage crisis.[63]

The above is an explanation of the great financial crisis (also known as the subprime mortgage crisis) of 2007–2008. Because the banks were issuing NINJA loans, when rough financial times came, those people could not pay back their loans and the whole house of cards in consumer lending was destroyed. Banks collapsed.

The preceding was a description of the cause of the great financial crisis. To continue the story: Once the crisis had started and big banks had started to fail—see narrative regarding Lehman Brothers in Chapter 2 (*How I Discovered the Secret to Wealth*)—the world's governments jumped in to bailout the banks. They gave money to the banks so that the banks wouldn't collapse. A big part of the bailout consisted of printing money.[64] The rest of the bailout came from the governments taking loans from investors around the world.[65] Research indicates that it is likely that much of this investor money also originated from the Fed's printing press.

Sadly, the printing of money has not stopped. As of 2013, the U.S. Fed continues to print money. It is on its third round of QE (quantitative easing, which means printing money)—QE3.

The point here is that the problem has not been solved, just postponed.

So, what you need to understand is that we are living in an illusory world. The money you are using, it's funny money. Your pension plan, it could fall a long way. The price of your house, it's on artificial respiration. The world is not real anymore. What if people and investors finally decided not to accept U.S. dollars? It has not happened yet even though it should have happened (it has not happened yet, because, for the time being, the U.S. dollar is the world's reserve currency). However, if it ever does come to pass that the world stops accepting the U.S. dollar, then the whole economic house of cards, worldwide, will be destroyed. The way to get safely out of the system is to not have bad debt, don't spend more than you make, create passive income. Also, at all times, have extra food in your house to last you at least a month. God, bless us all.

What is bankruptcy?

For example, let's say that I borrowed $100 from you, and I had promised to give it back to you a year later. However, one year later when you asked for the money back, I told you that I had spent it on buying chocolate and chewing gum. The money was all gone and I had no money to return to you. As a result, you said that you would take me to court. We went to court and the judge asked me to sell all of my personal belongings so that I could pay you back the $100. But all I had was the shirt on my back and the trousers on my legs. So the judge declared me bankrupt. You would lose your $100.

I, too, would have lost because my "normal" life was disrupted. In future, I would not be able to obtain a loan from anybody else because of my bankruptcy record. I probably would not be able to find a decent job, and could possibly be forced to hand back my professional designations. Hence, my income generation abilities could be curtailed. My bankruptcy record would haunt me for a good number of years, until my slate could be wiped clean, and I could start building my life all over again. Bankruptcy is a disaster all around. The bankruptcy could have been avoided though. Had you decided to check my financial situation before lending me the $100, and you had found out that I was on the verge of destitution, you probably would not have given me the money. Then I wouldn't have spent it indiscriminately. You would not have had to demand the money back, and I would not have had to declare bankruptcy.

What are taxes?

Tax is money that you have to pay to the government by law.

The most common form of tax is income tax. For example, if you earn $3,000 per month, you do not receive the full $3,000. You might only receive $2,700. The difference of $300 was deducted from your pay at source (your employer) and paid to the government.

Government needs the tax money to run the country. For example, tax money is used to provide police services and to repair the roads.

What is the difference between funds, capital, and revenue?

All three terms constitute money, but there is a fine distinction between funds/capital and revenue. If I have $100 in my bank account, I can say, "I have funds of $100 in the bank," or "I have capital of $100 in the bank." Both of these statements are applicable in this case. However, if I sold you a gadget for $150, then I'd say, "I earned revenue of $150."

What is retail?

If you needed to buy milk, you could go to a *wholesaler*. However, you would have to buy in bulk, for example, a box containing 100 individual cartons of milk. That may be more milk than you could use. Therefore, instead, you prefer to go to your local supermarket and purchase two or three individual cartons. The supermarket is a *retailer*. The manager buys in bulk from the wholesaler and then sells the individual cartons to his customers.

How does money in the bank depreciate?

This refers to the loss in value that cash in the bank can experience because of inflation. Assuming that the interest rate on the bank account is nil (as it is—today, 2013) and that inflation is five percent, then the following year your money will be worth 95 percent of what it was worth the previous year. If the same situation persists for the following year, two

years out your money will be (.95 × .95) 90 percent of what it was worth at
the start. And so on. Hence, cash lying in the bank can *depreciate*.

What is a market-timing fund?

In Chapter 7 (*How to Invest Money*) the DOW, a stock market index, was
introduced. It was shown that, over a period of twelve years, the DOW
started at 7,000 points, then hit a peak of 14,000 points somewhere in the
middle, and then came crashing back down to 7,000 points towards the
end of that period. What this means is that if you were invested in the
DOW at the start of that period, you would have made money until its
peak, but then you would have lost the gains as it came back down to
7,000 points.

If you had exited the stock market at the peak, or 14,000 points, you
would have been a big winner. You would have escaped the subsequent
losing period. You would have *crystallised* your gains. You would have
made money and avoided the losses.

In general, this is rather hard to do. No one can know when to exit the
market. What if, after you exited the market, it ran up another 50 percent?
You would have forsaken the additional returns. However, what if, just
after you exited the market, it dropped 50 percent? You would have saved
yourself from great losses. Additionally, consider the following: If the
market goes down 50 percent, it has to gain 100 percent just to break
even. See below.

Consider the following: You invested in October 2007 when the DOW
hit its high of 14,000 points. Thereafter, it lost 50 percent of its value; it
went down to 7,000 points. In order for it to get from 7,000 to 14,000
again, it would have to appreciate by (7,000 × 100%) 7,000 points. If the
starting value of 7,000 is added to the appreciation of 7,000, the total is
14,000, thereby showing that your investment needed to appreciate by 100

percent. This is an awfully hard thing to happen. You might have to wait years. In fact, the DOW only regained that level in approximately March 2013, about five and a half years later (if you factor in fees and inflation, your investment would still be down; it had not yet recovered it's full value). Hence, after five-and-a-half years, you are back to square one (and not even, if you factor in fees and inflation).

The above is an example of a *market-timing fund*: a fund that tries to ride the upswings of the stock market, but steps into cash (meaning, it's out of the stock market) before the stock market falls.

What is flipping, or buying houses with no money down?

This is a speculative investment strategy. It is highly risky and should be avoided. The idea is to buy a house with no money down, and then sell it for a capital gain. In theory, the way it works is that an investor borrows the full purchase price of a house, for example, if a house is selling for $100,000, the borrower requests $100,000 from the bank to purchase the house. The borrower maintains the house for a period of time, paying the monthly repayment, hoping to sell the house for a profit. If the borrower sells it for $105,000, he wins. After paying off the loan of $100,000, he pockets $ 5,000. But if the property value went down, forcing the borrower to sell for $95,000, he would lose $5,000. One should only buy real estate for the long term and for the cash flows. It is not a good idea to purchase real estate for the potential capital gains, as those "potential" capital gains may never materialise.

What are chequing, savings and fixed deposit accounts?

1. Chequing account vs. Savings account: When you open a bank account the bank offers you a choice of a chequing account (also known as a current account) or a savings account. The difference between the two is that with a chequing account you get a chequebook, but with a savings

account you don't. With a chequebook, you do not need physical cash to make payments; you can make payments by writing cheques. The chequing account is for your everyday use, meant for paying bills and buying groceries.

Both accounts are useful. You need the chequing account because it saves you from having to go to the ATM for cash. It also enables you to write a cheque for mail-in payments. A savings account on the other hand, is useful for the purpose of accumulating money, simply because it is a bit more difficult for you to access the cash. You don't have a chequebook, so you would have to get the cash from the bank or from an ATM. In this way a savings account creates a bit of distance between you and your money, encouraging you to save.

2. Fixed deposit account: A fixed deposit account pays a higher interest rate than a savings account, but it locks up your money for a certain period of time. This time period could range from one month to one year. The longer the period you select the higher the rate of interest. For example, a one-month fixed deposit may pay two percent interest, a three-month fixed deposit four percent and a one-year fixed deposit six percent.

These rates are calculated on an annualised basis. For the sake of convenience, let's just use simple interest rates, whereas in real-life banks may use compound interest rates. (For the purpose of our explanation the difference would be exiguous).

Hence, the one month fixed deposit would pay you two percent divided by twelve months (2/12) or approximately 0.17 percent after one month has expired. The three-month fixed deposit would pay you four percent divided by twelve months multiplied by three months (4/12 × 3) or approximately 0.99 percent after three months. And the one-year fixed deposit would pay you six percent after one year.

Appendix VIII: Summary of Acronyms

1. AMYAT (Route to Financial Success):

(Part II): A= **A**cquiring Financial Independence.

(Part III): M= **M**ind the Trap.

(Part IV): Y= What stage of the life cycle are **Y**OU in?

(Part V): A= Financial **A**dvice for Certain Groups of People

(Part VI): T= More **T**ips for Success.

For more details—see Chapter 3 (*Route to Financial Success—Summary of the Financial Solution*).

2. Four Steps Millionaire Formula (MSIP):

Step 1: M = **M**ake money.

Step 2: S = **S**ave.

Step 3: I = Invest in cash Flowing **I**nvestments.

Step 4: P = Generate **P**assive income in excess of Living Expenses.

For more details—see Chapter 4 (*The Four Steps Millionaire Formula*).

3. WFD:

Weapons of Financial Destruction (Includes credit cards, bad debt, mutual funds and bad advertising).

For more details—see Chapter 4 (*The Four Steps Millionaire Formula*).

4. LTV

Long-term view.

For more details—see Chapter 4 (*The Four Steps Millionaire Formula*).

5. SPO:

S = an entrepreneur is Self-reliant. He believes that it's up to him. He is responsible for the outcomes in his life.

P = an entrepreneur believes that he is not entitled to any compensation unless he Produces—that is, puts out something of value in the world.

O = an entrepreneur does not worry about guaranteed Outcomes. He lives with the risk of the unknown future as being part and parcel of the entrepreneurship strategy.

For more details—see Chapter 5 (*How to Make Money*).

6. Four Ways Business Formula (MSIPPS):

Step 1 (from Four Steps Millionaire Formula): M = Make money.

Step 2 (from Four Steps Millionaire Formula): S = Save

Step 3 (from Four Steps Millionaire Formula): I = Invest in Cash Flowing Investment

Step 4 (from Four Steps Millionaire Formula): P = Generate Passive income in excess of Living Expenses

Step 3 (from Four Ways Business Formula): P = Pretty up the business

Step 4 (from Four Ways Business Formula): S = Sell the business

For more details—see Chapter 5 (*How to Make Money*).

7. TAM (Entrepreneur Roadmap):

T: Embrace the Entrepreneurial Traits: You know them— "SPO."

A: Know the winning Attitude: It is—How to Win Big—as discussed in Chapter 8 (*How to Win Big*).

M: Master the Methodology: Know how to do a Business Plan— covered in Chapter 5 (*How to Make Money*).

For more details—see Chapter 8 (*How to Win Big*).

8. PPT:

Peer Pressure Trap

For more details—see Chapter 12 (*Trap #4: Your friends*).

9. LEAP:

L = Never **L**eave home when having a fight.

E = Have **E**xplicit trust in each other.

A = Never go to bed **A**ngry.

P = Have respect for each other in **P**ublic. Never fight with or make fun of your spouse in public.

For more details—see Chapter 16 (*Young Adult*).

10. CALS:

Centralised Assets and Liabilities Schedule.

For more details—see Chapter 17 (*Pre-retirement*).

11. EASy:

Estate Archive System.

For more details—see Chapter 17 (*Pre-retirement*).

Endnotes

[1] Watters, Graydon G. *Financial Pursuit*. North York, Ontario: Financial Knowledge Inc, 2002:193.

[2] Frank, Robert. *Does America Have Too Many Rich People?* June 15, 2011. blogs.wsj.com/wealth/2011/06/15/does-america-have-too-many-rich-people/ (accessed April 18, 2014).

[3] Moeng, Gothataone. *A tale of two cities*. October 19, 2012. www.mmegi.bw/index.php?sid=1&aid=235&dir=2012/October/Friday19 (accessed April 18, 2014).

[4] Franks, Sandy and Nunnally, Sara. *Barbarians of Wealth*. Hoboken, New Jersey: John Wiley & Sons Inc., 2011: 325.

[5] Tracy, Brian. *The 100 Absolutely Unbreakable Laws of Business Success*. San Francisco, CA: Berrett-Koehler Publishers, Inc., 2000:14.

[6] Nobelprize.org. *The integrated Circuit*. www.nobelprize.org/educational/physics/integrated_circuit/history (accessed March 13, 2014).

[7] Sullivan Dan, Smith Babs and Neray Michael. *The Great Crossover*. Toronto, Ontario: The Strategic Coach, 1994: 19.

[8] McGrath, Jane. *How has technology changed the way we conduct business*. money.howstuffworks.com/technology-changed-business1.htm (accessed Oct 23, 2104).

9 Johnston, Gretel and Bebiak, Emoke. *iol news*. December 31, 2012. www.iol.co.za/news/world/end-of-the-line-for-newsweek-1.1446497#.UylnaVGSxbV (accessed March 13, 2014).

10 Bloomberg. *Bloomberg Sustainability*. January 19, 2012. www.bloomberg.com/news/2012-01-19/kodak-photography-pioneer-files-for-bankruptcy-protection-1-.html (accessed February 23, 2014)

11 Duncan, Richard. *The New Depression*. Singapore: John Wiley & Sons Singapore Pte. Ltd, 2012:19-20.

12 Duncan, Richard. *The Dollar Crisis*. Singapore: John Wiley & Sons (Asia) Pte Ltd, 2005:18-22.

13 Guillen, Mauro F. *The Global Economic and Financial Crisis, A Timeline*. lauder.wharton.upenn.edu/pages/pdf/class_info/Chronology_Economic _Financial_Crisis.pdf (accessed February 24, 2014)

14 O'Brien, Timothy L. *Fortune's Fools: Why the Rich Go Broke*. September 17, 2006. www.nytimes.com/2006/09/17/business/yourmoney/17broke.html?page wanted=all&_r=1& (accessed November 1, 2014).

15 Quilty, David. *6 Bankrupt Celebrities who went from Rich to Broke*. www.moneycrashers.com/bankrupt-celebrities-rich-broke/ (accessed February 26, 2014)

16 Dyke, Barry James. *The Pirates of Manhattan*. Hampton, NH: 555 Publishing Inc, 2008: 65

[17] Bren School of Environmental Science and Management, YouTube video. *Why Accountants Don't Run Start-ups: Getting Eco-Entrepreneurship Right by Steve Blank*. April 20, 2011. www.youtube.com/watch?v=F1CGPdjQ_oo (accessed February 26, 2014)

[18] Raiz, Allon. *Developing an entrepreneurial mindset.* www.unleashingideas.org/global-entrepreneurship-library/sites/grl/files/developing_an_entrepreneurial_mindset.pdf (accessed Ocober 29, 2014).

[19] Gordley, James. *Good Faith and Profit Maximization*. www.stthomas.edu/CathStudies/cst/conferences/antwerp/papers/Gordley.pdf (accessed October 29, 2014).

[20] Founder institute. *How to Adopt an Entrepreneurial Mindset*. 08 07, 2014. fi.co/posts/8491 (accessed October 29, 2014).

[21] Finkel, David and Harness, Stephanie. *Build a Business, Not a Job!* Bradstreet and Sons, 2011: 31.

[22] Ibid., 73-75.

[23] Federal Reserve Board of Governors Report to the Congress on College Credit Card Agreements. *Federal Reserve Board of Governors Report to the Congress on College Credit Card Agreements*. 2010. www.federalreserve.gov/boarddocs/rptcongress/creditcard/2010/downloads/CCAP_October_web.pdf (accessed April 2, 2014).

[24] McKenna, Paul. *I can make you rich*. London: Transworld Publishers, 2008: 83.

[25] Aka, Mr. Jahangir. "Constructing Portfolios Aligned to Client Objectives." *Family Office and Wealth Preservation Conference.* Geneva: Financial Events International, 2006.

[26] Otar, Jim C. *Realistic Retirement.* November 2011. www.camagazine.com/archives/print-edition/2011/nov/regulars/camagazine53142.aspx (accessed March 08, 2014).

[27] Otar, Jim C. *Unveiling the Retirement Myth.* Jim C. Otar, 2009: 71.

[28] Dyke, Barry James. *The Pirates of Manhattan II.* Hampton, NH: Barry James Dyke, Castle Asset Management LLC, 2012: 161.

[29] Mooney, Manohar B. *Investing in Real Estate (Pocket Booklet).* Gaborone: Manhar B. Mooney, 2005.

[30] Benza, Brian. *IMF Warns on P15bn unsecured household debt.* July 19, 2013. www.mmegi.bw/index.php?sid=4&aid=1484&dir=2013/July/Friday19 (accessed February 28, 2014).

[31] Franks, Sandy and Nunnally, Sara. *Barbarians of Wealth.* Hoboken, New Jersey: John Wiley & Sons Inc., 2011: 132.

[32] Griffin, G. Edward. *The Creature from Jekyll Island.* Westlake Village, California: American Media, 2010: 25.

[33] Ibid: 17.

[34] Chris Martenson, PhD. *The Crash Course.* Hoboken, New Jersey: John Wiley & Sons, 2011: 49.

[35] Duncan, Richard. *The Dollar Crisis*. Singapore: John Wiley & Sons (Asia) Pte Ltd, 2005: 251.

[36] Ibid: 121.

[37] Duncan, Richard. *The Corruption of Capitalism*. Hong Kong: CLSA Books, 2009:5.

[38] Duncan, Richard. *The New Depression*. Singapore: John Wiley & Sons Singapore Pte. Ltd, 2012:70

[39] Keto, Jill. *Don't get caught with your skirt down*. New York, New York: Atria Paperback, 2008: 19-20.

[40] Franks, Sandy and Nunnally, Sara. *Barbarians of Wealth*. Hoboken, New Jersey: John Wiley & Sons Inc., 2011: 113.

[41] Duncan, Richard. *The Dollar Crisis*. Singapore: John Wiley & Sons (Asia) Pte Ltd, 2005: 120-121.

[42] Wright, Shawn. *What can Donald Trump teach you about filing bankruptcy?* March 14, 2011. www.pittsburgh-bankruptcy-law.com/blog/bid/60500/What-can-Donal-Trump-teach-you-about-filing-bankruptcy (accessed April 18, 2014).

[43] Tracy, Brian. "Get out of Debt Now." Compact Disc. Solana Beach, California.

[44] Ibid.

[45] Ramsey, Dave. "Dumping Debt." Compact Disc.

[46] Friedman, Thomas L. *The World is Flat*. New York, New York: Picador/Farrar, Strauss and Giroux, 2007: 53.

[47] Moshe A Milevsky, Ph.D. and Alexandra C. Macqueen CFP. *Pensionize your nest egg*. Mississauga, Ontario: John Wiley & Sons Canada, Ltd., 2010: 81.

[48] Ibid: 80.

[49] Franks, Sandy and Nunnally, Sara. *Barbarians of Wealth*. Hoboken, New Jersey: John Wiley & Sons Inc., 2011: 103.

[50] Rosplock, Kirby, PhD. *The Complete Family Office Handbook*. Hoboken, New Jersey: John Wiley & Sons, Inc., 2014: 20.

[51] Markowitz, Justine. "Keeping wealth in the Family." *Family Office and Wealth Preservation Conferece*. Geneva: Financial Events International, 2006.

[52] Wilson, Richard C. *The Family Office Book*. Hoboken, New Jersey: John Wiley & Sons, Inc., 2012: 261.

[53] Law, Mr. Andrew. "Structuring Family Offices in Offshore Locations." *Family Office and Wealth Preservation Conference*. Geneva: Financial Events International, 2006.

[54] Helmer, Bruce. "The Power of Two in Financial Planning." *The Register*, July 2006:11-12

[55] Burchard, Brendon. *The Charge*. London: Simon & Schuster UK Ltd, 2012: 128.

[56] Dyke, Barry James. *The Pirates of Manhattan II*. Hampton, NH: Barry James Dyke, Castle Asset Management LLC, 2012: 29.

[57] Chapra, M. Umer. *Towards a Just Monetary System*. London: The Islamic Foundation, 1985: 56.

[58] Ibid., 88.

[59] Canadian Securities Institute. "Professional Financial Planning." In *Professional Financial Planning*, by Canadian Securities Institute. Toronto: Canadian Securities Institute, 1996: Section 7, p.28.

[60] Ibid., Section 7, 29.

[61] Ibid., Section 7, 35.

[62] Radsch, Mrs. Pamela. "Control, Alt, Delete: A fresh Look at Managing Risk and Preserving Assets." *Family Office and Wealth Preservation Conference*. Geneva: Financial Events Internationa, 2006.

[63] Franks, Sandy and Nunnally, Sara. *Barbarians of Wealth*. Hoboken, New Jersey: John Wiley & Sons Inc., 2011: 229.

[64] Duncan, Richard. *The New Depression*. Singapore: John Wiley & Sons Singapore Pte. Ltd, 2012: 69-70.

[65] PBS. *PBS Newshour*. March 17, 2009. www.pbs.org/newshour/bb/business-jan-june09-solman_03-17/ (accessed April 16, 2014).

References

Aka, Mr. Jahangir. "Constructing Portfolios Aligned to Client Objectives." *Family Office and Wealth Preservation Conference.* Geneva: Financial Events International, 2006.

Benza, Brian. *IMF Warns on P15bn unsecured household debt.* July 19, 2013. www.mmegi.bw/index.php?sid=4&aid=1484&dir=2013/July/Friday19 (accessed February 28, 2014).

Bloomberg. *Bloomberg Sustainability.* January 19, 2012. www.bloomberg.com/news/2012-01-19/kodak-photography-pioneer-files-for-bankruptcy-protection-1-.html (accessed February 23, 2014).

Bren School of Environmental Science and Management, YouTube video. *Why Accountants Don't Run Start-ups: Getting Eco-Entrepreneurship Right by Steve Blank.* April 20, 2011. www.youtube.com/watch?v=F1CGPdjQ_oo (accessed February 26, 2014).

Burchard, Brendon. *The Charge.* London: Simon & Schuster UK Ltd, 2012.

Canadian Securities Institute. "Professional Financial Planning." In *Professional Financial Planning,* by Canadian Securities Institute. Toronto: Canadian Securities Institute, 1996.

Chapra, M. Umer. *Towards a Just Monetary System.* London: The Islamic Foundation, 1985.

Chris Martenson, PhD. *The Crash Course.* Hoboken, New Jersey: John Wiley & Sons, 2011.

Duncan, Richard. *The Corruption of Capitalism.* Hong Kong: CLSA Books, 2009.

—. *The Dollar Crisis.* Singapore: John Wiley & Sons (Asia) Pte Ltd, 2005.

—. *The New Depression.* Singapore: John Wiley & Sons Singapore Pte. Ltd, 2012.

Dyke, Barry James. *The Pirates of Manhattan.* Hampton, NH: 555 Publishing Inc, 2008.

—. *The Pirates of Manhattan II.* Hampton, NH: Barry James Dyke, Castle Asset Management LLC, 2012.

Federal Reserve Board of Governors Report to the Congress on College Credit Card Agreements. *Federal Reserve Board of Governors Report to the Congress on College Credit Card Agreements.* 2010. www.federalreserve.gov/boarddocs/rptcongress/creditcard/2010/downloads/CCAP_October_web.pdf (accessed April 2, 2014).

Finkel, David and Harness, Stephanie. *Build a Business, Not a Job!* Bradstreet and Sons, 2011.

Founder institute. *How to Adopt an Entrepreneurial Mindset.* 08 07, 2014. fi.co/posts/8491 (accessed October 29, 2014).

Frank, Robert. *Does America Have Too Many Rich People.* June 15, 2011. blogs.wsj.com/wealth/2011/06/15/does-america-have-too-many-rich-people/ (accessed April 18, 2014).

Franks, Sandy and Nunnally, Sara. *Barbarians of Wealth.* Hoboken, New Jersey: John Wiley & Sons Inc., 2011.

Friedman, Thomas L. *The World is Flat.* New York, New York: Picador/Farrar, Strauss and Giroux, 2007.

Gordley, James. *Good Faith and Profit Maximization.* www.stthomas.edu/CathStudies/cst/conferences/antwerp/papers/Gordley.pdf (accessed October 29, 2014).

Griffin, G. Edward. *The Creature from Jekyll Island.* Westlake Village, California: American Media, 2010.

Guillen, Mauro F. *The Global Economic and Financial Crisis, A Timeline.* lauder.wharton.upenn.edu/pages/pdf/class_info/Chronology_Economic _Financial_Crisis.pdf (accessed February 24, 2014).

Helmer, Bruce. "The Power of Two in Financial Planning." *The Register,* July 2006.

Johnston, Gretel and Bebiak, Emoke. *iol news.* December 31, 2012. www.iol.co.za/news/world/end-of-the-line-for-newsweek-1.1446497#.UylnaVGSxbV (accessed March 13, 2014).

Keto, Jill. *Don't get caught with your skirt down.* New York, New York: Atria Paperback, 2008.

Law, Mr. Andrew. "Structuring Family Offices in Offshore Locations." *Family Office and Wealth Preservation Conference.* Geneva: Financial Events International, 2006.

Markowitz, Justine. "Keeping wealth in the Family." *Family Office and Wealth Preservation Conferece.* Geneva: Financial Events International, 2006.

McGrath, Jane. *How has technology changed the way we conduct business.* money.howstuffworks.com/technology-changed-business1.htm (accessed Oct 23, 2104).

McKenna, Paul. *I can make you rich.* London: Transworld Publishers, 2008.

Moeng, Gothataone. *A tale of two cities.* October 19, 2012. www.mmegi.bw/index.php?sid=1&aid=235&dir=2012/October/Friday19 (accessed April 18, 2014).

Mooney, Manohar B. *Investing in Real Estate (Pocket Booklet)*. Gaborone: Manhar B. Mooney, 2005.

Moshe A Milevsky, Ph.D. and Alexandra C. Macqueen CFP. *Pensionize your nest egg*. Mississauga, Ontario: John Wiley & Sons Canada, Ltd., 2010.

Nobelprize.org. *The integrated Circuit*. www.nobelprize.org/educational/physics/integrated_circuit/history (accessed March 13, 2014).

O'Brien, Timothy L. *Fortune's Fools: Why the Rich Go Broke*. September 17, 2006. www.nytimes.com/2006/09/17/business/yourmoney/17broke.html?pagewanted=all&_r=1& (accessed November 1, 2014).

Otar, Jim C. *Realistic Retirement*. November 2011. www.camagazine.com/archives/print-edition/2011/nov/regulars/camagazine53142.aspx (accessed March 08, 2014).

Otar, Jim C. *Unveiling the Retirement Myth*. Jim C. Otar, 2009.

PBS. *PBS Newshour*. March 17, 2009. www.pbs.org/newshour/bb/business-jan-june09-solman_03-17/ (accessed April 16, 2014).

Quilty, David. *6 Bankrupt Celebrities who went from Rich to Broke*. www.moneycrashers.com/bankrupt-celebrities-rich-broke/ (accessed February 26, 2014).

Radsch, Mrs. Pamela. "Control, Alt, Delete: A fresh Look at Managing Risk and Preserving Assets." *Family Office and Wealth Preservation Conference*. Geneva: Financial Events International, 2006.

Raiz, Allon. *Developing an entrepreneurial mindset.*
www.unleashingideas.org/global-entrepreneurship-
library/sites/grl/files/developing_an_entrepreneurial_mindset.pdf
(accessed Ocober 29, 2014).

Ramsey, Dave. "Dumping Debt." Compact Disc.

Rosplock, Kirby, PhD. *The Complete Family Office Handbook.* Hoboken,
New Jersey: John Wiley & Sons, Inc., 2014.

Sullivan Dan, Smith Babs and Neray Michael. *The Great Crossover.*
Toronto, Ontario: The Strategic Coach, 1994.

Tracy, Brian. "Get out of Debt Now." Solana Beach, California. Compact
Disc.

—. *The 100 Absolutely Unbreakable Laws of Business Success.* San Francisco,
CA: Berrett-Koehler Publishers, Inc., 2000.

Watters, Graydon G. *Financial Pursuit.* North York, Ontario: Financial
Knowledge Inc, 2002.

Wilson, Richard C. *The Family Office Book.* Hoboken, New Jersey: John
Wiley & Sons, Inc., 2012.

Wright, Shawn. *What can Donald Trump teach you about filing bankruptcy?*
March 14, 2011. www.pittsburgh-bankruptcy-
law.com/blog/bid/60500/What-can-Donal-Trump-teach-you-about-filing-
bankruptcy (accessed April 18, 2014).

Index